CRIME SCIENTIST

The end of a wire noose used to strangle a pregnant girl; the torn piece of a man's shirt found at the scene of an assault; an imprint of the clothing of a victim on the bonnet of a hit-and-run car . . .

All vital evidence for Dr. John Thompson in his pursuit of crime in Rhodesia. *Crime Scientist* is the compelling story of criminal investigation by a man of unusual talents.

Dr. John Thompson trained as a scientist at London University and worked with ICI until the war when he gained valuable experience as an explosives expert. After a brief period of tobacco farming in Rhodesia he became first Director of the Police Forensic Science Laboratory in Salisbury, a post he held until his retirement in 1977.

CRIME SCIENTIST

John Thompson

A STAR BOOK

published by

the Paperback Division of
W. H. ALLEN & Co. Ltd

A Star Book

Published in 1982
by the Paperback Division of
W. H. Allen & Co. Ltd
A Howard and Wyndham Company
44 Hill Street, London W1X 8LB

First published in Great Britain by
George G. Harrap & Co. Ltd, 1980

Printed in Great Britain by
Cox & Wyman Ltd, Reading

ISBN 0 352 31238 6

CONTENTS

ILLUSTRATIONS

PREFACE

I VENTURED to write this book in the belief that I had something worth saying and some experiences sufficiently unusual to merit retelling. I am aware that this has been the proud boast of many a writer so captivated by feelings of uniqueness about his own life story that he has an embarrassing desire to share them with others. In the cold light of print, of course, many such claims fall short of the readers' expectations. I am conscious then of the pitfalls, as any scientist should be, but nevertheless have felt encouraged to proceed for at least two reasons. Firstly, I believe I can make a modest claim to have helped in furthering forensic science as a necessary discipline in the structure of law and order in Africa. And, secondly, I am firmly convinced of the gifts of science which, if properly nurtured in the vast continent of Africa, have such power for good as to be capable of disarming confrontation and enhancing human dignity.

Science proceeds by always applying the same rules. It is the demonstration of this which is the best hope of helping the African peoples to greater health and development. Of course, it might be thought that this is simply an example of pure arrogance in knowing what is best for the African. But there need be no doubt that in common with every other member of the human race he wants to be free of disease and he wants his crops to succeed. These are deep-seated human wants and as simple objectives require little sophistication—at least insofar as things go well. In face of adversity, however, the African has traditionally had no other recourse but to the witch-doctor and tribal culture. It will be seen from what follows in this book that by any objective judgment witchcraft is to a considerable extent an anti-social retrograde force.

In talking about the African as an individual I am aware of the enormous sensitivity which clouds understanding of the inter-racial conflict in Southern Africa. Throughout this book the references are always to the tribal African and it is important that there should be no misunderstanding about this. Where the account may be judged as critical, I can only say that I have tried to apply fairness and objectivity.

As a scientist, or indeed simply as an accountable observer, I feel it as appropriate to write about the tribal African in the same way that I would of, say, the tribesman of New Guinea or of the mountain dweller of the South American Andes, had my career been followed in those geographical domains.

There may be small differences between the black and white races although this is doubtful. Certainly there is no strength in the argument that whites are inherently superior and therefore entitled to privileged status. Indeed humanity is so variable that even the most biased person must admit that the most intelligent blacks are superior to most whites. Therefore the privileged white concept is nonsense.

On the other hand it is equally wrong to ignore the fact that man is largely a product of his environment. We inherit from the previous generation the language we speak and the writing we use together with a whole range of technical skills. We also acquire social attitudes, standards of behaviour, moral outlook, religious belief, superstitition and many life-forming habits.

The heritage of the tribal African is vastly different from that of a person born in Europe. He is raised in poverty in a thatched mud hut and has an income about one-tenth or one-twentieth of his European counterpart. His diet is mainly starch and sufficiently lacking in protein to lower his IQ by five points.

He lives in a society where the ideal is to be rather better than average—there is no drive to attain outstanding qualities. The competitive spirit is lacking, with the advantage that while he may not bask in great achievements, he does not suffer from ulcers or nervous disorders. Sleeping pills and tranquillizers, so much a feature of high-pressure European life, are not needed in tribal society.

He lives in an intensely conservative community in which a high standard of courtesy is normal, where precedent governs most actions and where a clearly defined social order is recognized—

females occupy the lower social ranks and are regarded as minors all their lives. They may not own property or sue in the courts unless represented by a male relative.

Above all the tribal African lives in fear and awe of spirits and witchcraft. Illnesses and misfortunes are attributed to the influence of spirits, particularly those of departed parents and grandparents. He does not understand germs or organic disease and cannot conceive of their causing illness. Consequently, not seeing the need for prevention, he almost certainly suffers from one or more of the parasitic diseases, such as malaria, bilharzia or hookworm. But he is not stupid—a black herdsman in charge of two hundred oxen will probably not be able to count beyond twelve, but if one animal goes missing he is aware of the fact and will be able to give an accurate description of the beast. What he lacks in education he compensates for by the sharpening of other senses, especially visual ability.

I count it as my fortune to have spent a large part of my professional life in Africa. The scientific work I had a hand in starting goes on and will evolve in ways appropriate to the needs of African development. Forensic science is after all but one of the human disciplines woven into the fabric of good government designed to protect the innocent and to identify the offender without prejudice.

The experiences related in this book are minute steps in the advancement of science in the cauldron of Africa. But they encapsulate examples and practices which may profit the imagination and understanding of others. The virtue of that, however, must be for the reader to decide.

In these days when the police are referred to as fuzz and pigs I should like to pay tribute to the British South Africa Police. In spite of the name there is no connection with the Republic of South Africa and the name will probably disappear in the near future. This is a pity as, in police circles, the British South Africa Police are recognized as an elite body ranking with such forces as the Royal Canadian Mounted Police. The most efficient and capable men I have met in my working life served with the BSAP and did difficult work with judgment and humanity and I consider it a privilege to have served with them.

This account would never have seen the light of day without the co-operation of Mr Robin Odell who put it into readable shape. It was a pleasure to work with him.

Finally all the cases mentioned actually happened but some details have been altered to avoid possible embarrassment to individuals.

Chapter One
BEGINNINGS

ALL the African villagers were gathered in the compound to attend a trial by ordeal presided over by the witch-doctor. The clapping of hands and stamping of feet announced their belief that the spirit of Matope would be avenged. The witch-doctor appeared and started to prepare a potion. He sprinkled crushed leaves and ground roots into a rough pot of thick porridge. Stirring slowly and mumbling magical incantations, he approached the row of nine suspects squatting on the ground before him.

The first man trembled but without hesitation swallowed the spoonful of porridge pressed to his lips. The witch-doctor passed onto the next man, and the next. All accepted the concoction without mishap. At length the witch-doctor reached the ninth and last man. He stirred his brew and pushed a spoonful between the man's clenched jaws. Terrified, the villagers watched as the man quivered violently, lurched to his feet, staggered and with a cry fell dead to the ground. Terror then gave way to joy and admiration at this dramatic demonstration of the witch-doctor's power.

Trials by ordeal in the African bush might not conform to the accepted view of what constitutes a forensic scientist's job. Certainly I had no idea when I went to Southern Africa at the end of the Second World War that I should find myself pitting science against witchcraft. But then I only became a forensic scientist by accident, as I shall explain.

Death by witchcraft is not uncommon in Africa. I have come across several instances where the victims were so firmly convinced that they had been bewitched and were doomed to die, that of course they did. The process is not particularly difficult to understand. The terrifyingly intense belief in the power of a fatal spell puts the victim off his food, profoundly depresses him and causes loss of vitality so that death intervenes within a few months. This is really death from fear and, influenced by the sinister potency of witchcraft, it is often a slow, drawn-out affair.

Matope was a greatly respected village elder and it was his misfortune when he fell sick to be attended by a witch-doctor called in by his worried relatives. Initially, the old man responded to the witch-doctor's ministrations, but family rejoicing at his recovery was premature for Matope suddenly became worse and died.

His daughters and grand-daughters were distraught. It is commonly believed that death and disease result from the displeasure of one's ancestors or from witchcraft inspired by an enemy. So that, when a parent dies, the cause of death must be established and, if necessary, suitable action must be taken to appease the spirits. Failure to do this is likely to incur further demonstrations of anger on the part of the spirit and more misery will follow.

Matope's relatives found it difficult to believe that he had died from natural causes and the longer they grieved the more convinced they became that he had been bewitched. They put this to the witch-doctor and asked for his help. He was inclined to accept the suggestion favourably and agreed that Matope's demise was inexplicable, especially as he himself had prescribed the potions which had been so effective during the early part of his illness. After much consideration he concluded that death must have been wrought through black magic. He said that he would prove through his own powers that Matope had been murdered and forecast that the murderer would be one of nine men whom he already held under suspicion. The dead man's grieving relatives so appreciated this offer of help that they presented an ox to the witch-doctor by way of advance payment for his services.

The witch-doctor then staged his trial by ordeal with its dramatic denunciation of the ninth suspect as the murderer of Matope. Seemingly, his standing as a magician was greatly enhanced—but the story did not end there. Such is the ferment of ideas in Africa that the dead suspect's favourite daughter, a fifteen-year-old who had attended the local mission school, was not disposed to believe the witch-doctor's explanation. This girl had learned to read and write and had come into contact with new ideas—she had developed a mind of her own. African children are brought up strictly in accordance with rigid tribal lore and codes of conduct. Penalties for disobedience are severe to the point of shameful cruelty. It would be difficult to find a parallel in western society to illustrate adequately the courage of this brave girl in the action which she now took.

Believing that her father had been murdered and remaining unconvinced by the witch-doctor's solution, she defied village opinion and went to the police. With incredible pluck she flew in the face of all the tribal standards held by her fellow-villagers, virtually denouncing the witch-doctor and condemning his trial by ordeal of the nine suspects.

It was at this point that I came into the story. An important feature of the incident was the sudden, almost immediate, death of the witch-doctor's ninth suspect. There was no lingering demise so characteristic of death by bewitchment—this looked to me like a straightforward case of poisoning. Only one common poison produces such rapid results—cyanide. It was significant that potassium cyanide was used extensively in the local gold-mining industry and thus was likely to be fairly readily available. Of course, this was just an educated guess without supporting evidence.

The difficulty with cyanide is that it tends to disappear very quickly from the stomach and organs of the victim. Fortunately in this case, an astute police officer, on hearing of the girl's account of the trial by ordeal, summoned the help of a doctor who removed tissues from the corpse for possible later examination. These were refrigerated and when analysed showed beyond all doubt that the death of the victim had been caused by cyanide poisoning.

After this it was not difficult to tie up the witch-doctor's guilt. Traces of cyanide were found in the pocket of the old army greatcoat which he wore during the trial by ordeal. This proved sufficient to convict him and he was eventually hanged—a rare occurrence because of the difficulty of persuading the rural African to overcome his fear of witch-doctors sufficiently to give evidence in court.

The witch-doctor was undoubtedly a skilled conjuror and he had carefully stage-managed the whole affair with sufficient drama to beguile his audience. With dexterous fingers he slipped some cyanide into the still sticky spoon with which he had served the previous suspect. Then, scooping up a little porridge from his bowl, he administered the fatal concoction to the ninth suspect.

Any one of the suspects would probably have served the purpose but his selection of the unfortunate ninth man allowed him to build up the tension and play the situation for all it was worth. By supposedly having found and punished the man who had bewitched Matope he had manifestly proved his power and strengthened his reputation beyond measure.

It was later proved that there was nothing the least sinister about Matope's death—he had simply died of natural causes. So by seeking to enhance his self-esteem, the witch-doctor had merely contributed to his own downfall aided by the spirited intervention of the dead man's daughter and the application of a little science.

▼▼▼▼▼▼

I became a forensic scientist by accident and had the good fortune to start this new career in Africa. In the early 1960s crime detection in Rhodesia had reached a point where it was clear that forensic science methods should be put on an organized footing. Consequently, in January 1963, I became the first Director of the British South Africa Police Forensic Science Laboratory in Salisbury.

Thus I embarked on a fresh career at the age of forty-nine and faced the challenge of building-up a new laboratory to aid the police in their pursuit of crime. The prospect was an exciting one. Professionally, there was the opportunity to achieve standards of forensic work which would be the equal of those in Europe. Intellectually, there was the challenge of pursuing this in Africa where modern society confronts the tribal community and culture.

The application of science to the crime resulting from this confrontation produced a wealth of cases which Sherlock Holmes might have called 'singular'. Because of the African dimension they may fairly be called unique. The years which followed my appointment were rich in forensic experience, involving murder, witchcraft, robbery, fraud and forgery. They are among the happiest and most rewarding years of my life.

My world was that of the laboratory detective. I functioned as an impartial scientist producing information and evidence by applying scientific methods to crime materials. It was the microscopic world of identifying and comparing hairs, fibres, chips of paint, particles of dust, slivers of glass and specimens of soil, sand and rock found in all manner of places but usually associated with criminal acts. It was also the world of advanced equipment used to analyse chemical traces, to match bullets to the guns which fired them and to compare knives and clubs with the injuries they made.

But the laboratory is not the sole domain of the forensic scientist.

He also carries the responsiblility of performing in the role of expert, which means making judgments the quality and reliability of which can be tested in court.

I well remember the very first case I dealt with for the police. It ended up with my giving expert evidence in court and splitting my trousers into the bargain. I had been asked to identify some home-made bullets fired from a revolver in the furtherance of robbery. The bullets were composed of solder which is known to contain several impurities. I obtained forty different samples of solder and analysed them for silver, arsenic, bismuth, antimony, copper, zinc and cadmium. Of the forty samples, one only had the level of two impurities agreeing with the crime samples and all the rest had either one level or none at all. The crime sample extracted from the wounded victim agreed in all seven levels.

It is the common practice for experts to swear that two samples of material are identical. I doubted the validity of such claims. After all, if a hundred coins straight from the mint are examined visually they will be seen as identical. But when each coin is weighed on a sensitive balance it will be found to have an individual weight. Thus, a claim that the coins are identical depends on the method of examination used.

So when asked in court during my first appearance as an expert if the solder samples were identical, I refused to answer and gave instead an explanation of the principle involved. I failed to convince some members of the court and was recalled at a later date to repeat the evidence. This entailed a 500-mile journey but I was rewarded when the court professed its understanding and I established myself as a reliable witness with an original approach. I did not escape entirely unscathed though, for while giving evidence I balanced some documents on the edge of the witness box and, as I was talking, one of the papers fluttered to the floor. I swooped down to retrieve it only to hear an awesome tearing sound as the back seam of my trousers split asunder.

The tension of making my first court appearance was anxiety enough without problems of this sort. I remember standing very upright with my feet close together, embarrassed beyond description. I was subsequently rescued by a helpful policewoman who provided some small safety pins which saw me home without further difficulty.

This stand on a matter of principle with its undignified sequel marked my baptism as a forensic expert. What led to my appearing in the witness box in the first place was due to the workings of chance.

▾▾▾▾▾▾

I was born in Harrogate where I had a vast number of aunts and uncles and a correspondingly large number of cousins scattered around Yorkshire. My parents left Harrogate when I was quite young and my childhood was spent in South London with two older sisters and a younger brother. Mother was determined that her children should do well and it was due to her encouragement that we all won scholarships and benefited from a good education.

Father was a professional musician before he married but his father-in-law insisted that a musician's income did not provide a sufficiently reliable basis for marriage. Reluctantly he gave up music for accountancy although he practised daily at the piano throughout his life. To his sorrow none of his children showed any ability to play a musical instrument although we each loved music.

My maternal grandfather was an outstanding character and Yorkshireman. Even when we moved to London we kept in close contact with the family and spent our holidays in Yorkshire whenever we could. Grandfather Rudd was a joiner and carpenter and his loving wife Mary bore him nine children. The story goes that as a young man he turned up for work suffering from the effects of the previous night's carousing and was summarily sacked. He joined the Quakers and never touched another drop of alcohol.

Work was difficult to find in the 1870s, but with an astute eye for business grandfather borrowed some money and made a hundred coffins of varying size and quality. So far as I know he was the first man in England to start an 'off-the-peg' coffin business. This made good sense, for the standard procedure at the time was for the undertaker to measure the deceased and then have the coffin made —an arrangement which could take up to four days. Grandfather could guarantee delivery within hours with his made-to-measure service.

Although he continued to make coffins he developed the wholesale supply of timber as his main business. He bought a three-ton Fiat lorry and hired Bill Nutter, whom I count as a life-long friend, as driver. Bill was immensely proud of his lorry and worked on it in the evenings polishing the copper radiator until it shone like a mirror. Grandfather had a coach body made which could be bolted to the lorry chassis. Once a year, the entire family—some thirty adults and children—piled into the Fiat and we drove off to Scarborough for a day's outing at the seaside.

When we children went to stay with grandfather on holiday he allowed us to ride in the lorry when he made deliveries. I particularly remember one visit when I was about five years old and we were delivering mineral waters to the army camp at Catterick near York. It was a very hot day and to our fiendish delight the bottles of mineral water began to burst due to the heat and the shaking up they received in the lorry. The entire journey was punctuated with loud explosions followed by shrieks of boyish laughter.

Grandfather was devoted to his wife and when she died in 1935 he was heartbroken. His final tribute to her was a magnificently carved Burma teak coffin with solid silver handles and a double lead lining with upholstery in pure silk. It was a wonderful piece of craftsmanship. I shall never forget the funeral and the sight of eight strong men staggering through the churchyard to the graveside under the weight of this enormous coffin. One of the bearers was my Uncle Edwin, who had a scandalous reputation, despite which he was grandmother's favourite child. I remember noticing that Uncle Edwin appeared to be particularly distressed at the funeral but what I took for grief was in reality severe pain. As a result of being called upon to act as a coffin bearer the poor man had ruptured himself. Grandfather Rudd died a few months after his wife.

Perhaps because of my close association with grandfather and his joinery trade I have nurtured vague aspirations to work with wood. Only much later in my life have I found the time to devote to woodcarving which has proved a satisfying and therapeutic hobby. There are fewer stories to tell on the other side of my family although it is perhaps worthy of note that my paternal grandfather caused a disruption to parliamentary business. He was a type-setter for a London daily newspaper and also president of the printer's trade union. During a printing dispute he called out on strike the men who printed the daily order papers for the Houses of Parliament. The dispute was apparently shortlived but grandfather lost his job.

In due course I was educated at Alleyns School, Dulwich, and an early adventure into the realms of practical chemistry possibly pointed to my future career. I discovered that a very satisfactory bang could be gained from an experiment using my mother's cut-glass scent bottle, which had a ground-glass stopper. I put some granulated zinc in the bottle, added some spirits of salts and rammed the stopper home. It took about five minutes for the pressure of the gas to build up while tension mounted for the young experimenter and his watchful spectators. Finally, the bang came and the stopper flew thirty or more feet into the air. One day, I rammed the stopper in too hard and, instead of joyfully observing its familiar flight-path, there was an impressively loud explosion and the whole bottle disintegrated. All that was left was a ball of thick mist and no glass fragments to be found anywhere. My mother accepted the loss of her scent bottle with equanimity but it was a dangerous game to play.

I went on to University College, London, where I read a degree in chemistry and also managed to make my mark in an explosive fashion. This occurred during my last year in the Chemistry Department which was on one side of a quadrangle with the Slade School of Fine Art on the opposite side. At that time men were only a small fraction of the Slade School's student population. The majority were young women who seemed to apply their artistic talents to their appearance rather more enthusiastically than they did to their work. They were a gorgeous bunch, particularly compared to the small number of female students of chemistry who were earnest, hard-working girls with their noses firmly on the grindstone. This produced a situation in which the Slade School men obviously 'had it made', an advantage which they emphasized by parading in the quadrangle during the morning break, each man accompanied by several admiring girls.

The tables were turned on this display of oneupmanship on the day that I decided to dispose of some unwanted ether. I had half a gallon of ether which had been used as a solvent. I distilled it and let the vapour go down the drain from the laboratory sink which was not fitted with an elbow, liquid trap. I did not know it at the time but the drain fed into the system which went under the centre of the quadrangle and was fitted with heavy, cast-iron manhole covers at regular intervals. The result of my action was that the whole drain system became filled with ether vapour. My fund of knowledge was soon to be increased with the information that five pounds of ether vapour mixed with air has an explosive energy equal to that of ten pounds of TNT.

All that was required to release that energy was an igniting spark. This was unwittingly provided by a fellow-student who happened to dispose of some potassium metal down his laboratory sink. Now, when potassium comes into contact with water a flame is produced and in the presence of ether an explosion is inevitable. There was a heavy, dull thud and I turned to look out of the window in time to see several cast-iron manhole covers sailing through the air, breaking as they landed on the hard concrete of the quadrangle. The decorum of the Slade School men parading there with their consorts was completely shattered and the area was cleared in seconds with the manly escorts in most cases well in front of the flight to safety.

Fortunately, no one was hurt and I quickly realized that my carelessness was mainly responsible for the incident. I hastily dismantled my apparatus and looked as innocent as possible while I joined my chemistry colleagues in expressing delight at the way in which the Slade School boys had been routed by a few manhole covers. It was a temptation to boast of my part in the affair but I prudently kept my mouth shut and shared the secret with no one.

In 1936 I gained a doctorate, also at London, for a thesis on physical chemistry. In the course of this postgraduate work I worked with one of the earliest samples of heavy water ever produced. Heavy water contains hydrogen atoms which have two protons in the nucleus instead of the usual one proton, and each atom of 'heavy' hydrogen, known as deuterium, is twice the weight of a normal hydrogen atom. Water formed from deuterium is heavy water. All natural water contains a small proportion of heavy water but it is not easy to isolate it. During the war heavy water figured so much in the production of atom bombs that a large air raid was organized to destroy the heavy water plant in Norway.

I started my first job in 1937 as a research chemist with Imperial Chemical Industries where I worked on the development of chlorinated rubber as a paint base. The first large-scale application of this material was on the new Mersey tunnel.

The urge to broaden my experience and to see something of the world excited me and I applied for a job in Southern Africa. I landed a position as research chemist with the Tobacco Research Board at Trelawney in Rhodesia but before I could start my new employment the Second World War caught me in its net. Like most young men of the day, my ambitions were curtailed, at least temporarily, and I found myself in uniform.

September 1939 saw me sitting on a gun site on Merseyside as an anti-aircraft gunnery officer. After a few months the powers-that-be wisely decided that I was a pretty poor regimental officer and would be of more use to my country's war effort employed in the technical field.

I was transferred to the Royal Army Ordnance Corps and assigned the duties of explosives expert, which included bomb disposal.

Personal survival is a matter of some concern in this job and I adopted a mental approach which saw me through and also helped later on in my career. Many academically trained persons acquire the faculty of concentrating on the matter in hand and ignoring all other issues. Hence the proverbial absent-minded professor type who is not so much absent-minded as single-minded—pursuing one line of thought to the exclusion of all else.

This is a fatal weakness in any administrative work where attention has to be given over a wide field but it is an essential attribute in the bomb-disposal officer. If he is burdened with anxiety about being blown to pieces he will not be able to focus adequately on the technical details of the matter in hand and his effectiveness—not to say his life expectancy—is diminished.

One of my most vivid memories of this period of the war was of removing 800 pounds of gelignite from a bombed-out suburb in Birmingham with orders to dispose of it. This large quantity of gelignite had been requisitioned by a bomb disposal unit who required an eight-ounce stick each time they disposed of an unexploded bomb. After eighteen months' operations they had used so little of their generous stock that what was left had deteriorated to a highly dangerous condition.

Gelignite is a mixture of ammonium nitrate, nitro-glycerine and a little nitro-cellulose to waterproof it. Ammonium nitrate is a salt-like substance which strongly attracts water. When gelignite picks up moisture from the atmosphere the water is taken up by the ammonium nitrate and the nitro-glycerine separates out as an oily liquid which is highly sensitive and may detonate without warning. Horrifying tales, many of them invented, I suspect, are told by explosives experts about accidents with weeping gelignite. What is certain is that the immediate witnesses and most of the physical evidence would be destroyed in the explosion.

The gelignite I was confronted with in Birmingham was weeping very badly—it was in a worse condition than any I had seen before or since. I was equipped with a one-ton Austin van and assisted by two soldiers. We placed two layers of sacks on the floor of the van and, having changed our ammunition boots for plimsolls, started to load the boxes of gelignite. We finished this task at about 5.0 p.m. and I decided to set off at once for the quarry, a short distance out of the city, where the gelignite would be either burned or blown-up.

Strictly speaking I should have waited until there was little traffic about and I should have asked for a police escort. But at the age of twenty-eight I was impatient to get on with the job and, throwing caution to the winds, started up the Austin van and got under way. I reassured myself that no questions would be asked if nothing went wrong and if it did I wouldn't be around anyway. It was a headstrong decision.

As soon as we got onto the Hagley Road we found ourselves in the midst of the evening rush-hour traffic, caught up in a stream of buses and trolley-buses. In those days Hagley Road had a wood-block surface which was greasy after a three weeks' dry spell. Suddenly the heavens opened and, to my horror, I saw the road surface change to an oily, slippery nightmare. Some two hundred yards from the next junction, the traffic lights turned to red and although I applied the brakes gently, the van went into a wild skid. I managed to correct this, narrowly missing an oncoming trolley-bus, only to start another skid as I had over-compensated. We careered wildly from side-to-side and the boxes of gelignite began crashing about in the back of the van. I really thought my number was up!

It was with enormous relief that we got the vehicle under control and pulled up safely beyond the traffic lights. We were sweating as much as the gelignite by that time! I remember getting out of the van and pacing up and down by the roadside for several minutes berating myself for a foolhardy decision which had imperilled the lives of my two companions and subjected many innocent passers-by to danger. I vowed never again to take unnecessary chances with explosives.

After two-and-a-half years as an explosives expert with the RAOC I went to the Royal Military College of Science as a technical staff officer. I took a six-month course there which amounted to an engineering degree with a military slant, and was then posted to the Department of Tank Design at Chobham where I spent the rest of the war. I found myself testing armour plate in work which eventually was incorporated in the design of the famous Centurion tank.

One of my jobs was to study the optimum distribution of armour on a tank. It is not possible to give full all-round protection to a tank as it would then weigh some 150 tons and would drop through the first bridge it attempted to cross. The question had to be settled whether it was better to have vertical or sloping armour-plate covering the frontal area of the tank and, if sloping, how steep? And was it preferable to have two separate plates with a gap in between or just one solid plate? It was also important to determine the range and angles at which British guns could knock holes in German tanks and vice versa. If an armour-piercing shot strikes at an angle, the gun has to be fired from a closer range than if the shot strikes the armour at right-angles. Our findings were greatly in favour of the Germans who at that time had the best steel-makers in the world. Both their armour and armour-piercing shot were about ten per cent better weight for weight than the best of their rivals. The German 88 mm was a magnificent gun with a supremely accurate sight and a shot that could knock a hole in armour eight inches thick.

In the routine testing of armour-plate the object was to find a shot velocity which just failed to penetrate the armour. A proportion of the cordite explosive charge was removed from the shell case in order to control the velocity of the shot. Velocity was measured by means of two photo-electric cells placed fifty feet apart. The time taken for the shot to pass over these cells was measured by apparatus using a form of transistor. This device was probably one of the earliest computers used in England.

The next step was to find a shot velocity which just penetrated the plate. The results yielded by these two phases of testing could be used to assess the quality of the armour-plate. It was an expensive method of testing and only about two per cent of the plate used in tank construction could be tested in this way. I carried out some successful work aimed at improving testing procedures. This was based on relating the properties of small test samples of plate to their ability to keep out armour-piercing shot.

These developments were, of course, top secret at the time. But the results of these and other investigations were incorporated in British tank design including the Centurion which saw successful active service in various parts of the world until replaced by the more advanced Chieftain in the late 1960s.

Since then I have seen the latest British tanks on television fitted with 'Chobham' armour and the brief glimpse seemed to show that the same basic ideas are still current.

It was while I was engaged in testing armour-plate for tanks in 1942 that I met Mollie, who was to become my wife. Some of the test firings were carried out in a quarry at a village near Sheffield. I was billetted locally with Mollie's mother. Eight years younger than me and the only child of devoted parents, Mollie was a smiling girl with a great sense of humour and the ability to laugh at herself. We were instantly attracted to one another although we were both married. Like many young adults during the war years we had been swept along on a tidal wave of war emotions and made marriages which were doomed even before they started.

Our friendship was therefore the briefest of brief encounters. We enjoyed the companionship provided by a few dances, walks and bicycle rides and learned a little about each other. Mollie had three loves in her life—animals, music and ballet. She was on the verge of a possible career in ballet when the war intervened and she settled down to do a useful job as a secretary.

The war drew to a close and we parted to go our separate ways. Mollie continued as a secretary and I went to Africa to take up the appointment which the Tobacco Research Board in Rhodesia had kept open for me. Demobilization saw me sailing for Africa on a converted troopship—a nightmare journey made no easier by the depressing thought that I was leaving Mollie behind.

But my initial gloom lifted with the excitement of arriving in Africa. I thought then that Salisbury was the most beautiful town I had ever seen. Cecil Rhodes had given instructions that the city's streets were to be made sufficiently wide to allow a 'U'-turn to be made by a wagon pulled by eight pairs of oxen. These wide streets, spotlessly clean and lined with jacaranda trees covered with bluebell-coloured blooms, were unforgettable.

The parks and open spaces were even more attractive. Although some of the older buildings had something of the look of a wild west film set about them, the shops and cinemas were very English in appearance. The people were cheerful and friendly and it seems to me that there was a relaxed relationship between the races. I have crossed the Rhodesian border into South Africa many times and although it may be pure imagination I always sensed a change there. The atmosphere was recognizably different and it could be felt as soon as the border was crossed.

African roads were a new experience for me. The first few miles of the main roads out of Salisbury were ordinary tar macadam but they soon turned into strip roads. A strip road consists of two strips of tarred road about eighteen inches wide and spaced to take the wheels of a car. When two cars approached from opposing directions it was customary for each to pull over to the side of the road keeping two wheels on one of the strips with the nearside wheels kicking up clouds of dust. This manoeuvre was usually performed without reducing speed. If a driver had nerves of steel, not to mention a complete lack of courtesy, he would keep his car on the strips and force the oncoming vehicle into the ditch.

Driving on such roads at night further taxed one's judgment for it was difficult to estimate the distance of an approaching car. To judge the correct moment to pull over, I developed a visual rule of thumb whereby I gauged the distance by the space separating the headlamps of the oncoming car. This worked well until I encountered a French-built car whose designer had thoughtlessly placed the headlamps some fifteen inches apart instead of the more usual four feet. This led me to over-estimate the distance of the approaching car by a factor of about three and nearly produced a head-on collision at sixty miles an hour.

The dirt roads which branched off the main routes also required a special driving technique. To overcome the unbelievably shaky ride produced by travelling over the corrugated surface of a dirt road it was necessary to drive at such a speed, usually between forty and fifty miles an hour, that would bounce the wheels from crest to crest. Braking on such surfaces was attended by all manner of unexpected results. Various hazards such as heavy rains also helped enliven car journeys. I discovered that many minor roads were not provided with bridges over the rivers. Instead, the river bed was floored with a concrete 'drift'. Judgment was again put to the test when the rivers were swollen with flood water and the depth of water to be forded had to be estimated. Many times I have seen cars forging across flooded rivers with the doors on both sides open and the river flowing through the car.

This was my introduction to Africa and I pondered my future as I drove out of Salisbury heading towards Northern Rhodesia or Zambia as it now is. My destination was the tobacco research station near Trelawney, a small bush village some sixty miles north of Salisbury where I was to spend the next four years as a research chemist. I arrived in a somewhat idealistic frame of mind hoping that I could contribute to the prosperity of the country and help alleviate the poverty which I saw was the lot of the majority of its inhabitants.

It seemed to me that my career in science up to that time had been directed mainly to destructive ends. The chlorinated rubber plant I had worked on in the 1930s had been put to wartime use and my work with explosives and tank design could hardly be described as peaceful. So I went into tobacco production, which was an important plank in Rhodesia's economy.

My chief contribution was to show that crop yields could be improved by using large amounts of fertilizer. Until then, the usual quantity of fertilizer applied was about 100 to 200 pounds per acre. I initiated field trials using up to 1,000 pounds per acre. The old hands told me I was mad and merely wasting government money. However, my trials proved that one pound of fertilizer costing three pence produced rather more than one pound of tobacco worth in those days about twenty-four pence. Thus, increased doses of fertilizer proved to be sound investment. Within a year or two fertilizer applications on Rhodesia's tobacco farms doubled and so did the crop yields per acre.

Elated with the success of growing some high-yielding tobacco crops for the Research Board I grew restless and began to reason that I could do so equally profitably for myself. In other words I was smitten by the 'get rich quick' bug. My first wife had left me by this time and, abandoning all caution, I scraped together every penny I had and invested it in a tobacco farm. Then I cabled Mollie and asked her to marry me.

I had hesitated to contact Mollie after my wife left me. Four years had passed since our brief encounter in Yorkshire and I knew nothing of her circumstances now. What I was to learn later was that a month after my departure from England she had separated from her husband and was then divorced. She changed her name by deed poll and steered clear of any attachments, believing in her darkest moments that our wartime song 'I'll see you again' would come true.

It nearly didn't. I did not write directly to Mollie but to her mother enclosing a letter to her daughter to be passed on if she thought this was the right thing to do. Several weeks passed without reply and my hopes began to sink. I was not to know that Mollie's mother was going through an agony of indecision about passing the letter on. She kept it for two months before giving it to her daughter, fearful of re-opening wounds which she hoped had begun to heal.

I followed my marriage proposal with a letter containing an engagement ring dubiously concealed in a pair of stockings. This was further proof to Mollie that I had gone quite mad, for she already believed I had lost my reason in forsaking science for farming. Happily, she accepted my proposal but told me quite bluntly that if I wanted her to come to Africa I should have to send the fare. I rapidly sent a money draft and with all her worldly wealth—five pounds—Mollie boarded the *Edinburgh Castle* and sailed for South Africa.

In early November 1950 I travelled the 1,600 miles by train to meet her in Cape Town. The long-awaited romantic reunion turned into something of a farce when Mollie was asked about her financial position by immigration officials. She told them brightly that she would check and counted out the contents of her purse which totalled the grand sum of seven shillings and four pence. The officials laughed uproariously and inquired about bank accounts. It slowly dawned on them that the passenger in question indeed possessed no other assets than the declared seven shillings and four pence and an impatient fiancé who had been waiting at dockside since day-break.

About midday Mollie was hauled to the top of the ship's gangway by immigration officers whom I informed by shouting from the quayside that I was indeed going to marry her. Eventually she was allowed to disembark and we left the docks with a stern warning from officialdom ringing in our ears, 'Marry that woman or back she goes—no room for penniless females here'.

We were married on 17th November, having had to delay the ceremony until I had planted my first tobacco crop. In those days tobacco seedlings were taken from the seed beds and planted during the first days of the rainy season, usually in early November. The best crops resulted from early planting and so I set about the urgent task of planting out some 300,000 seedlings. This done, we were married and immediately went to work as farmers.

Mollie was soon confronted with the everyday phenomena of her new life in Africa. A few days after our wedding, the wife of one of my labourers came to us for help—she was in the final stages of labour. Mollie offered to drive her to the local clinic but before she could get the car ready the baby was born with the mother squatting on two bricks on the garage floor. To Mollie's shocked surprise the African women in attendance insisted that the placenta must come away before the cord was cut and they left the new-born infant lying on the cement floor for almost thirty minutes until the afterbirth was produced.

My tobacco farming days proved to be short-lived and my get rich quick scheme flopped badly. I was simply not cut out to be a farmer. We had lost money and spirits were low but Mollie gently yet firmly guided me back to science where she had always known I belonged. I took a job as spectroscopist with the Federal Ministry of Agriculture's Department of Research and Specialist Services in Salisbury. It is interesting to reflect that had I been a successful tobacco farmer I would never have become a forensic scientist. That disaster and the accident of becoming a researcher again led me into the realm of crime detection.

Spectroscopy is a method of analysis by which the elements present in a sample are identified. The sample is vaporized to an incandescent gas or vapour which emits radiation at wavelengths corresponding to the elements present. The spectrum of rays produced may be viewed directly or it can be recorded on a photographic plate. The fact that each element emits a unique pattern of wavelengths enables the composition of, for example, a paint sample, to be determined. I used spectrographic analysis in my work to study trace element deficiencies in crops. This research was fascinating in itself but the variety of problems broadened when I began to receive requests from the police to analyse crime samples. Spectrography was widely used in forensic laboratories around the world and it was only natural that the police authority, having no forensic science facilities of its own, should seek assistance from a government department. Several Salisbury doctors also gave specialist advice to the police and the idea began to grow that the Criminal Investigation Department should have its own laboratory.

The number of requests coming to me for forensic investigations gradually built up to the point where I was doing more work for the police than for the Department of Agriculture. So when it was finally decided that the British South Africa Police should set up a forensic science laboratory, I applied for the advertised post of Director. My application was accepted and thus on 1st January 1963 I became a civilian attached to the Criminal Investigation Department.

In those early days at the laboratory, it seemed as though Rhodesia's criminal elements were doing their utmost to put me to the test. I was often called out at night; the telephone would ring in the small hours and Mollie, a light sleeper, would field the calls. 'May I speak to the doctor please?' was the opening gambit for many a murder investigation or hit-and-run case. By the time I had showered and dressed Mollie had organized toast and coffee and the laboratory car was waiting outside. The car was usually driven by my Forensic Science Liaison Officer (FLSO), a police inspector, who had already called at the laboratory and picked up 'Doc's murder bag'.

One of the routine requirements of the job was to see and handle dead and injured bodies in the search for trace evidence. Ascertaining cause of death and interpreting injuries was of course the province of the medical men but early forensic examination of the crime scene before anything was disturbed was important. In this way a picture could be built up of what had happened. The difference between accident, murder and suicide is not always apparent at first—it is the detailed forensic work which helps to make the distinction.

I was called out at first light one morning and driven to a spot on the Bulawayo road some twenty miles from Salisbury where a dead coloured man had been found. The police-officer who arrived first on the scene saw the man's head injuries and thought he was faced with a murder or hit-and-run case. The body was lying near a tree and there was an ugly bruise with broken skin on the forehead close to the hairline. Using a small lens I discovered fragments of tree bark in the wound and a careful examination of the nearby tree led to the discovery of a clump of hair and skin embedded in the tree bark about thirty inches from the ground.

The post-mortem clearly showed that death had been caused by the man's head striking the tree but was this an accident or could it have resulted from an assault? There were no other injuries on the body and there was an absence of footprints or signs of a struggle. However, the dead man reeked of methylated spirit, and a whisky bottle found near by had a little meths left in it. It later became known that the man was a confirmed alcoholic and it was evident that he had died not as a murder victim but accidently by falling against the tree while stumbling about in an alcoholic stupor.

The single-minded approach which had served me well as a war-time explosives expert was equally effective in those aspects of my new job which involved examining dead bodies. When confronted with a mutiliated body lying at the centre of a crime scene it is necessary to concentrate on the technical details and to remain completely impersonal. Children and young persons who meet violent deaths threaten to penetrate one's defence mechanism and I can remember one instance in which it was positively breached.

A young woman had committed suicide by shooting herself in the head and it was necessary for me to confirm suicide by establishing the range at which the shot had been fired. Now a live person blinks every few seconds and this action keeps the eyeball moist and clear. If a person dies with the eyes open they dry out and become very dull. This makes them look lifeless and it requires no effort of imagination to regard the person as dead. When I attended at the mortuary the dead girl was brought out of a freezing chamber and I saw at once that she was a most beautiful girl despite a hideous bullet wound at the side of the head just inside the hairline. Her eyes were closed.

As I was bending down to gather some hair from around the wound in order to make tests for cordite residues, the mortuary attendant moved the girl's body with the result that her head fell back. With my face about two feet from hers I watched in horror as her eyes opened—it was as if she were alive and looking straight at me. My defence mechanism was completely shattered, giving me a moment of sheer horror that I shall never forget.

After the first year of its existence, the forensic laboratory's work was described by the Commissioner of the British South Africa Police as paying 'handsome dividends in supplying evidence of a scientific nature resulting in court convictions in cases which might otherwise have gone by default'. And within two years we were dealing with over 700 crime cases annually, including over twenty murders and involving some 3000 examinations of trace evidence. These beginnings taxed every facet of my varied technical background, and my wartime knowledge of explosives and military matters proved useful. The liaison aspects of forensic work, so often criticized in other countries, were a strong feature from the start in Rhodesia and the quality of the work carried out reaped the benefits accordingly.

In addition to pursuing crime cases with the police, I also had the pleasure of building up the laboratory's facilities and of extending the range of investigations and services offered to the police. One of my prized pieces of equipment in the early days was a powerful quartz spectrograph and associated instruments which were housed in the chemical laboratory. There was also a microscopical laboratory and photographic darkroom. The latter was the province of a loyal helper and versatile photographer Frederica (Ricky) Coates. This was an important feature of our work for much of the scientific presentation of our findings was achieved by the use of photographs in court.

Crime exhibits, such as evidence found at the scenes of murder, hit-and-run incidents, petrol bomb attacks and robberies, were taken in and documented in a reception area presided over by my secretary, who delighted in the apt-sounding name of Peggy Scull. This housekeeping side of the business was also important, for each polythene bag containing samples of soil, glass or less mentionable materials had to be properly recorded. We also built up our own Black Museum of crime exhibits. Some were mildly exotic, like the teddy bear stuffed with pound notes which featured in a famous Rhodesian robbery trial. But most of the exhibits were of the more conventional but violent kind—knives, guns, clubs and the like.

Over the years, the Salisbury forensic laboratory gained a modest reputation for the good-standing of its work. We also developed methods for our own use and some, such as the matching of broken glass fragments, have gained international acceptance.

▼▼▼▼▼▼

From the standpoint of western society and behind the safety curtain of the welfare state it is easy to lose sight of the struggle for life which is still fought in the developing parts of the world. In Central and Southern Africa life is often primitive and conforms to Thomas Hobbes's description as 'solitary, poor, nasty, brutish and short'.

Under primitive conditions, infant mortality, disease, lack of medical care, malnutrition and petty warfare all take their grim toll. The individual who survives to the age of thirty can count himself among the fortunate minority. It is inevitable therefore that his outlook on life should be profoundly affected. In face of the terrifying dangers of nature, and to enhance his slim chance of survival against them, he seeks comfort and reassurance from ritual and superstition. Guidance is sought from the spirits of his immediate ancestors and charms are used for protection.

For the sake of preserving the community, the individual accepts a social discipline which is more rigid and comprehensive than that imposed in modern western societies where the threat of disaster is more remote. An important facet of this social discipline is that a man has a much greater sense of responsibility to his family and immediate nieghbours than his more sophisticated western brother.

But at the same time this sense of responsibility is narrow. It stops at the boundaries of his community because that is where his world finishes—there is no contact with the world at large. Consequently, wider loyalties and concern for mankind in general are alien concepts, being the products of travel and communication. This is certainly part of the reason why it is so difficult to eliminate bribery and corruption from developing countries. The African official who takes a bribe is merely putting his own interests and those of his family before those of the community. He will not necessarily be blamed for this, as many will see it as the most obvious and natural thing to do. It appeals to instincts of self-preservation lying deep within them.

Another manifestation of his narrow responsibility is that most Africans will show a degree of regard for the welfare of their relatives that is excessive by European standards. For instance, the farmer with a good crop and a surplus above and beyond his minimum requirements is expected to hand this over to his less industrious or less fortunate relatives. Some successful African farmers have tempered this custom with a different outlook. They harvest only half of their crops because they have no real wish to labour and bring in surplus crops to support their sponging relatives.

While the majority of Africans are prepared to help their own relatives they are capable of being utterly callous and indifferent to the sufferings of fellow, unrelated Africans. Some of the most appalling crimes and cruelties are committed in this context with the perpetrators showing no remorse afterwards. An example of this cruel and barbarous behaviour occurred in a case I was concerned with in which an African consulted a witch-doctor about his gambling losses. The man wanted to improve his luck and asked for a charm for that purpose. The witch-doctor agreed on condition that his client provided the necessary ingredients, which were the blood of a young girl, part of her ear, and part of her brain mixed with the man's semen. With neither qualm nor quibble the man deliberately assaulted a girl who was a complete stranger, raped her and bludgeoned her to death. He then collected the ingredients as prescribed by his witch-doctor.

The man was caught by the police before he could mix his evil potion and his presence at the scene of the crime was confirmed by footprint impressions. Several footprints made by a shoe with a complicated pattern on the sole were found beside the body of the murdered girl. The unlucky gambler was found to own such a pair of shoes and the pattern of wear matched that of the impressions. In marked contrast to this callous behaviour is the African who commits a serious offence against tribal morality and hangs himself. The inclination to use fencing wire for this purpose often has unfortunate consequences for those who find a body with the head severed as a result of the thin wire ligature.

▼▼▼▼▼▼

Forensic science is not a specialized discipline in its own right like physics or biology. Rather it is a collection of scientific methods adapted for use in the investigation of trace evidence. Its materials are the unthought-of debris and unnoticed contact traces of human activities which indicate involvement with crime. Hence, my varied technical experience in paint research, explosives, military science and microscopy provided a good background for my emergence as a forensic scientist.

The pursuit of crime in Africa takes on a unique dimension because of the collision of cultures. In western society the average wrongdoer knows something of what he is up against in terms of crime detection. Criminal and detective speak a common language and there is a sense of one trying to outwit the other in sophistication of method. But in Africa there is often a different morality at work and, consequently, disagreement about what constitutes a criminal offence. It is witchcraft and bone pointing versus microscope and analysis in a fascinating conflict of ideas.

This is the backdrop to the greatest variety of technical challenges I had ever met. It is also my life in Africa for fourteen years, each crowded with unusual crime cases with surprise and excitement as rewards.

Chapter Two

WITCHCRAFT AND MURDER

TRIBAL magic is still a force to be reckoned with in modern Africa. The ideas of western civilization may appear established but their penetration is not deep enough to unbalance the old customs which leap out to confront dazzling new technology.

The witch-doctor, wily practitioner of tribal magic, rules in many African communities; he takes what he needs from the new culture and grafts on pieces of the old. He is quite capable, for example, of conjuring up a traditional charm to assist an African who wishes to succeed in business administration studies. He exercises considerable power in all matters. Advising community elders, administering justice, treating the sick and banishing evil doing. All these activities may contribute to the successful standing of his village.

Magical thinking is a dynamic force in the life of the tribal African who believes broadly in an animistic or spirit world. Death, disease and ill-fortune are attributed to the workings of this spirit world. But the witch-doctor professes the power to communicate with the spirits and to be able to drive away disease and to induce good fortune by means of charms, potions and fetish. It is not always the Africans only who are the believers. I remember the story of a white farmer who, driven desperate by the sight of his crops wilting and dying for lack of rain, paid the local witch-doctor to conjure up a cloud burst. Perhaps, the farmer lacked true faith or possibly the witch-doctor was incompetent for there was no rain.

There are many kinds of witch-doctor but generally speaking they can be put into two classes according to whether they practise black or white magic. The Black Magician works in the realm of misfortune and death. A man wishing to be rid of an enemy will consult such a witch-doctor, who places a charm in a position where it will do most harm to the victim. It may be buried along a path regularly used by the victim or be hung above the door of his hut. The idea is for the charm to be very near to him although he does not necessarily have to see it. If he does, the sight holds such terror as to reduce a man to a state of apathy and despair. When a man is told that charms have been hidden to bewitch him, he is inevitably overtaken by some disaster.

Charms are not essential to the witch-doctor—he can equally demonstrate his power by calling down a vile and terrifying curse on the head of his intended victim. These curses are most effective when something personal has been taken from the enemy. The more intimate the article, the more effective it is—finger-nail trimmings, hair, underclothes, urine, faeces, for example.

Because of the magical environment in which he lives, the tribal African is anxious never to leave lying around anything which might be used to harm him. Consequently, for his own safety, he tends to relieve himself in streams and rivers so that no witch-doctor can fasten on to his body waste with evil intent.

Unfortunately, this form of protection against black magic encourages the spread of tropical disease, notably bilharzia which affects over 90 per cent of the black African population. Bilharzia is a water-borne disease perpetuated by a flatworm which for part of its life cycle uses a particular variety of water snail as an intermediate host. Adult parasites develop in the snails and emerge in a swimming form. Human infection occurs either through the skin while bathing in infected water or by drinking the water.

Infection causes fever, diarrhoea, bladder disorders and anaemia. There is a general loss of vitality and often a slow death. Eggs of the parasite exit from the body through the bladder or rectum. Consequently the use of streams and rivers to dispose of human waste has the effect of recycling the parasite and passing on the infection. I have often thought that one of the most evil results of black magic is not the immediate effect on the individuals concerned but its secondary effect in spreading debilitating disease.

White magic, on the other hand, is used for constructive ends and to meet social needs. The practice of white magic is to improve the human lot by weaving magical influence over vital forces such as birth, marriage and fertility. The White Magician's control over nature is achieved by incantation, ceremony and mystery rooted in the belief that a desired effect can be achieved by imitation. Thus the ritual kill is designed to assist the hunter.

The practitioners of white magic fall into two groups—the diviners and the herbalists. Diviners are mediums through which the spirit world communicates with man. They determine which spirits have been offended and advise how to appease them. Then there are the herbalists and fortune-tellers famous for predicting the future by throwing the bones. The bones are really pieces of wood carved with mysterious markings. Before throwing them, the witch-doctor goes into a ritual, rubbing, breathing and mumbling over the bones like a crap player about to shoot dice. After he has thrown them he carefully studies the pattern created before making his prognostications.

The herbalist combines magic with healing powers. He carries with him a collection of remedies contained in numerous animal horns which are stoppered with corks like medicine bottles. Only the horns of small animals are believed to assist the healing process. When treating his patient, the witch-doctor keeps his medicine bottles out of sight, mysteriously conjuring them up as if from out of the ground or from the affected part of his patient's body. This is a part of his act, which enraptures patient and audience alike and confirms their faith in the witch-doctor.

A great deal of the witch-doctor's activities are designed to feed that most ancient of human appetites—self-esteem. So long as he can compel his followers' faith in his abilities by sheer magnetism, by sleight of hand or by other trickery, he will retain power and influence. The price of failure is loss of face and diminished status. This is perhaps when the witch-doctor is at his most sinister and dangerous as some of the following incidents demonstrate.

▼▼▼▼▼▼

Trial by ordeal was a common practice in Europe during the Dark Ages having been adopted from pagan rites by the Church. The principle was simple. An accused person was required to plunge his hand into a bowl of boiling water and retrieve a stone from the bottom. Evidence of scalding after three days constituted proof of guilt. Walking on red-hot ploughshares or grasping a piece of red-hot iron in the hand without the flesh being burned were variations on the theme. Such practices were abolished in England in 1219 but the custom prevailed in Africa before colonization. As the story of Matope and the nine suspects illustrates, the tradition dies hard.

I recall the downfall of a witch-doctor in a Malawi village who also attempted a trial by ordeal in a case of bewitchment. A villager by the name of Matthew Selemani was affiicted with painful, suppurating sores on his face. His neighbours were horrified at his condition and, in the absence of any obvious reason for his suffering, decided that he had been bewitched.

Myesi, the local witch-doctor, was called in. He confirmed the villagers' diagnosis and said he would round up a number of suspects and denounce the guilty party at a trial by ordeal. Such is the awe of the witch-doctor that Myesi had no difficulty in gathering together a number of willing suspects. Those designated, while feeling they are innocent, are apprehensive lest an angry spirit might be working through them. It is even thought possible for a man to bewitch himself without realizing it—he might become possessed by an angry spirit urging him to destroy himself. Consequently, it is easy to enrol candidates for trial by ordeal and there is even kudos to be gained from taking part and being declared innocent.

Myesi was a shrewd, seasoned campaigner. He picked fifteen villagers as suspects and added Matthew Selemani, the complainant, to their number. He began the proceedings by gouging short, deep cuts in each of their faces. Then, having rubbed some white powder into the fresh wounds, he made them drink a concoction made from tree bark.

Unfortunately, his magic did not work. Instead of one of the suspects dropping dead in a dramatic demonstration of his guilt, all sixteen were taken violently ill. Twelve were rushed to hospital and four of them died. The survivors were skilfully treated in hospital for poisoning. This was a remarkable feat for all the vomiting and incoherent patients could tell the doctors was that they had taken 'mooti'. This word is lingua franca in Southern Africa meaning both 'tree' and 'medicine'. Consequently, its utterance by the stricken patients offered no help to the doctors in their search for an antidote. Moreover, there is a wide variety of plant poisons in Africa and even today antidotes are not known for all of them.

The experienced witch-doctor should know that the use of plant poisons is a tricky business. The extent to which a plant is poisonous depends on such variants as the weather, locality and its age. And, of course, the dosage must be accurately judged. In conducting a trial by ordeal the witch-doctor relies on two factors; that one of his suspects will be more sensitive than the others to the poison he has selected and that one of them will be so overcome psychologically as events unfold that he will collapse from shock. Myesi was either unlucky or incompetent. He killed four people and the toll could easily have been worse. He was convicted and sent to prison for his crime but worse, from his point of view, was the ignominy of losing face.

The powers of witch-doctors are seemingly endless and while, as in the case of Myesi, somewhat transparent, other incidents are more mystifying. There is a belief that some witch-doctors can render themselves, and others, invisible and are able to travel by supernatural means. A senior police-officer I knew in Rhodesia and whom I would put in the hard-bitten class, told me an unusual travel story.

As a comparatively young inspector stationed at Odzi, a fairly remote bush station, it fell to him to arrest a witch-doctor on a swindling charge. Two Africans had paid out the equivalent of one month's wages for a charm to bring them luck at gambling. Believing firmly in the efficiency of the charm, they had borrowed as much money as they could, added their savings to it and embarked on a weekend's gambling spree. It proved a disaster—they ended up deep in debt, having lost everything including their blankets.

They decided that the charm had been defective and that they had been swindled by the witch-doctor. Their anger overcame their fear of witchcraft and they took the unusual step of making a formal complaint to the police. My police inspector friend took a statement from the couple which they duly signed. All that remained to do was to find the witch-doctor and arrest him. For the first time in his police career my friend thought he had a case which would lead to the conviction of a witch-doctor.

His quarry lived in a village some twenty-five miles distant but at that moment he was apparently staying with some relatives closer to hand. Together with an African sergeant the inspector set off in a Land Rover to make the arrest. They found the witch-doctor without difficulty and returned with him to the police station where he was put in a cell.

The African sergeant was obviously unhappy about having a witch-doctor in his cells. He pointed out that the prisoner had with him an elaborately carved walking stick. This was a stick of office which the sergeant declared was no ordinary stick. It had magical properties not least of which was the power to let its owner fly. He strongly urged the inspector to confiscate the stick.

My friend responded to this idea with laughter and roundly rejected the whole idea. Nonetheless, he felt a little edgy about his prisoner and to make sure there could be no deception, bribery or corruption, he put the only two keys to the cell in his uniform pocket. No more than fifteen minutes later the sergeant appeared with a somewhat smug expression on his face to report that he had checked the cells and as far as he could see their prisoner had escaped. Understandably, the inspector was dumbfounded. He checked the cell himself and to his utter dismay confirmed that it was indeed empty. Putting aside the question of how the witch-doctor had escaped from a locked cell, he reasoned that the man would probably try to return to his home village.

He decided to drive immediately to the village with a constable with the intention of leaving the officer there to re-arrest the escapee when he arrived home through the bush. Imagine his shock, when, having driven to the village at speed in a police Land Rover, he saw the witch-doctor calmly sitting outside his hut tucking into a hearty meal. There was only one road giving vehicular access to the village. This was of dirt construction and, as it had rained heavily the previous night, the inspector believed he would find track marks of a vehicle other than his own which would show how the witch-doctor had travelled home so quickly. But he was disappointed—the only tyre marks were those made by his Land Rover.

The inspector was angry at having been hoodwinked. There was no question of anyone acting as stand-in for the witch-doctor as fingerprints taken when he was first arrested matched those made on his re-arrest. Conceivably, the wily old man could have escaped from the police cell if he had managed to obtain a third key but this hardly seemed likely in view of the precautions taken. Setting the escape apart, there was the puzzle of how he had contrived to travel twenty-five miles in an hour and a quarter on his feet. For he had no transport whatever, apart from his walking stick of course!

In the event, the effort to re-arrest this escape artiste was wasted. After this marvellous demonstration of magical power no one, least of all the original complainants, would dare to give evidence against him in court.

It is difficult to find a rational explanation for these events and, in spite of the old European tradition of witches riding on broomsticks, I cannot believe it really is possible.

The inspector concerned worked with me for two years and he was one of the most competent and able men I have ever met. I am sure his version of the facts was reliable. It is possible that the witch-doctor was one of identical twins who usually have fingerprints which are so similar that the difference can only be detected by an expert who has spent most of his working life classifying fingerprints, so there is the possibility of a mistake in identifying the prints. Obviously a pair of identical twins in the witch-doctor business would have tremendous opportunities for producing spectacular effects. This explanation is basically improbable and to add to the improbability is the fact that in tribal African society twins are regarded as being very unlucky and usually measures are taken to ensure that only one survives.

Another explanation could be that it was some sort of conjuring trick. Considering the marvellous and apparently inexplicable results produced by stage magicians it seems most likely that the explanations lies along these lines; but as to how the trick was worked, I have no idea whatever.

As far as opening the locked cell door and locking it shut again is concerned, there are several possible explanations. One of the keys to the other cells might have fitted the lock in question, or one of the warders might have copied the original key. The warders' fear of the witch-doctor would almost certainly be greater than his respect for authority and, given the chance, he would release such a powerful prisoner.

In prisons generally there is sometimes a remarkable array of talents. I know of one man in Khami prison, one of the main prisons of the country, where a locksmith prisoner merely caught sight of the master key on the Governor's desk. He returned to his cell and broke the handle off an aluminium mug and, using part of a broken hacksaw blade which he had lifted from the workshop, he reproduced the key which opened the doors leading out of the prison. At a suitable moment he unlocked the doors and calmly walked out. Unfortunately for him his planning was not nearly as good as his craftsmanship and about three hundred yards from the prison gate he walked slap into a warder coming on duty. He was back inside within minutes of leaving!

▼▼▼▼▼▼

Witchcraft and murder become related in a continuation of time-honoured practices in these incidents. But modern Africa's political and military difficulties provide a new dimension for the witch-doctor's involvement, often with tragic consequences.

Numbers of Africans receive training in the arts of guerilla warfare in other countries. Despite exposure to months of rigid military discipline and training in the use of modern weaponry and tactics, many of these men return home believing as strongly as ever in the powers of witchcraft.

I became involved in the aftermath of such an incident which began when a group of eight such men crossed into Rhodesia from Zambia. One of these men suggested to his companions that they pay a visit to a famous and well-respected witch-doctor whom he knew in the area. The idea was to seek a charm which would provide invisibility and hence protection against the security forces.

Because of the witch-doctor's eminence it was necessary for the guerrillas to negotiate their request through an intermediary. In Africa, as in the East, lengthy preliminaries are an essential part of the way of life. Inquiries are made as to the health and welfare of the parties concerned, their relatives and mutual acquaintances; the state of the crops and weather conditions are touched on and any topic of local interest. Each inquiry is concluded by hand-clapping. Time is of no consequence while these protocols are being observed.

The preliminaries in this instance went on throughout the day and into the night. After a few hours sleep the parties re-convened to get down to the serious business of negotiations. The guerrillas made an offer for the invisibility charms which they were after. The intermediary passed their proposal to the witch-doctor who countered with a blunt demand for one of the guerrillas' rifles as payment.

These rifles were Chinese copies of the AK47 Russian assault weapon. They are highly prized and the witch-doctor no doubt thought that he was on to a good thing if he could trade his charms for one of these guns. The group were not in a strong position to argue. They had the choice of keeping their weapons and forsaking the protection which they so dearly wanted or they could disarm one of their number and trade his rifle for an assurance that they would become invisible and avoid the security patrols. They knew the witch-doctor had made them an offer they could not refuse.

Solemnly, a rifle was handed over in exchange for the precious charms which consisted of ground roots, leaves and snake bones sewn up in a small piece of brown cloth. Alas, within three weeks, the whole group had been accounted for by the security forces, some were killed, the remainder being captured. That was the end of the story for them but it was only just beginning for the witch-doctor.

The precious rifle, carefully wrapped in a cloth, had been hidden by the witch-doctor in a hollow tree. It was probably only his intention to produce it on special occasions for display to his admirers, and possibly his doubters, in order to re-affirm his status. News of an illegal transaction involving a Russian-type rifle had reached the police who followed up with the usual inquiries. Their investigation was hampered by the customary lack of co-operation where witch-doctors were concerned, with the added difficulty in this case that like everyone else they had to work through the great man's intermediary. The result was that the existence of the rifle was kept secret from the authorities.

All would have been well for the witch-doctor had he not allowed jealousy to pierce his supernatural powers. Although quite elderly, he had recently acquired a fourth wife. Young Esther was a beautiful, vigorous woman and in a very short time became bored with the old man. She decided to enter more romantic spheres by taking as her lover a local lad delighting in the name of Sixpence. Quite simply the old witch-doctor had been cuckolded.

The rules governing African marriage are such that nothing delights a father more than to be blessed with many daughters. While sons are welcome, it is the daughters who bring in the money. When a man chooses the girl he wants to marry he is obliged to pay her father a sum of money known as 'lobola'. If the girl is a virgin, handsome and a good daughter, the lobola can entail payment of a considerable sum of money with several head of cattle thrown in for good measure. The total sum may be the equivalent of what a young man might hope to earn in one or even two years. As this level of payment can involve several years of hardship and saving, it is customary for parents to help out by advancing a loan. They, of course, are only able to do this on account of lobola paid to them for their daughters. In this way, the lobola payments are recycled within the community.

But a young man who has the misfortune to be an only child, or worse, comes from a family of many sons and no daughters, knows that his chances of acquiring a wife are remote. This was Sixpence's predicament—he had six brothers but not a single sister and therefore little hope of marrying. Consequently, when Esther, the bored witch-doctor's wife, offered him love and consolation, he, not surprisingly, responded to the temptation.

In the way of these things, this illicit liaison quickly reached the ears of the witch-doctor. Now a cuckolded husband is one thing but a witch-doctor so affected is really another. The furious husband raged and ranted and brought down curses on the heads of Esther and Sixpence. But all his antics proved ineffective as the young lovers continued to defy him.

With his pride severely injured and desperate to defend his waning reputation, the witch-doctor thought of the rifle which he had wheedled out of the guerrillas and hidden away. Thought turned to action and he retrieved the weapon from the hollow tree and loaded it in readiness to follow Esther to her lover's tryst. Unaware that she was being followed, the girl led her husband to her assignation with Sixpence. The witch-doctor surprised the couple and without hesitation shot them dead, firing several times into the boy's head and the girl's body.

News of the shooting and its circumstances quickly reached the police. Far from enhancing his reputation, the witch-doctor's actions earned him only the contempt of those he sought to impress. He had failed to use his alleged powers to solve his problems and instead had to resort to alien technology. Any lingering respect he may have commanded now completely vanished.

Police investigations turned up overwhelming evidence against the witch-doctor. The most damning of which was the matching ballistics of the bullets removed from the murdered couple's bodies with the rifle still in his possession. Esther's family proved to be helpful witnesses and the murderer was tried and convicted for his crimes.

The once powerful witch-doctor was brought low by the most human of passions—jealousy and loss of face. Once he had resorted to such commonplace solutions as the use of firearms he forfeited his magic and laid a trail for his detection. I suppose the moral is that the good witch-doctor really believes in himself!

▼▼▼▼▼▼

The African continent is made up of a tilted tableland with the higher edge running some two or three hundred miles inland from the east coast. In Rhodesia, part of this region is known as Inyanga which means 'Place of the witch-doctors'. The mountains, green hills and valleys are reminiscent of England's Lake District although on a somewhat grander scale. There are those who believe that the source of the 'Gold of Ophir', mentioned in the Bible, was located in Inyanga. Certainly, there are many traces of ancient gold workings in this part of Africa.

Inyanga is noted for its association with the practice of witchcraft and the existence of weird superstitions. An air of mystery attaches to the isolated communities of this region and some of the worst murders with magical overtones have been committed there. One of these involved a forensic investigation by my laboratory and I vividly remember the rather unusual exhibits of the case.

Late one Saturday night in the early 'sixties on a farm in one of Inyanga's fertile valleys, Elias, the foreman, was awakened by loud knocking on the door of his hut. Reluctantly, he left his bed to see who this late caller was. Standing smiling on the doorstep was Mynhezi, one of the herdsmen employed on the farm. He was holding a parcel wrapped in newspaper. He handed this to Elias explaining that it contained a gift of meat which he had cut from a dead Klipspringer buck which he had found. Elias, who was nursing a hangover from a night's heavy drinking, showed little sign of appreciation for the gift. He thanked Mynhezi rather ungraciously and put the parcel on the floor of his hut. He then returned to his bed.

The following morning, still feeling a little under the weather, Elias picked up the parcel and pulled out a piece of liver which he gave to his wife to cook for breakfast. While he was waiting, he sorted through the remaining contents of the parcel, reeling back in horror when he found two human fingers and an ear. Despite the shock of his discovery and his fragile state of health, Elias had sufficient presence of mind to rush off and inform his employer who called the police.

The herdsman was quickly found and questioned. The discovery of a virtual chamber of horrors at his home was all that was required to ensure that he was locked up. Even the police were shocked at what they found. The main room of Mynhezi's house was festooned with strips of human flesh rather like macabre Christmas decorations. In his bedroom were a dried human heart and a set of male genital organs while a number of assorted human vertebrae and long bones were found buried outside the house. But the most gruesome discovery was made further away from the house hidden in a small outcrop of rocks. Here was unearthed a complete human skin, all in one piece including the head. There was a hole in the skin of the forehead through which, it was later proved, the brains had been extracted. This grisly cache of human remains also included some lengths of human intestines.

The strips of flesh in Mynhezi's house had been salted and hung up to dry—he was apparently preparing 'biltong', African-style dried meat. It was technically a simple matter to prove that these strips were human rather than animal flesh using the precipitin test. There is structurally little difference between human and animal flesh so that blood tests are virtually the only way of telling them apart. The precipitin test is based on the fact that the blood of each animal species is unique as regards the properties of its serum proteins. A highly sensitive anti-sera prepared from rabbits is used in the test. This turns cloudy when it touches human blood.

With terrifying confidence, not to say callousness, Mynhezi owned up to the revolting crime he had committed and related the whole story to the police. He admitted deciding to kill a fellow-herdsman, a man called Tobias, in order to make charms from various parts of his body and to turn the remaining meat into biltong which he proposed to sell as butchers' meat. His plan was to wait until after sundown when darkness would draw a veil over his evil intentions. The day before the murder he deliberately broke a fence post on the farm's cattle kraal with an axe. This premeditated act gave him the excuse he wanted to trap his victim. The following day as the two young herdsmen were finishing work in the twilight and about to set off home, Mynhezi pointed out the broken post. Tobias, a conscientious worker, agreed that it was their duty to stay and repair the damage. By the time they had finished darkness had fallen.

As they were wending their way home, Mynhezi lashed out at Tobias with his knobkerry knocking him to the ground. He stunned him with further blows to the head and dragged his body some thirty yards from the road where he calmly cut his throat and proceeded to skin the body. He also dissected the corpse, hiding or burying organs and bones which he did not immediately want. What was left of the still warm remains of his former workmate he took home. This task probably necessitated several trips.

It was then that the murderer began to make mistakes. While cutting the flesh into strips for biltong he was overtaken by feelings of generosity and decided to make a gift of some of the meat to his foreman. He busily made two butchered heaps, one consisting of odds and ends such as ears, fingers and genitalia which he could use later as ingredients for magical charms, and another of titbits for Elias. Before he could finish this work his candle died and he was obliged to complete his gruesome butchery by the feeble light of a smouldering fire. Probably tired by his exertions, he carelessly threw an ear and a couple of fingers onto the pile destined for Elias.

An earlier mistake had been the deliberate chopping down of the kraal fence post. Mynhezi had been seen wielding his axe and a reliable witness came forward to say so. Examination of the post showed that it had been almost completely cut through. That Mynhezi's axe had been used for this purpose was put beyond reasonable doubt when it was proved that the tool marks on the wooden fence post matched indentations in the axe's cutting edge.

The police were unable to obtain an admission from Mynhezi that he was in any way involved with witchcraft although he admitted everything else in connection with the murder. He maintained silence on this question despite the grim evidence of the dried-up organs found in his home. It can be safely assumed that these had been collected in order to concoct a charm for protection or good fortune, probably on the instructions of a witch-doctor.

There is no agreement among the practitioners of witchcraft as to which parts of the body make the most effective charms. No doubt this is a vital part of the craft's mystery. Murder victims are occasionally found with various organs and appendages missing from their bodies but what is removed varies from case to case. When this occurs in southern Africa it is generally believed that the victims have fallen prey to the procurers of organs for the purpose of witchcraft. Of course it is not murder victims in this part of the world alone whose bodies are so desecrated. Two of Jack the Ripper's victims in London in 1888 had organs removed and witchcraft was among the motives imputed to the murderer!

As a rule I can say that I am not particularly concerned about the outcome of criminal trials in cases that I have been involved in. My job was to present the facts as I found them and leave it to the workings of the courts to pronounce judgment. In the case of Mynhezi, though, I confess that the eventual guilty verdict caused me no anguish. A defence plea of insanity was put up on his behalf but the court did not feel moved by it. Mynhezi was convicted of murder and received the death sentence.

Apart from the terrible nature of the crime itself, its implications were so grim. Interestingly enough, although Mynhezi had worked in extremely poor light he had made a very competent job of dissecting the body. For example, the bones of the hands and feet, the metacarpals and metatarsals, had been separated with particular skill, suggesting the possibility of previous practice.

▼▼▼▼▼▼

Some elderly people seem to have a mystique all of their own. In Africa, if this aura of age has slightly sinister connotations, accusations of witchcraft are never far away.

African elderly folk are generally treated with great respect and deference because it is believed that the spirits of a person's immediate ancestors play a large part in his life. Consequently, the not-so-old tend to keep sight of the fact that their elderly relatives are soon to become powerful spirits. Nevertheless, when a witch-hunt is in progress it is the old and infirm who frequently are singled out as suspects, no doubt because of their physical vulnerability. This also happens because it is thought that an old person convicted as a witch forfeits power in the next world. Thus, stripped of power in the spirit world, an old person poses no threat. It can be seen that this kind of logic provides a welcome loophole for those wishing to shed responsibility for looking after an aged relative.

Taken to extremes this type of thinking can lead to murder.

Large anthills are a common sight in Rhodesia and are large cones of earth up to ten feet in height and thirty feet in diameter. Many areas are covered in these anthills with a distance of 100 or 200 yards between them. An animal known as an ant bear lives on the ants (or more correctly, termites) and digs holes about fifteen inches in diameter and up to six feet in depth in order to feed on the insects, so most of the anthills have several ant-bear holes in them.

Near a village about twelve miles from Hartley in the Rhodesian Midland Province an anthill was found with eleven ant-bear holes in it and each hole was found to contain the corpse of an old person who had been strangled. In the face of complete non co-operation of the local villagers it was not possible to identify the bodies and no prosecution resulted, but the investigating officers were convinced that it was a case where old people had been accused of witchcraft and then quietly disposed of.

In 1965 I came across a case of matricide which resulted in tribal cunning being outwitted by forensic botany. Most of the African-held land is under the control of the local chiefs, who allocate available land to particular individual farmers. A man named Fiyu was one of these farmers; he lived with his wife and their four children with his mother completing the family unit. This happy domestic arrangement suddenly broke up when Fiyu accused his mother of casting spells over one of his children. The poor old woman was partially blind and only able to walk short distances with the aid of a stick.

Following this accusation Fiyu's mother disappeared. Eventually rumours reached the police of sinister circumstances surrounding the missing woman. The chief informer was one of Fiyu's own children who, with an adult witness, reported seeing Fiyu leading his aged mother into the bush near the village. They had not seen the old lady since. When questioned, Fiyu hesitatingly told a story of being worried one evening when his mother failed to appear at supper-time. He went off in search of her and to his horror found her hanging from a tree near the village. Shocked and very frightened, he said he took the body down and placed it in a river close by—he was afraid the authorities would not believe that he had accidently found the body.

Fiyu displayed unusual eagerness to co-operate with the police and showed investigating officers the exact spot where he claimed to have discovered the body. He pointed out a very tall tree whose lowest branches were some fifteen feet above the ground. It was difficult to imagine that even the most agile old lady could have climbed such a tree in order to hang herself. With her poor eyesight and lack of mobility, Fiyu's mother hardly qualified for such a feat.

Moreover, the branch from which he said he had found his mother hanging was covered on its upper surfaces with lichen which showed no sign at all of having been disturbed. A rope fixed to the branch and supporting the weight of a body would certainly have left its mark. To counter this line of inquiry it was suggested that the lichen would have grown sufficiently to cover up any tell-tale marks. I was able to dismiss this idea by pointing out that lichen grows extremely slowly.

Despite a thorough search no body was found, but Fiyu maintained his story about panicking and putting the corpse into the river. A further search was therefore made several weeks later when the river had largely dried up, but again without results. The investigation was dropped only to be re-opened dramatically six months later when a skeleton was found in the bush several miles from Fiyu's village. It was a female skeleton identified as Fiyu's mother by remnants of clothing and by a string of beads of the type which African women commonly wear around the waist next to the skin. Three pieces of mopani tree bark were also found near the neck of the skeleton. This was an important discovery for mopani bark is a type that is often used as a rope. Were these pieces of bark the remains of a noose?

I took the bark back to the laboratory to consider the question of whether the three pieces had been formed into a loop with a knot. The fact that mopani bark is made up of five layers proved to be of great assistance. Microscopical examination showed that, at each break, five of these layers had been fractured and we were able to match and fit each of the layers together. All the ten breaks matched equally well. Clearly, the three pieces of bark had originally been one length measuring twenty-two inches overall.

Owing to its layered structure this type of bark frays badly when twisted. While the longest of the three pieces had not frayed, the two shorter lengths had chaffed badly. The long piece measured eleven inches, as did the two short pieces when put end-to-end. This seemed to support the theory that a loop had been put around the woman's neck, with the slack then being tightened by twisting the rope and resulting in death by strangulation. The finger of suspicion thus strongly pointed at Fiyu and, of course, the tree did not feature in the incident at all except in his fictional account.

Although the only exhibits found were an undamaged skeleton, the remains of clothing and three pieces of bark rope, it was possible to produce evidence strongly suggesting murder. At the magistrates court hearing, the two witnesses gave evidence that Fiyu had admitted to them that he had strangled his mother and the evidence of the bark clearly supported this statement. During the inevitable delay before the High Court hearing the witnesses retracted their story and the case against Fiyu collapsed and he never went before a judge. What made the witnesses go back on their original story never came to light. They might have been lying in the first place but it is more likely that some sort of pressure was brought to bear. In the intensely conservative African tribal life, family influence and fear of witchcraft are very great and, while it is not possible to say what actually happened, there is no doubt that witnesses are much more liable to be influenced than in a more sophisticated community.

The premature disposal of old people is more common in Africa than is realized and my case files included a number of such occurrences. One particular incident sticks in mind because of its similarity with a well-known English murder which took place at Bath in 1933. Reginald Ivor Hinks made several attempts to kill his father-in-law, eventually gassing the old man and arranging his death to look like suicide. In my story, Dyson, an ambitious young African, found his style too cramped by having to look after Isaac, his enfeebled old father who lived with him.

Like Hinks, Dyson resolved to get rid of the old man. His first attempt involved pushing his father in front of a bus, but the driver reacted with commendable skill and managed to swerve and avoid knocking him down. Undeterred, Dyson tried another ploy. This time he pushed his father over a bridge into a river in flood. Incredibly, old Isaac survived once again and struggled to the safety of the river bank. Perhaps relenting a little at his father's seeming indestructibility, Dyson packed the old man off to stay with some relatives. They quickly tired of their new charge, however, and in due course, Isaac was shunted back to live with his son.

Shortly after his return Isaac was admitted to hospital suffering from severe burns. His son said that the old man was lighting a cigarette at a wood stove when his clothing caught fire. He died ten days later from his injuries and thus his persecution was ended although Dyson's explanation did not readily account for the severity of the burns. The bereaved son now embarked on a ruthless plan to draw any suspicion away from himself. He found out that another elderly man had died in that hospital on the same day as his father. Cunningly, he persuaded this man's relatives to accept money in return for which they would claim Isaac as their dead relative. The way was thus clear for Dyson to identify the other, unmarked body, as his father's.

Unfortunately for him, because of the mysterious circumstances of his father's death, the hospital authorities decided to carry out a post-mortem. Imagine the pathologist's astonishment when he could find not so much as a single mark on a body supposed to have been badly burned. Slowly, the sequence of events was unravelled and Isaac's body was eventually exhumed.

Traces of paraffin were found in what remained of the dead man's clothing. By a stroke of good luck these had not been destroyed after his death and the shape of the burns on the jacket indicated that it had been splashed with paraffin and then set alight. My suspicions were heightened when I examined the corpse's beard—the hairs under the chin were singed but those on the sides of the chin and cheeks were untouched. If the old man had indeed been lighting a cigarette over a wood stove when his clothes caught fire, one would have expected his beard to have been singed more evenly.

The forensic evidence suggested it was more likely that paraffin had been poured over the old man while he was lying down and that he had been set alight while in that position. Later it was learned that, when admitted to hospital, Isaac had told a nurse that his sons' account of the incident was untrue. He claimed that Dyson deliberately poured paraffin over him and set light to his clothes.

The nurse, for some inexplicable reason, failed to notify the authorities of this conversation. As it happened, the statement was not admissible as evidence in a court of law anyway. Courts will only accept as evidence the declaration of a dying man if he knows at the time of making it that he is dying. Old Isaac's story did not qualify as evidence, for when he first entered hospital he was not expected to die.

Consequently, with a combination of mere circumstantial and inadmissible evidence connecting him with his father's death, the worthless Dyson was convicted only of fiddling the funeral arrangements and got away with six month's imprisonment. Unlike Reginald Hinks, who met his end on the gallows, Dyson escaped the worst of temporal punishments. But who can tell how old Isaac's spirit eventually avenged itself?

▼▼▼▼▼▼

Witchcraft remains a powerful influence in the thought and life of Africa. While it achieves some good things, even some remarkable cures in the psychiatric field, it must also be held accountable for many retrograde practices. It is generally held that most witch-doctor's remedies and procedures have no effect at all and, while a few do some good, many cause real harm. I referred earlier to bilharzia and the manner in which it is spread through fear of magic. Regrettably, it is also true that witch-doctors exacerbate that other scourge of Africa, trachoma. This is the world's greatest single cause of loss of eyesight, affecting some 400 million sufferers in tropical and sub-tropical countries. It is a severe and chronic form of conjunctivitis and is one of the oldest known eye diseases. It is difficult to cure and leads to partial blindness due to impairment of the cornea. I have seen a number of children blinded for life as a result of witch-doctors treating them for this eye disease.

Witch-doctors are probably also largely responsible for the African's terror of hospitals. In earlier days, after the dubious ministrations of their witch-doctors, patients found themselves in hospital, frequently more dead than alive and beyond the reach of any treatment save miracles. As a result, a hospital came to be regarded as a place to die and, no matter how ill, many Africans would simply refuse to be sent to hospital.

I encountered this attitude with dramatic force a few weeks after I first arrived in Rhodesia. Ignorant about the relationships between old customs and new ideas, I witnessed the phenomenon of a man literally frightened to death. A man in a gang of labourers working on my farm was involved in an accident when the calf of his leg was badly gashed by an axe. It was hardly a dangerous injury, but it certainly needed some stitches.

I pointed out the dangers of infection which would result from failure to treat the wound properly not to mention the necessity of stitching it up. Confident that I knew what was best. I thrust the injured workman into my car and drove him to the nearest hospital where he was duly admitted.

One week later I learned with incredulity that he had died from 'unknown causes'. Doctors with whom I discussed the incident spoke from a wide knowledge of similar cases although this did not lessen my feelings of guilt and sorrow. In the years that followed I had to deal with many such situations but never again did I insist on taking anyone to hospital against his will. It was bad enough that the witch-doctors' hold on people's minds was strong enough to kill them without the intervention of well-meaning outsiders.

The temptation to play the magician and overthrow the witch-doctor is ever present, especially when his influence is brought to one's own doorstep. One day, our cook, Gatsi, arrived home distraught and trembling, clutching a bracelet of glass beads in his hand. He told me that he had found the bracelet—obviously a death charm—hanging on the door of his house.

Gatsi's fear was almost tangible and I knew it was pointless trying to reason him out of it or to try to find out why he thought someone was wanting to get rid of him. As it happened I had been carrying out some experiments using magnesium ribbon. Suddenly, I had an idea. I told Gatsi that I was a very good magician myself and that if he would trust me I should be able to help him. I suggested he carried on his normal duties until nightfall that evening.

When it was dark I wrapped the bracelet in magnesium ribbon, carefully put it in my pocket and went off to fetch Gatsi at his house. There, with suitable ceremony and solemnity, I placed the magnesium-covered bracelet on the floor and set fire to it. For added effect I recited excerpts from Coleridge's *The Ancient Mariner*, hoping that it sounded impressive. As I spoke, the intense white heat of the burning magnesium reduced the glass beads of the bracelet to powder—they had effectively disappeared.

To rid Gatsi of any lingering doubts about the now defunct death charm, I gave him a piece of soap which I had treated with a green dye. I told him to go to a particular waterfall at daybreak and when the sun appeared over the horizon to wash himself carefully with the magic soap. If he turned green that would be a sure sign that the magic had worked and that the death charm no longer had the power to harm him.

Gatsi experienced no further trouble—my magic had outwitted that of the witch-doctor. What I had not reckoned with was the speed at which news of this sort travelled. My fame spread abroad and in no time at all I was being asked to repeat the trick. Spurred on by Gatsi's unbounded joy and relief at having the death curse removed, I repeated the performance on several other occasions, all with complete success.

One of the prerequisites of good magic is that there must always be a plentiful supply of ingredients. For the African witch-doctor, this poses no problem but in my case the time came when my stock of magnesium ribbon ran out and fresh supplies were difficult to obtain. I therefore had to refuse to perform the ceremony and I turned away a man who in desperation offered me two month's wages to help him. Of course I had never accepted payment of any kind and I regretted not being able to help this man who seemed so fearful. My misery in this case was completed two months later when I learned that he had died.

This was another instance of death by frightening and I suppose another triumph for witchcraft. For my part I had learned the perils of setting up in opposition.

There is some evidence that death from fear is due to an instinct deeply rooted in some animals. Hares, mice and wild birds die from rough handling and humans have died from fright while being given injections. In a series of experiments performed at the Johns Hopkins Medical School in Baltimore, rats were subjected to stress by forcing them to swim in narrow-mouthed jars from which there was no possibility of escape. Domestic white rats survived for days while freshly captured wild brown rats died in a matter of minutes. If the brown rats were removed from the water just before they died they recovered quickly and having learned in this way that the situation was not entirely hopeless they swam for much longer when returned to the jar. It seems that humans under a death curse behave in the same way and die of hopelessness, but if any man can survive the ordeal he is in a much better position to avoid becoming the victim of a second attempt.

Perhaps my activities in this field produced long-term benefits for my clients!

Chapter Three
SEX AND MURDER

SEX murders always make large headlines. Mollie commented on this phenomenon at breakfast one morning following my return from Bulawayo where I had been called to a particularly unpleasant murder which had been committed on a train travelling to Wankie.

On arrival at Bulawayo the overnight train from Wankie was checked through by the conductor as part of his normal routine. To his horror he found the body of a young woman in one of the sleeping compartments—she had been savagely beaten in what looked like a sexual murder. The police were called immediately and it was soon established that the girl had been strangled and raped. A desperate struggle had evidently taken place as the girl, a European nurse, tried vainly to fend off her assailant as the train rushed through the night.

The conductor told police that he remembered seeing a man who occupied the adjoining compartment talking to the girl. The man was known by name to the conductor for he was a young, married railway trainee. Within an hour of the train pulling into Bulawayo station police officers were knocking on the door of the young man's house. They had to knock loud and long for their suspect was sound asleep. It seemed incredible to think that anyone could have committed such a dreadful act as that which had occurred on the train and then gone home and, completely undisturbed, fallen asleep so quickly.

In answer to questions the man admitted talking to the girl and said that she had invited him into her compartment. After some petting she resisted his further advances and he put his hand over her mouth to stop her shouting—but he denied killing her. The medical report confirmed that the girl had been raped, an act which had been carried out on her unconscious, or dead, body. The girl had been returning from leave to resume her nursing duties in Bulawayo. She was known as a deeply religious person and was highly regarded for her moral behaviour by all who were acquainted with her. It seemed, therefore, extremely unlikely that she would have indulged in promiscuous sexual relations.

Smear marks found on the outside of the train indicated that someone had climbed out of the window in the compartment occupied by the suspect and entered the victim's compartment, also by the window. The girl's injuries included facial bruises and the clear imprint of a woollen sock could be seen near the ear. This indicated a savage kick by a stockinged foot, a theory which was borne out by a bruise on the opposite side of the face caused by the head striking against a hard object.

The head hair which grows just in front of a woman's ears is characteristically fine hair and is usually uncut with tapered ends. Three such hairs were found on the toe of one of the woollen socks worn by the suspect on the night of the murder. These hairs matched for type, colour, thickness and scale pattern the head hair of the victim. This was vital evidence linking suspect and victim. Evidence of the struggle which had taken place was found under the girl's finger-nails in the form of numerous white cotton fibres. These indicated that she had clawed frantically at the sheets on her bunk and was consistent with her having been surprised while she lay asleep.

The young railway trainee was sent for trial, and the savagery of the crime combined with compelling evidence persuaded the jury of his guilt. He was convicted of murder and sentence of death was duly carried out.

In Africa, as elsewhere, sexual crimes occupy a prominent place in the catalogue of violence which the forensic scientist has to deal with. Rape, adultery, prostitution, venereal disease, abortion and simple jealousy provide the ingredients for many sexually motivated crimes. Add the distinctive seasoning of tribal morality and you are left with a potent mixture.

▼▼▼▼▼▼

The European attitude to rape is rather different from that of the tribal African whose main considerations are financial and material. To start with the traditional African attitude to marriage is vastly different. An African's wife costs her husband the equivalent of one or even two years' wages; so she represents a considerable investment.

Frequently the girl is not consulted as to whom she will marry and is expected to respond passively to the arrangements made for her by her parents. Usually, though, boy meets girl in the normal sequence of events and the boy uses an intermediary to approach the girl's father to plead his case. At this stage the girl's father can veto the whole thing. As discussions have been conducted through the intermediary, there is no direct insult to the boy. This practice is in keeping with the strict conventions which govern behaviour in African tribal life. Moreover, it is part of the high standard of courtesy and good manners to which the tribal African subscribes. He normally behaves with a politeness and urbanity which is an example to his European contemporaries.

If the girl's father agrees to open negotiations in earnest, the boy's father takes over from the intermediary. The serious business of deciding the details of how much cash is to be paid, how many cattle are to change hands, what is to be paid in cash or kind to the girl's mother and a host of other matters is then begun. These negotiations can go on for days or even weeks. Naturally, the prospective bride's father drives as hard a bargain as he can for his own sake, since he is the main recipient, but also for his daughter's benefit as she derives status and personal satisfaction from a higher than average settlement.

Wives are a good investment and, in addition to normal household duties, may be expected to work the land and carry burdens. It is a common sight for an African man to walk along carrying nothing but his own weight while his wife staggers behind carrying an enormous burden on her head as well as managing an infant strapped to her back. Husbands hope too that their wives will bear female children who in due course will bring in handsome marriage settlements.

As I mentioned in the previous chapter, this payment for brides is known as 'lobola'. Many Europeans, and Africans too, regard it as a stabilizing influence in African society as it tends to preserve marriage and protect the children. The husband, having invested a large amount of money in his wife, does his best to protect his investment and to avoid the necessity of re-investment. The father-in-law also wishes the marriage to hold up since if his daughter runs home to mother he is expected to make a refund. Understandably, therefore, a wife is not encouraged to leave her husband.

Polygamy is accepted and this contributes to the low status of women. As decent wives are so expensive only the richer African can afford several, but the economic temptation, to mention no other, is ever present. Curiously enough, an African woman who marries without being paid for often feels degraded and to the older generation she is no better than a prostitute. As urbanized Africans are shaking loose from the bonds of tribal morality, often without adopting any other standards, the lobola system is seen in a good light despite its tendency to lower the status of women. There is a small swing to European attitudes among town-dwelling Africans but the old ideas are still strong, especially in the country districts. Lobola will probably be paid for many generations to come, but one of its side effects is an appallingly high proportion of illegitimate children in African townships.

An African has the choice of being married under tribal law or according to European custom. One of the consequences of being married under tribal law is that adultery becomes a criminal offence entitling the injured party to redress through the tribal courts. On the other hand, tribal law permits easy and inexpensive divorce.

There is usually little or no recognizable wedding ceremony when a tribal marriage takes place but a series of customs are observed. It is quite common for half the lobola to be paid when the couple start living together, the remaining half being paid on the birth of the first child. If the woman fails to produce a child she can be returned to her family and the amount of lobola already paid is refunded. Alternatively, the wife's sister may be offered as a substitute.

If a wife is returned to her parents her life becomes unenviable. She is despised and frequently ill-treated. In despair, these rejected wives often end up as prostitutes.

▼▼▼▼▼▼

African prostitutes are quite often fierce and rather vindictive ladies. One one occasion during my tobacco farming days one of my workmen came to me after a weekend beer-drinking session with a wound over his left eye. It was an unusual-looking wound, a piece having been gouged out of the forehead together with part of the eyebrow, leaving the bone of the skull exposed at the base of the hole. As I was unable to decide how the wound had been inflicted I questioned the sufferer, who proved less than forthcoming with an answer.

Reluctantly, he related the sorry aftermath of his liaison with a lady of doubtful character. He had enjoyed her favours for an agreed price of four shillings. When the time came to pay up he offered the woman only three shillings and sixpence. She decided she was being insulted and furiously lashed out at her client. In the ensuing altercation she latched on to him and bit out a piece over his left eye. The wounded man's companions thought that he had really got what he deserved for trying to cheat the prostitute. But their ribald laughter turned to horror when, after the combatants were separated, the woman sat on the ground and calmly chewed the piece of flesh and swallowed it.

The wound healed well in due course but the left eyebrow was permanently divided, giving its owner a perpetually surprised expression. No doubt the sight of this in the mirror served as an ever-present reminder of his folly not to say meanness. It is quite common for prostitutes to get their teeth into their customers. A particularly vulnerable piece of the anatomy is the lip. This is certainly unfortunate for the injured party because the features are permanently marred by an obvious scar. Moreover, the bitten lip is viewed as a disgrace in African society as such a scar is regarded as the badge of the rapist.

Understandably, nothing annoys the world's oldest profession more than the inability or unwillingness of the customer to pay up. African prostitutes are no exception and have been known to take knives to defaulting customers. I was called to a lonely spot near the little town of Hartley early one chilly May morning where a dead man had been found in a parked car. He had sustained thirty-five stab wounds, many of them on his face and others on his arms and body.

I quickly established from the nature of the wounds that they had been inflicted with an ordinary short-bladed penknife. A wound penetrating the left eye suggsted that the man had been blinded early on in the assault making subsequent self-defence difficult. It was quite clear that a tremendous struggle had taken place as there were stab marks on the front seats of the car and slashes in the roof-lining.

The man was without his trousers and the evidence of the scene suggested that he had clearly been consorting with a woman. Independent evidence indicated that the man may not have been carrying any cash with him and a cheque book and pen lying on the floor of the car suggested a non-cash payment. Assuming that his consort was indeed a prostitute, the crime scene had all the makings of a violent row over money.

The dead man's trousers were not just missing from his body, they were absent altogether. It was established that the trousers matched the jacket he was still wearing and it was assumed that the prostitute might have taken the garment by way of payment. Painstaking inquiries by CID officers at laundries and dry cleaners in the locale eventually succeeded in locating the missing garment. After this discovery it was an easy matter for the police to sit back and wait for the trousers to be collected.

In due course a prostitute called at the dry cleaners for the trousers and she was promptly arrested. Two witnesses reported seeing her in the company of the dead man. What really clinched her guilt was the penknife still in her possession. This was undoubtedly the murder weapon as traces of blood, skin and hair found on it matched those of the murdered man. The prostitute's foolish action in taking the man's trousers had led to her conviction and a sentence of ten years imprisonment.

▼▼▼▼▼▼

While they may be passive in their domestic role, African women have some highly effective ways of dealing with lusting, cheating males. I came across one such method during the investigation of two cases, one of murder and one of attempted rape.

A young man, Rabson, and his girl friend were seen drinking in a beerhall on a warm muggy October evening in the African township of Sinoia. They appeared to be engaged in a mild quarrel and were seen leaving together.

The following morning the girl's body was found lying near a path leading from the beerhall. She had been stabbed to death. There were ample signs that a struggle had taken place—her clothing was in disarray and her blood-stained handbag was found some twelve yards from the body. The girl had sustained two stab wounds in the chest, one by the second button of her coat and another two inches to the right.

The dead girl's boy friend, Rabson, was quickly rounded-up and categorically denied any knowledge of the killing. His denial was soon put in another light when he was searched and a knife bearing traces of blood was found in his pocket. The amount of blood was sufficient to establish that it was group 'A' human blood. What proved more revealing was a collection of small fibres found on the knife blade.

Fibres from textile materials are one of the forms of trace evidence most commonly encountered by the forensic scientist. Since most people, even in hot climates, wear clothing of one sort or another, there is inevitably some transfer of individual fibres in nearly every crime incident. Our clothes are wearing out all the time and we go through life leaving a trail of fibres behind us, most of which are identifiable. The transfer may be by contact between the participants —criminal and victim—or between the participants and the environment, both indoors and outdoors. Fibres may be rubbed off during a struggle, transferred on footwear or simply rubbed off by coming into contact with a piece of furniture or a moving vehicle. As carpets, upholstery, house-furnishings and many ordinary domestic articles such as string and sacking are made from threads or textiles, the forensic investigator at a crime scene is often presented with a rich harvest.

Many different kinds of fibres are used in textile manufacture, both natural, such as cotton, wool and silk; and man-made, such as nylon and Terylene. These may come from animal or vegetable sources or be entirely synthetic. Most of these fibres have individual characteristics which may be identified under a microscope. Single fibres can be characterized by their material and colour but, where fragments of material are available, many other features such as pattern, weave, and colours of warp and weft may be considered.

In the case of the stabbed girl I was able to examine her coat in the laboratory. It was made of brown wool with a lining material which had a brown rayon weft (the thread running across the length of the cloth) and a grey cotton warp (the thread running parallel to the length of the cloth). In between the inner and outer edges of the coat was some stiffened blue cotton material which had been used to strengthen the sewing of the buttons. At this point I felt rising excitement for here was some highly identifiable material. The first thrust of the assailant's knife had penetrated the brown wool of the coat and the stiffened blue cotton while the second blow had gone through the brown rayon and grey cotton lining. The knife had therefore cut through four types of fibre.

Detailed examination of the fibres discovered on the blood-stained knife showed that all four types of fibre were present. Moreover, they matched those of the coat for colour and thickness. The knife also bore traces of human blood of Group A which is characteristic of about 1 in 25 of the population. The knife was without doubt the weapon which had been used to stab the girl and its blade had one more clue to offer. It had cut through the girl's ribs leaving striation lines (marks made by small imperfections in the steel of the cutting edge) on the bone which were matched to lines on experimental cuts made with the knife.

Strangely enough, the more customary type of identification made through fingerprint examination proved inconclusive in this case. A fingerprint found in the blood-staining of the handbag belonged neither to the dead girl nor to her suspected assailant. This impression was never identified and most probably belonged to some passer-by who handled the bag before the body was found.

The total evidence was strong enough to obtain a conviction for murder in spite of the continuing denials on the part of the accused man. Before passing sentence, the judge, according to custom, asked the prisoner if he had anything to say why sentence should not be passed upon him. This opportunity is afforded a convicted person not so that fresh evidence may be produced but simply to make possible a plea in mitigation. To the utter amazement of the court, the prisoner stood up and declared that while making love to the girl she had gripped his testicles so fiercely that in his agony he drew out his knife and stabbed her.

While he was conceivably impressed by the ingenunity of this plea, the judge would not admit the statement as evidence. Accordingly, he proceeded to pass sentence of death. Subsequently, the appeal court overruled this decision, taking the view that the statement should have been considered. The trial was therefore re-opened to admit Rabson's final piece of evidence. He was still found guilty of murder but experienced the rare distinction of being sentenced twice in the same court for the same crime.

During the time which elapsed before the hearing of the appeal another case involving this gripping technique occurred. A respectable African girl had been walking home after work one evening when she was accosted by a young man who suggested a romp in the long grass. The girl refused in no uncertain way but the man, bent on his lust and refusing to accept no for an answer, hit her on the head with a piece of wood. He dragged her unconscious body into the surrounding bush and was about to commit rape when the girl revived.

With great presence of mind, and to the complete surprise of her assailant, the girl gripped his testicles in a manner commonly described in army barrack-rooms but seldom used in practice. According to her subsequent account she squeezed, pulled and twisted as hard as she could until the would-be rapist, howling in agony, passed out. Sensibly, the girl reported the incident to the police and she returned to the scene with two officers. By this time her assailant had fled but a visit to a nearby hostel for single men quickly produced the wanted man.

Trace evidence provided by clothing fibres and hair played an important part in confirming the girl's story. The man she identified at the hostel was wearing a shirt with one torn sleeve. A small piece of cloth picked up at the scene of the assault by an alert constable was found to fit exactly along the edge of the ragged sleeve. In addition, some of the girl's head hairs were found on the piece of wood which the man had discarded in the grass after using it to knock her unconscious. The hairs were flattened at one end and when viewed microscopically they looked like the squashed ends of sticks of celery. This was clear evidence of a heavy blow on the head, as hair is relatively tough material being made from keratin, the same protein as that which forms finger-nails. The evidence was rounded off by the identification of some fibres from the girl's clothing found on the bushes through which she had been dragged. The would-be rapist, brought low by the vice-like grip of his intended victim, was sent for trial and convicted of attempted rape.

The occurrence of these two cases in a relatively short time was intriguing and it appeared that a little research into the matter was indicated. Inquiries showed that in some African communities it is considered to be a useful part of a girl's education to acquire this technique for use in emergency. In five cases where men had been subjected to this treatment three had dropped unconscious and two had paid the ultimate price for their sins by dropping dead from shock.

Though new to me at the time, I learned that this method of self-defence is well known in some of Europe's more isolated communities in the mountains of Greece and Rumania. It is medically documented also, and it appears that it is the final twisting motion following a squeeze and pull which is the killing part of the action.

This information put a very different light on the degree of provocation endured by Rabson, and the Appeal Court reduced his sentence to two years imprisonment for culpable homicide. He might have got off scot-free if he had stated that he considered his life was in danger and he was forced to defend himself.

Another murder case in which one of the participants had a similar 'gripping experience' was an eternal triangle affair. Generally speaking, moral standards in tribal Africa are higher than those in many European communities. This may be partly due to the memories of savage punishments meted out to offenders only a couple of generations ago. It may also be associated with the innately conservative outlook of the tribal African.

The story began in a tribal trust area in the Victoria Falls district when rumours reached local police that a man had been murdered. The missing man was named as Myita and gossip linked his wife Ida with another man known as Karikoga. A search was mounted which resulted in Myita's body being found at the bottom of a disused well along with the frame of his bicycle. Cause of death was strangulation as evinced by the cord which was still around his neck.

Myita had been a well-built man known for his strength and enviable reputation with the ladies. Significantly, his right ear had been cut off and his right eye gouged out—the traditional African punishment for adultery. It looked as if his murder was a family affair. A search was made of his wife's hut and also of the hut in which lived Karikoga, the man associated with her by gossip. The burnt remains of an army cap belonging to Myita were found in Ida's hut, and later more telling remains came to light hidden in the hut's thatched roof where the police discovered a human ear and eye.

Ida now told the story of the intricate eternal triangle which had trapped her. Even though they accept polygamy, African women bitterly resent extra-marital relationships. Ida's husband, as I have described, was a big, handsome man with a fatal fascination for the opposite sex. He indulged in numerous affairs which, not surprisingly, aroused Ida's wrath and indignation. She resolved, by way of teaching Myita a lesson, to form a liaison with another man. She chose Karikoga, a rather small and ugly man but possessed of sufficient charm to capture her love.

The affair between Ida and Karikoga was ardently pursued to the point where they wished to marry. Unfortunately the path of their desire harboured a seemingly insurmountable obstacle, Ida's husband, Myita. Quite simply, the lovers decided to overcome this difficulty by murdering him.

One Saturday evening Ida put on a show of affection so convincing that Myita was lured into a lonely banana plantation for the apparent purpose of sexual indulgence. There, in hiding, was Karikoga. Myita, his inflated ego boosted by Ida's warm embraces, had his passion shattered when his partner's mood changed suddenly and she gripped his genitals with such violence as to disable him. While faint with pain Myita was pounced on by the lurking Karikoga who put a noose around his neck and strangled him. The cord used for this purpose was the belt worn by Ida.

Myita's eye and ear were removed with a penknife and the dead man's body was left where it lay. It was necessary to dispose of Myita's bicycle, so Karikoga stripped it, burying all the parts except the frame which he threw down a disused well. The two lovers then went home, Ida foolishly decided to take her late husband's army cap with her. On reaching home she burned the cap but recognizable portions of it, included the buttons and badge, survived the fire.

Ida and Karikoga studiously avoided seeing each other during the following day. Both showed signs of desperate anxiety in fearful anticipation of the body being found. When the body was not discovered, their nerves reached breaking-point and they returned to the scene of murder after nightfall with a sack, bent on disposing of the corpse. They placed the body in the sack and carried it to the well shaft where it was thrown in to join its late owner's bicycle.

In rural Africa, as in village life anywhere, everyone knows everything about everyone—nothing happens without its being well known. Ida and Karikoga had committed a serious offence against tribal morality and it was not long before news of it reached the ears of the authorities. The lovers were questioned and the eternal triangle was exposed. Karikoga's knife carried traces of human blood and eyelashes which bore out the details of Ida's confession. The couple were sent for trial and were found guilty of murder, but in view of Myita's loose ways, sentence of death was commuted to life imprisonment.

▼▼▼▼▼▼

Embarrassingly practical solutions are often found by the African to solve marital problems. As I have explained earlier, children are of great importance to the African family, one son being necessary to carry out the duties owed to the ancestral spirits and as many daughters as possible are desired in order to provide an old-age pension in the form of lobola.

The eternal triangle seems inevitably to end up in tragedy and to create forensic headaches. One of these situations led to a logical but fateful solution applied in the case of a childless African couple.

After three years of marriage they had failed to produce any offspring and the matter was discussed at a family conference in the traditional African manner. What was after all a delicate problem was debated at great length and in a spirit of freedom and attention to detail which would have made even a lady of doubtful virtue blush.

One possibility was for Mary, the wife, to be returned to her family and, as she had no sisters to be offered in her place, it would have been necessary for her father to return the lobola. Mary, however, was a woman of strong personality and she managed to persuade the family conference that the lack of children was due to her husband's failure rather than her own. She argued that even if she went back to her family and her husband gained another wife by re-investing the returned lobola, the marriage would fail to produce children. After many hours of discussion the family conference decided that the husband's brother, Toby, should sleep with Mary for a trial period. In view of the over-riding necessity to produce a child, this arrangement was regarded as perfectly respectable.

After twelve months of putting this procedure to the test, the wife and brother-in-law liaison failed to produce evidence of pregnancy. Understandably, the husband began to grow resentful, particularly in view of the false reports he received from his wife about her condition. Following several loud and bitter quarrels, in which the husband firmly demanded his marital rights, Mary agreed to share his bed once more. Nevertheless, she had decided that she preferred the attentions of Toby. As African tribal law decrees that on the death of her husband a widow becomes the property and responsibility of his brother, it was clear that the only impediment lying between Mary and her ambition was the life of her husband.

Exploiting all her feminine guile in the ageless practice of sexual intrigue, Mary, with murder in her heart, coyly invited her husband to make love to her. He readily agreed and she led him to a secluded, treeshaded spot in the bush near their village. As the love-making began Toby emerged from his hiding-place and slipped a wire noose around his brother's neck. A wild chase ensued with the snared man trying to loosen the wire while Toby pulled harder and harder. Finally, the poor husband collapsed and died of strangulation.

The murderous pair decided to fake a suicide by hanging the body from the branch of a tree. In their first attempt Mary lifted the body while Toby pulled on the wire to raise it. This sort of operation is easy in theory but exceedingly difficult in practice. At the second attempt, having reversed their positions, the pair succeeded in suspending the body from the tree. They were not adept at this kind of deceit for they neglected to replace the husband's trousers which he had discarded near by in anticipation of sexual activity. A suicide who removes his trousers before hanging himself is not a common occurrence!

This was another instance of an offence against tribal morality and every man's hand was against the guilty parties. Despite the apparent emptiness of the African countryside, the local population became aware very quickly of practically everything that happens in the district. The bush telegraph is efficient, ubiquitous and mysterious. In no time at all news of the crime and its perpetrators reached the police. Neither Mary nor Toby elected to commit suicide, which is frequently the way out for offenders against tribal law. The vehement disapproval of their peers, however, completely shattered their morale and they both readily gave an account of what had taken place.

The killing had been unwitnessed save for the murderers themselves and at first there was no evidence to corroborate their story. As it is not possible to convict a person solely on his own testimony, it was desirable to secure some supporting evidence. This came from an examination of the branch from which the body had been suspended. Two twigs could be seen growing from the same point on top of the branch and forming a 'v'-shape. It appeared that the wire had become caught in this notch during the first attempt at hanging the body up. This thesis was confirmed by microscopic studies of the two grooves in the bark formed by the wire during the process of hauling up the body. The bark fibres in one groove were all pushed in one direction by the wire sliding over them. The surface fibres in the other groove were not disturbed in this way, indicating one successful and one unsuccessful attempt. It was clear that the wire had not first been tied round the branch and then the weight suspended from it as would have been the case if death had been due to suicide. This evidence, while not strong, did support the defendant's guilty plea and they were duly convicted and each sentenced to five years' imprisonment.

Another 'eternal triangle' case arose in a remote, lonely part of Rhodesia where an aggrieved husband made his living by shooting game with an old 'Tower' musket. This was a weapon in common use over a hundred years ago and was a muzzle-loading gun with a bore about 7/8 inch. The gunpowder was made from charcoal and saltpetre produced locally by a technique handed down from the Arab slave-traders. Some of the salt lakes in the district contain a small proportion of saltpetre which is very soluble in hot water but much less so in cold water. The solubility of salt itself, in contrast, is much the same in hot or cold water. The method used to extract the saltpetre is to stir some of the salt deposit at the edge of the lake with very hot water and this is poured into another vessel. The liquid is boiled to reduce the volume and then it is allowed to cool and the saltpetre crystallizes out. Mixed with charcoal and carefully ground an adequate gunpowder can be produced in spite of the lack of sulphur which is usually considered an essential ingredient.

This man made his bullets from short half-inch bolts which, using his considerable skill as a blacksmith, he hammered into balls which would fit into the gun. They were ominous-looking things almost like junior cannon balls.

One day, returning from hunting with his gun still loaded, he caught his wife in bed with a neighbour and he promptly shot the man through the heart with his musket. The ball went right through the victim's body, came out the other side and buried itself three inches deep in a brick wall, which, to my mind, was a belated but remarkable tribute to the technical efficiency of Arab slave-traders!

A charge of murder was brought against the owner of the musket but his African counsel was arrested the day before the trial on a charge of subversion. The judge considered that this showed disrespect for his court and quite rightly gave considerable assistance to the new defence counsel who had insufficient time to prepare his case. The case against the accused was not very strong and depended mainly on my evidence showing that the fatal ball was of the same origin as other balls in possession of the accused. They had all been made from short half-inch bolts and certain faults in the hammer used to make them were imprinted on them all. His wife could not give evidence against her husband and the only other witnesses were very indirect. The end result was that the man was acquitted.

In similar circumstances the outraged husband was a fisherman who used a fishing spear, which is a six-foot-long spear with a head about ten inches long fitted with large barbs about three-quarters-of-an-inch in length along both edges. He struck the offender with his spear, which entered into his face about 1½ inches below his left eye, went right through his head and two inches of the spear protruded behind his left ear. The injured man walked six miles to the nearest hospital with a friend walking in front supporting the handle of the spear. To add to the difficulties they had to ford a breast-high river on the way.

The doctors at the hospital found it was impossible to pull the spear out owing to the fearsome barbs, so the spear handle was cut off and the spear head pulled right through.

It is difficult to believe but the injured man made a complete recovery and was discharged after six weeks in hospital by which time the only effect of the injury was that he occasionally suffered a slight headache.

The victim refused to give evidence and in the absence of witnesses no charge could be brought against the husband.

The use of wire nooses in Africa in the commission of suicide and murder is a method which had results more ghastly than the imagined consequences of hanging. Thin steel wire of the type used for reinforcing the rims of bicycle tyres is commonly used in African villages for a variety of domestic purposes. It also comes in handy for suicide with unfortunate consequences for those who find the body. The thin wire, bearing the weight of the body, slowly cuts through the neck and, if suspension is longer than twenty-four hours, severs the head completely. The decapitated body drops to the ground with the head rolling away like a football.

It is a maxim in forensic work that things are not always as they seem. This was true of an apparent suicide in which a nineteen-year-old pregnant girl hanged herself from a roof beam by a steel wire. The family who found the body pulled it down, breaking the wire in the process, and called the police.

It appeared that the father of the unborn child was unable to provide the bride money and as a result her family had been giving her a hard time because of her lost market value. In the circumstances suicide seemed a reasonable possibility—at least until the wire was examined in the laboratory.

There are two ways of breaking wire. The first is by a straight pull which leaves the ends tapered and square. The second is to form a loop or kink in the wire and to pull it apart leaving the broken ends bent at right angles. The breaking action twists the ends and usually a rough break forms with no signs of tapering.

Tests were made with some pieces of wire found lying about in the hut. The wire had evidently been obtained by burning the rubber off a bicycle tyre. This had weakened it so that with a straight pull the breaking strain was one hundred and twenty pounds, but once looped or kinked the wire would only bear thirty pounds weight. The wire noose from around the dead girl's neck had broken about nine inches above the knot and the end was bent over, obviously broken by looping and pulling.

The wire from the beam was the same and the break was rough and uneven, indicating that it had not been part of the noose. The breaking strain of this wire was only thirty pounds and clearly could not have supported a person's weight. Obviously, those who claimed to have found the body hanging from the hut beam were lying. Significantly, among the assortment of wire found in the hut was one piece which did fit the noose wire and which was coiled in a manner suggesting it had been wrapped round someone's hand. There was good reason therefore to conclude that a wire noose had been put around the girl's neck to strangle her. In spite of this evidence the police were unable to bring a prosecution.

Violence as a solution to marital disagreements ranks as one of the foremost reasons for murder. I was called in to assist the investigation of a rather distasteful axe murder which occurred in June 1971 near the Zambian border. A married couple had run into difficulty when the horrified wife discovered that she had contracted gonorrhoea. Turning on her husband, she accused him of indulging in extra-marital relationships, of contracting venereal disease and passing it on to her. The husband vehemently denied the allegation and, screaming abuse at his accuser, asserted that she had picked up the disease herself by her associations with other men.

The row gathered momentum and finally the enraged husband took up an axe and with a blow to the head felled his wife. She was dead when she hit the floor. The husband, in common with generations of murderers, was confronted with the disposal of the corpse. His solution was to bury the body and to chop down a tree so that it fell on the grave and thereby disguised it. This seemed a perfectly foolproof solution to the problem, but secret disposal of the dead is not that easy as it is virtually impossible to hide a grave. In the first place the vegetation is disturbed, leaving an obvious scar on the ground, and differently coloured sub-soil is brought to the surface. Secondly, it is never possible to return all the soil to the original hole. The only material which lends itself to the successful hiding of a grave is sand. There is usually little to no vegetation, no difference in colour between top and sub-soils, and surplus sand can be spread around the grave—it becomes unnoticeable when dried out. This secret was known to the ancients and is contained in the Biblical account of Moses slaying an Egyptian on behalf of two enslaved Hebrews and burying his body in the sand.

As usual, gossip was the criminal's enemy and rumours of murder circulated at once and duly reached the ears of the police. A European sergeant and two African constables were dispatched to investigate. The husband meantime escaped into exile in the bush leaving his axe behind. This was sent for examination to my laboratory together with the base of the cut-down tree. Experimental cuts made with the axe showed striation characteristics matching those of the cuts on the tree. It is an interesting phenomenon that no European has such skilful mastery with an axe as an African. In order to reproduce the marks made by an African cutting wood it is always necessary to employ another African. This was done in this instance and the result left no doubt that the husband's axe had been used to fell the tree over his murdered wife's grave.

The murder investigation in this case produced no result—the wanted husband had simply disappeared into the bush. The story had an extraordinary sequel, however, which developed twelve years later. A violent patient escaped from a Bulawayo mental institute and wandered into a barren bush area where he died from thirst and exposure. His body was found three months later in a mummified condition caused by the dry environment. Fingerprints were taken from the dried-up corpse and the records were searched in order to establish identity. In addition to being identified as the escaped mental patient it was proved that the corpse was that of the missing axe murderer.

Domestic disputes are often heightened by alcohol and the African beerhall with its scenes of weekend drinking is frequently the touchstone for violence. The usual Saturday night jollifications were taking place in one of Salisbury's beerhalls in June 1974 when a couple drew attention to themselves by the volume of their argument. A number of people observed this fierce row between Bovril and his wife Constance and she was seen to leave in a fit of temper. After an hour or so Bovril followed her home.

The next time they were seen was when an ambulance called at their home about two hours later to collect Constance and rush her to hospital. She was found to be dead on arrival from head injuries. A post-mortem examination showed that the back of her skull was fractured and that she had also received a severe blow to the side of the head, probably a kick, causing a sub-dural haemorrhage inside the skull. Death had been caused by the blow to the back of the head which might have resulted from falling backward onto a hard floor. Bovril admitted that he had beaten his wife but he denied knocking her down and kicking her. His shoes, together with a sample of Constance's hair, were sent for forensic examination.

Hair is another highly identifiable material. Most human individuals have up to eight different types of hair in their heads—on the basis of colour, thickness and cross-sectional shape—and the proportion of each type is fairly constant all over the head. Colour is a variable feature and, even though all African hair looks black, individual hairs viewed under the microscope show a gradation of colour through a series of brown and ginger hues. The degree of curl or the condition of the roots and ends can be distinctive and cut hair can give away the nature of the barbering—whether by razor, scissors or singeing. The core or medulla of individual hairs can be continuous, interrupted or broken in various degrees or be absent altogether. All hairs have a scale pattern—the number of scales per millimetre being constant for each type on an individual but varying widely from person to person.

Lodged between the upper and lower sole of the toe of Bovril's right shoe we found two hairs which corresponded with the head hair of his wife. Constance's head hair was of two distinct types as regards thickness, both of which were matched in the hairs in the shoe. The scale patterns of the two hair types were photographed and again the number of scales per millimetre corresponded with those of the dead woman's head hair.

A significant observation was that the thinner of the two hairs found on the shoe had been pulled out by the root. Compared to European hair African hair is extraordinarily firmly rooted in the scalp. Hats worn by most Europeans will have loose hairs from the wearer's head clinging inside the hat. This is not the case with the African. The only time hair is found inside his headgear is when its owner has visited the barber and hair trimmings invariably find their way onto the inside of the hat. Rooted African hair is therefore unlikely to be picked up by accident.

The conclusion that Bovril had kicked his wife in the head, the toe of his shoe pulling a hair out by its root, seemed irresistible. The evidence connecting him with the blow she received on the back of the head was less clear-cut. Although there was grave suspicion of Bovril, he was acquitted of the charge of murder.

Hair evidence played a significant role in a similar case in which death resulted following a quarrel between a European couple. I was called at home late one evening in November 1975 and asked to attend a case of assault near Umtali. I was told that the couple had been seen drinking in the local hotel and that, on leaving, the wife had fallen down the steps at the entrance. Although shaken, she seemed unharmed and drove off with her husband.

About forty-five minutes later the husband drove his wife to the nearby hospital where it was found that she was in a bad way and nearly unconscious. Closer examination revealed that she was extensively bruised over the top half of her body and that most of her hair had been torn out. She was admitted to hospital but died ten days later. The hospital doctors, believing that she had been the victim of a vicious assault, informed the police. Investigations in and around the hotel and its environs led to the discovery of a spot some two miles away where a car had pulled off the road and where handfuls of head hair matching that of the dead woman were found.

The hair had been bleached, growing about two inches afterwards. When hair is bleached it is weakened and the maximum loss of strength is near the scalp where rinsing is least effective. Because of this, when the hair was pulled from the head of the victim each hair broke at the junction of the bleached and unbleached sections so that the hair which came away was a different colour to that left on her head. When she was admitted to hospital her hair was tidied up by cutting away the remaining bleached strands, so that by the time she died all the hair remaining on her scalp appeared to be a different colour to that found at the roadside crime scene. Nevertheless, her head hair consisted of three distinct types which, apart from differences in colour, corresponded in every feature with the hair found two miles away from the place where she had been seen to fall.

It proved impossible to determine to what extent the dead woman had been injured by falling down the hotel steps and, despite the strength of the hair evidence, it was equally difficult to assess what had happened at the roadside where large amounts of her hair were found. Already shaken from the earlier fall, she might have been dragged from the car by her hair and further assaulted by her husband, the injuries being so severe as to cause her death in hospital. But that is speculation—not a realm for the forensic scientist to indulge in except in his more idle moments.

The facts of the case were sufficient to convict the husband of assault only, for which he was sentenced to six months' imprisonment. He reaped a kind of rough justice though, for he was killed in a drunken brawl following his release from prison.

▼▼▼▼▼▼

Angry and vengeful women sometimes resort to poison as the instrument of murder. Tradition has it that poison is a woman's weapon because they lack the physical strength to use other, more violent methods of committing murder. The annals of crime show that overall there have been more men than women poisoners but, as a class, poisoners form the greatest proportion of female murderers.

It is commonly believed that powdered glass may be used as a poison. This is a misconception, however, for glass ground to a fine powder may be eaten by the spoonful with no ill effects. The effectiveness of glass as a poison depends on the sharp cutting edges which are formed when it is broken. Glass breaks with a conchoidal fracture resulting in curved break surfaces. Where these meet a flat surface obliquely, a razor-sharp edge is formed. It is these edges which are potentially so damaging but it is the administration of such lethal material which proves difficult. To be effective the glass particles must be no smaller than a sand particle. It is a common experience that a single grain of sand in a sandwich at a beach picnic brings itself uncomfortably to the attention of the person eating it. For this reason there is no record anywhere of a successful murder achieved by poisoning with powdered glass. Indeed, Edith Thompson in the notable English murder case which made headlines in 1922, complained to her lover that the glass she put into her husband's food did not work. It is also a matter of record that Nelson's sea captains were in the habit of demonstrating their toughness by drinking a toast and then chewing the wine glass. Most of these hardy men got away with it, although a few fatalities occurred among the less careful sea dogs.

It is possible to poison dogs with glass as their tendency to gulp their food makes them less aware of any sharp pieces in it. There are also a few cases of suicide reported from India where slow and painful death, taking as long as two weeks, has resulted from poisoning with glass.

Though unsubtle and ineffective, powdered glass is still occasionally favoured as a means of attempting murder. Several such cases were added to my forensic casebook during my time in Africa. The first involved a wife who doctored some mealie meal with powdered glass. It seemed she was having an affair with another man which cast her husband and the other man's wife, Sarah, in the role of suspects. On preliminary examination the glass in question appeared to be of the kind used in the manufacture of beer bottles; and a sample of the meal, together with two broken beer bottles found behind Sarah's home, were sent to my laboratory for examination.

The glass was separated from the foodstuff and put under the microscope. Examination showed that it was not the same as that of the broken bottles. This in itself was not surprising for the glass used in the manufacture of beer bottles varies widely between batches. The regular size of the glass particles indicated that they had been passed through a sieve about mosquito-net size. The food also contained small pieces of magnetite, the blue oxide which forms on iron when it is heated to white heat.

This suggested that the glass had possibly been ground to pieces using an iron fire bar. Moreover, the lack of rock traces in the glass indicated that the grinding process had been carried out in a metal container and not, as is traditional for grinding mealies, on a flat rock.

I therefore advised the police-officers on the case to look for a sieve, an iron bar and a strong, metal pot. Not surprisingly, all these articles were discovered in Sarah's possession and in due course found their way to the laboratory. Examination of the sieve turned up twelve fragments of beer bottle glass corresponding in size, density, refractive index and colour to the glass particles found in the mealie meal. Embedded in the iron bar were fragments of the same glass, and the metal pot also carried tell-tale traces of broken glass. Sarah was charged with attempted murder even though the method she had chosen was most unlikely to have succeeded. Her desire to regain her husband's affection earned her two year's imprisonment.

An attempt at poisoning with glass was made in another case of disturbed marital equilibrium when the somewhat unsavoury evidence ended up under my microscope. Dismas had the great good fortune to possess two wives. Well, it was good for him but perhaps less welcome to the ladies in question who competed for his attention. Sylvia, the senior of the two wives, who had borne Dismas one child after ten years of marriage, became jealous of her younger rival. Miriam, the second wife, had the attraction of youth and after only six years of marriage had produced four children. It was Miriam who almost exclusively shared Dismas's bed and sexual favours.

Consumed with jealousy and bitterness at the way she was being ousted, Sylvia sought revenge. Quite cold-bloodedly she decided to murder Miriam's children using broken glass. She retired to a secluded wood where her actions would be unobserved and pounded an old glass scent bottle to powder. Wrapping the powdered glass in a piece of newspaper and tucking it into her handbag, she returned home. At a convenient moment during the family's meal preparation she added some powdered glass to the children's sadza, a type of stiff porridge.

After a few hours the children were taken ill and their father rushed them to hospital. Doctors forced the children to vomit and some of the offending material was retained for examination. Glass particles were found in the vomit and, when details of the family marital situation became known, suspicion focused on Sylvia. Her handbag was searched and several particles of glass were found. The glass, which was of an unusual kind, clearly connected the handbag with the poisoning of the children, who fortunately made a rapid and complete recovery.

Sylvia was confronted with the facts. She was shown the glass particles retrieved from her handbag together with those found in the sadza and vomit. The laboratory tests which had established the common origin of the glass were explained to her but I doubt that she was too impressed with talk about refractive indices and Becke lines. The force of evidence was not lost on her however and, in common with many suspects embroiled in domestic disputes where jealousy is the driving emotion, she developed an urge to confess and tell the whole story. Her case was heard in the courts in due time and she received a three years suspended sentence. This seemed to me to be a humane way of dealing with a matter for which a heavy sentence would have had no deterrent effect whatsoever. If it proved anything it was the inadequacy of glass as a lethal medium.

▼▼▼▼▼▼

Criminal abortion cases usually form part of the routine work for police doctors. In the main, of course, the need is for strictly medical expertise but occasionally the forensic scientist is called in, especially if trace evidence is an important feature. Early on in my African experience I discovered that abortion as a population-limiting device was practised quite naturally by African women. During my tobacco farming days in the early 1950s I pricked up my ears when I heard some of my workmen grumbling to one another about their wives' child-bearing capabilities. The main cause of complaint seemed to be that in several instances a wife had produced one child and payment of outstanding lobola was made in the customary manner. But, since then, no further children had been produced. The men were indignant but I suspected that a quietly efficient abortion service may have been operating. I had seen a black fungus growing on some of the local grasses similar to that which is found on rye in Europe. Ergot of rye was identified in 1597 as the agent present in bread made from blighted rye which, among other harmful effects, caused pregnant women to abort. In the eighteenth century, midwives had sufficiently mastered the use of ergot to employ its power to contract the uterus to check haemorrhage and speed-up childbirth.

I tried a shot in the dark and asked my complaining workmen if their wives ever used fungus-affected grasses to produce abortions. They were taken by surprise but nevertheless my intervention was welcomed and they freely discussed their problems. It was well known that when their women wished to abort they gathered affected grass heads from six different areas, mixed them together with warm water, and drank the brew. What was interesting about this practice was that none of the men would accept that their wives indulged in it although they were quite prepared to believe that other women did.

Tests have shown that the ergot activity of affected grasses varies widely. Ergot is dangerous stuff and can cause severe illness, gangrene and death if taken in excessive quantities. This was the fate of many sufferers of 'St Anthony's fire', as ergotism was known in medieval Europe. Over many generations intuition, combined with the experience of many disasters, taught the African how to use ergot. It was safer to take the ergot not from one source alone but from several, thereby increasing the chance of striking a reasonable average dose. Until the women had acquired this knowledge for themselves, those seeking an abortion usually visited a witch-doctor who, for a considerable sum of money, would procure the desired result. Once the women knew what to do, it was easy for them to make their own arrangements to dispel unwanted pregnancies. The resultant reduction in the birth rate, however, made the men feel they were being swindled out of their old age comforts.

Criminal abortion, of course, is another matter, and the saddest case I can recollect involved an African doctor and nurse. The doctor came from a relatively poor family who must have made heroic financial sacrifices to help him in his studies. With such a background his own efforts must also have been prodigious in order to qualify. He met a young African nurse whom he made pregnant and, as he did not want to marry her, he decided to use his medical knowledge in the procurement of an abortion.

He used a method which involved pumping air into the womb and thus dilating it to such an extent that the blood-vessels connecting the foetus to the mother are broken and the foetus comes away. The broken blood-vessels are obviously connected to the woman's blood system, but as long as she is lying on her back the air in the womb is prevented from entering the bloodstream. But as soon as she sits up, it is possible for the air to be drawn up into the blood supply. When the air reaches the heart she dies of an air embolism.

The doctor carried out such an abortion on the nurse in her room and after she had rested in bed for a while he foolishly took her out for a ride in his car. They stopped at a local beauty spot to admire the scene when the girl suddenly collapsed—her heart had stopped beating. He gave her mouth-to-mouth resuscitation but to no avail. Desperate to try to restore the heartbeat he took a razor blade from his pocket and opened the chest cavity to massage the heart. Sadly, all his efforts failed and he took the girl's body to the hospital where he worked.

He admitted carrying out an emergency operation to restart the heart but denied performing the abortion. There were numerous indications in the dead girl's room that an abortion had been carried out there. As in so many crime cases it was trace evidence which provided proof of the doctor's presence in that room. On the bed was an unusual mohair blanket from which dozens of distinctive fibres had rubbed off onto the knees of the doctor's trousers.

The doctor was brought to court and found guilty of performing a criminal abortion. He was given only a nominal sentence, for the real tragedy and punishment was the loss of a potentially able doctor to a community in dire need of medical services.

▼▼▼▼▼▼

Hand-grenades and sex hardly seem a likely combination but the perils of inexperienced weapon handling can have unforeseen consequences. In the early 1960s Russian-made percussion hand-grenades were introduced into Rhodesia. These consisted of a thin-shelled body which housed the firing mechanism. The striker, the initiating assembly and unusually large detonator were formed in one piece which was screwed into the body of the grenade before use.

The handle is held down by a pin and, in use, the grenade is gripped in the usual manner—handle held down—and the pin is then pulled out. This position can be maintained indefinitely but the act of throwing releases the handle and three seconds later the grenade explodes.

In the course of a subversive operation near Salisbury an African guerrilla was given one of these grenades with instructions to throw it into a passenger train. He was taken to a point on the railway track just outside the city where trains usually stopped. He had the workings of the grenade explained to him and was told how to screw in the detonator. When the train was due he was to grip the grenade in the prescribed manner, pull the pin and keep the handle held down. As the train started to move away he was to throw the grenade into one of the compartments.

The guerrilla went down to the railway line and, squatting on his heels, tried to remember what he had been told. He had the grenade in one pocket and the detonator in another. Taking out the grenade he carelessly removed the pin and then started to screw in the detonator. After a single turn, the handle slipped and he dropped the grenade. There was a popping noise like an air rifle going off—this was caused by the striker coming down and firing the cap. Three seconds was all that now separated the luckless terrorist from the explosion. Petrified with fright he remained squatting exactly where he was. An explosion followed but it was not as expected.

The grenade was filled with high-quality TNT, a relatively stable material which requires a large detonator to set it off. As the detonator in the hands of this bungling operator had not been screwed right home, there was a gap between it and the body of the grenade. Consequently, the detonator discharged but the explosive in the grenade failed to go off. The result was that detonator and grenade parted company, each component flying off in opposite directions. Unfortunately, for the bemused and still squatting guerrilla the detonator assembly passed between his legs missing his thighs but damaging his testicles beyond repair.

The injured man's story came to light when the need to be patched up caused him to seek medical aid. An intensive search was made of the area near the railway line where the man claimed the accident occurred but neither grenade nor detonator could be found. The only piece of evidence supporting his story was a small particle of paint found in the torn crutch of his trousers which matched the paint used on the Russian grenade type in question. No prosecution was brought against the man. Perhaps the authorities thought he had been punished enough. Certainly his sexual proclivities had taken a knock!

Chapter Four
SUDDEN DEATH

DEATH can strike in many unexpected ways and it is its suddenness which shocks and causes man to reflect. The safety laws of most countries have been built up from many years of experience. The poison laws, for example, are the result of numerous fatalities and are framed to protect users of all kinds both from themselves and also from ill-doers. Sudden death encompasses natural causes, suicide, accident and murder. Unexpected death may appear to have an obvious cause which may actually disguise the true cause—accident, for example, may disguise secret murder. It is the job of the legal authorities to determine cause of death, to account properly for a spent life, to root out any wrong-doing and to add to the sum of knowledge.

A great many accidental deaths arise from ignorance and misjudgment and we have all experienced the near accident. I recall my student days and camping holidays spent in Scotland. In 1930 it was possible for the princely sum of twelve shillings and sixpence to travel by sea from London to Dundee. I made this journey one summer with a friend; we took our own food and travelled in the bows of the ship. After landing at Dundee we used our feet to journey across to the opposite coast. The last part of our itinerary was the most adventurous—it took us from near Balmoral to the coast in three days by foot. There were no roads, no houses and no signs of habitation. With food and tents packed on our backs, we navigated by map and compass.

At the start of this part of the journey we came across a shooting party and the gamekeepers brought us before a very haughty lady perched on a shooting-stick who demanded to know where we were going. We told her and she declared: 'You are quite mad. You will never make it. You will only get lost and make a nuisance of yourselves.' She pointed out a track which led back to a road and told us to follow it. With the cleverness of youth we did as we were told until we were out of sight and then doubled back on our original course. We ran into some remarkably inhospitable country in the mountains and were confronted by boggy terrain with long, wide, deep cracks in the ground half-filled with black, sinister-looking water. Skirting these obstacles slowed us down considerably. We managed to cross this unfriendly territory just as night fell and were forced to make camp higher up than we planned. It was extremely cold at night up in the hills and we would have much preferred to pitch camp in the valley. Rather apprehensively we unpacked our tent high up the mountainside and took our chances with the cold. We cut wads of heather to put under the groundsheet to keep out the chill rising from the damp ground and gratefully retired under canvas. Snug inside the tent and with the flaps tightly closed we cooked a meal over our primus stove and enjoyed mugs of steaming hot tea in the warm, homely fug now developing. We then slid into our sleeping bags with the hoods pulled up well over heads and went to sleep, using boots and heather wrapped in a towel as a pillow.

What I remember most of that escapade is how the cold exceeded my worst expectations—my boots and socks were frozen solid in the morning and there was hoar-frost on my sleeping bag. But the memory of discomfort is nothing compared to the horror of my later realization that it is practically suicidal to use a primus stove in a small, tightly enclosed tent. Later, I was to deal with many cases where Africans had brought a brazier into a closed room on a cold winter's night and succumbed to carbon monoxide poisoning. The porous roof of the grass huts in which they had lived for centuries provided sufficient ventilation to prevent a dangerous build-up of poisonous fumes, but the transition to huts with corrugated iron roofs and closed windows made the indoor brazier lethal. As far as my youthful camping episode was concerned, we were lucky to escape the consequences of our misjudgment and ignorance.

Very often only a hairsbreadth separates disaster and survival, and I was reminded of my own experience years later following the tragic death of a man and wife on a caravan holiday near Lake Kariba. A couple travelling in a large caravan made an overnight stop near the lake and the following morning bought some fish which they intended to store in readiness for a meal later in their journey. To keep the fish fresh they put them into the caravan's refrigerator. This was a gas-burning model and was kept running when in transit. On arrival at their next stop the couple decided to eat out and when they returned went straight to bed in the caravan. The wife woke up during the night and realized that something was wrong with her husband. She tried to drag him out of the caravan but after moving him a few feet, almost to the door, she collapsed on top of him. Both died of carbon monoxide poisoning.

The caravan was hermetically sealed to keep the dust out and the gas refrigerator had been running sufficiently to create a lethal build-up of carbon monoxide. The blood of both victims of this accident was over fifty per cent saturated with carbon monoxide. Tests on the tightly closed caravan showed that, if the refrigerator was left on for sixteen hours, there was a lethal accumulation of poisonous fumes. The small flame of that refrigerator had caused two tragic deaths. Men, on the whole, breathe more rapidly than women, and for this reason the woman was less affected than the man. In the frantic effort to get him outside she breathed heavily and was herself overcome.

Most of us can recall some such narrow escape where a small change in circumstances might have proved fatal. Of course it is not possible to take precautions against every conceivable disaster but it is sensible to avoid carelessness, lazy judgment and ill-considered risks. Safety procedures are often regarded as a bore and many individuals react as if they were impervious to mortal weakness. It is also a fatal human tendency to dice with death, often unwittingly, out of familiarity with circumstances. This is never more true than in deaths resulting from motor accidents.

Sudden deaths, whether from carbon monoxide poisoning, snake bite, hit-and-run injury, suicide or murder with intent, all have to be investigated. It is, of course, the province of the physician to examine persons who die unexpectedly in order to determine cause of death from the medical evidence. But the circumstances of death and the scene of its occurrence usually offer a wealth of evidence which enables the forensic scientist to play his part in reconstructing fatal events. He can help put the nature of sudden death beyond doubt and provide evidence assisting in the resolution of insurance and compensation problems.

▼▼▼▼▼▼

Snakes have the potential for causing sudden death but this is possibly rooted more in fear than in reality. In nearly thirty years in Africa I have only seen three persons bitten by snakes and I have never heard of anyone dying from snake bite apart from a European electrician who jumped from a pylon on which he had been working and had the misfortune to land on a cobra six feet long.

Granite outcrops are a common and often dominating feature of the landscape in eastern parts of Africa. Indeed many suburban houses have large groups of boulders in their gardens which are permanent features as they are too large to be moved. The cracks in these rocks tend to harbour snakes which, almost without exception, are shy, timid creatures. They fear and dislike man every bit as much as he fears and reviles them. Snakes hibernate during the cold season and they are seen most frequently when they are either entering or leaving the hibernation phase. Sometimes they find a warm spot for the winter in the foundations of a house and they are tempted to overcome their natural dislike of man and tolerate him as a neighbour.

On emerging from hibernation they usually lie around in the sun for a day or two until their winter sluggishness evaporates. Then they set about the serious business of life—hunting and mating. It is during this coming to and going from winter quarters that snakes are accidentally stumbled on and most bites occur at this time. I have killed scores of snakes as I believe they can be dangerous and the only good snake is a dead one.

A boulder-strewn suburban garden in Bulawayo which provided a refuge for snakes led to sudden death not from snake bite but as the result of an explosion. I was called to the scene of the explosion in April 1966. At its centre was a disintegrated brick-built garden shed and the shattered body of its owner together with a broken .22 rifle. After any big explosion the physical evidence is largely destroyed and, of course, the most direct witnesses are unavailable, having been blown to pieces in the blast. All that the neighbours were able to say was that at about 7.0 in the morning there had been the most tremendous explosion with the results which I was now contemplating. In such circumstances the best one can usually do is to make an intelligent guess as to the cause of the explosion.

The garden in which the shed stood had been made to look particularly attractive with its piled-up rock formations and it was apparent that the owner had a pronounced liking for garden bamboo plants which, in effect, are simply a very large variety of grass. The clumps of bamboo are shaped like tufts of grass but they grow to a height of about thirty or forty feet. The stalks are over two inches in diameter and at ground level the whole tuft is about six or eight feet wide and forms an impenetrable thicket. In this garden the bamboos, with their graceful, drooping curves over the large boulders, formed an attractive and idyllic setting. Unfortunately this bamboo and boulder glade offered an ideal refuge for snakes and it was well known that the owner was in the habit of killing some twenty snakes a year. He shot them with a .22 rifle kept specially for the purpose. As a sideline, the householder was also a well sinker and kept anything up to a hundred pounds of dynamite in his garden shed.

Possible causes of the explosion were beginning to form in my mind and I turned my attention to the broken rifle found in the debris. It had the usual wooden butt and stock which extended to a wooden support half way along the barrel. Embedded in the end of the wooden support, directly facing the target, I found fifteen fragments of aluminium. These turned out to be pieces of detonator casing. From the distribution of the fragments it was clear that the rifle was aimed directly at the detonator when it exploded. The cross-sectional area of the wooden support facing the target was only about one inch square, yet this small area had been hit by fifteen flying metal fragments. This suggested that a considerable number of detonators was involved at a very close range. There were even two detonator fragments inside the barrel of the rifle.

The total amount of damage caused by the explosion could not have been caused by a single box of detonators—or even by two boxes. It was clear that an explosive store had gone up. The evidence provided by the rifle indicated that the explosion had most likely started by a bullet from the rifle striking a box of detonators which in turn triggered off the main supply of explosives stored in the shed. For this to have happened, the box of detonators must have been directly on top of one of the boxes of explosives. Another theory was that the explosive, which was most probably dynamite, was old and in poor condition having become damp and weeping. The touchy and sensitive properties of nitro-glycerine are well known and weeping dynamite is a most dangerous and unpredictable material. However, this was ruled out when it became known that the dead man had bought a new stock of dynamite only a few days before the explosion. It was also possible that the explosion resulted from an elaborate but original form of suicide. It would certainly have been quick and painless, but inquiries showed no reason why a man known to be healthy, comfortably off and judged to be happy in his personal relations should take his own life in such a manner. Moreover there was no suicide note which is a feature in many cases.

I had to look elsewhere for an explanation and returned to the snakes in the garden. Considering the available evidence it seemed most likely that the man saw a snake in his explosives shed, took up his .22 rifle and, concentrating exclusively on his victim, ignored the box of detonators on which the offending reptile was crawling. He must have scored a direct hit and not a ricochet because the detonator fragments in the wooden barrel support of the rifle showed that the weapon was pointing directly at the box at the moment of the explosion. The detonators exploded in turn setting off the bulk supply of dynamite. Indeed witnesses came forward to state that the dead man quite often left detonators standing on boxes of explosives.

In circles where explosives are handled regularly it is regarded as bad practice to store detonators and supplies of explosives together. It appeared that this man, with a penchant for hunting snakes, ignored this elementary safety precaution and paid for it with his life. This highlights the problem of familiarity for anyone regularly dealings with dangerous materials. This tragic accident brought back to my mind the large notice over the blackboard when I attended a bomb disposal course during the Second World War. It read simply and boldly 'NEVER FORGET THE PURPOSE OF AN EXPLOSIVE IS TO EXPLODE'.

Like most people who have lived in Africa away from the towns I have had the occasional dramatic encounter with snakes. While driving a three-ton Chevrolet truck on a cold winter morning I became dissatisfied with the way the vehicle was pulling. I stopped the engine and lifted the bonnet to see if there was any obvious reason for the lack of power. The Chevrolet was designed so that either the left half of the bonnet or the right half could be lifted, but not both together. Lifting up one of the sections I put my head under the bonnet and immediately heard an unusual but quite loud hissing noise. This was odd as the engine was not running so I decided to look for the source of the noise. After a minute or so I realized the hiss was coming from a cobra which lay coiled up in the space between the bonnet and the radiator. It's head was less than a foot from my left ear. I jerked back and shouted out to my workmen to stand clear. The snake, having been disturbed, decided to make off which it did by cunningly sliding along the chassis of the truck and dropping to the ground at the back of the vehicle. The last I saw of it was its shape disappearing into the long grass by the roadside.

Snakes usually bite on a narrow part of the body such as the edge of the hand or the foot as they can sink their fangs in more successfully in those parts. If the cobra had struck at me the narrowest target in sight would have been my left ear. At least I was able to boast a narrow escape.

Another narrow escape but of more hair-raising proportions concerned a three-year-old child who lived on a farm. Philip liked to play at the bottom of the garden where he had a secret hiding-place. He would scamper off telling his parents, 'I am going to play with my friend'. He would amuse himself for an hour or so and then return to the house full of the joys of boyhood.

Intrigued by her son's talk of his 'friend', Philip's mother followed him one morning to his special play area. There on a patch of sandy soil the boy had made a long, narrow ditch about two inches wide in the form of a rough circle some three feet in diameter. Philip sat in the middle of this circle where he was joined by a puff adder, a short, fat and rather ugly snake with a large head and a venomous bite. The snake slid into the ditch made by the child and began slithering along it as if it were a race-track. When the snake stopped, Philip prodded it and it would go on again. The watching mother was too terrified to interfere—she knew that one bite from that particular snake would have meant certain death for her child. Finally, the snake grew tired of the little boy's game and took itself off into the grass.

When questioned, the boy said that he had been playing with the snake for some time. The snake was quickly found and dispatched without the child's knowledge and he soon accepted that his playmate was gone. His childhood sorrows were infinitely preferable to the danger which he had innocently conjured up for himself.

▼▼▼▼▼▼

Many sudden deaths result from lack of judgment and feelings of immunity to danger which cause accidents. Others offer happy release following a prolonged period of pain or suffering. All are tragedies even though they may have an explanation in logic. A third category is the unrelieved tragedy which results from the perverse workings of fate, leaving nothing but heartache, sorrow and hardship in its wake.

I was called in to examine a specimen of handwriting which featured in such a case in a small town in 1968. The central participants were a couple who had been married for ten years without having any children. They appeared to their friends to be happy and to be leading useful lives. They attended a Saturday afternoon wedding and, as is customary on such occasions, had a good deal to drink although not to an excessive degree. The husband had been suffering from mild insomnia and his doctor had prescribed a two-week course of sleeping tablets to break the habit of waking up too early. On returning home from the wedding celebration the couple decided to retire straight away. Before going to bed the husband took his sleeping tablets but, being a little befuddled with alcohol, he took a double dose. In most instances alcohol and barbiturates taken together reinforce and increase the effect of each other. In some persons this reinforcing effect is much greater than others. The husband must have been one of this group, for when his wife woke at about 8.0 a.m. the following morning he was in such a deep sleep that she thought he was dead.

Shocked and heart-broken at the loss of the man she loved deeply, she decided that her own life no longer had meaning. She wrote a note explaining that she no longer wished to live and then slashed her wrists with determined, devastating cuts. Tidy to the bitter, bloody end, she lay on the bed with her wrists held over a plastic bucket.

The husband woke from his deep sleep a few hours later to be confronted by the sight of his dead wife. Not only did he have his grief to bear but he also had to deal with a police inquiry. The suicide note was in his wife's handwriting and displayed all the characteristics of her hand. Her fingerprints were on the paper and no other impressions were found. The letter certainly appeared genuine, lacking any of the usual indications of forgery. While it is possible to forge a signature so that it will pass at quick examination, it is practically impossible to forge successfully the body of a handwritten letter as there is simply too much to write. In this case there was no doubt that the suicide note was genuine.

So quickly can sorrow turn to joy that the bereaved husband remarried four months later. He took as his bride a girl he had first met a few weeks after his wife's tragic death. The lack of previous acquaintance was discreetly checked and amply confirmed.

▼▼▼▼▼▼

To many, of course, death comes as a kind and beneficent friend. I am referring to the old and lonely whom circumstances detach from the real world and who live in solitary, often pitiful degradation. This happens all too often in towns and cities where, despite the presence of large number of people, the elderly find themselves abandoned to their fate. The usual pattern is a gradual letting go of standards which gives way to personal neglect and malnutrition. Eventually health breaks down and death intervenes, often in the form of pneumonia, 'the old man's friend'.

This type of death is more the province of the forensic pathologist and usually the circumstances and cause of death are all too obvious. The lonely demise of old people in this manner is almost entirely confined to western society and perhaps to urban Africans who have shed their tribal affiliations. The rural African, with his strong family ties, readily accepts responsibility for old and enfeebled relatives. The only excuse accepted for not assuming this responsibility is where the old person is a witch. Then the rules allow the responsible relative to murder the offender. Otherwise African society operates a sort of 'built-in' old-age protection scheme which largely eliminates the tragedy of lonely and destitute old age. The care given to the great majority of elderly Africans is genuinely kind and considerate, lending a stability to rural family life which is envied elsewhere. It probably also helps to explain the low incidence of mental illness among Africans.

The forensic scientist is called in when deaths of the elderly are not straightforward and when there is doubt as to the cause. I was asked to examine the evidence in such a case in 1972. An elderly man whose financial affairs had become hopelessly tangled had separated from his wife and family and ended his days as a down-and-out. His body was found on a piece of waste land near Salisbury. He had been dead for two or three days and on-the-spot examination showed a trickle of dried blood running down from the right side of his mouth. A .32 automatic pistol lay on the ground on the right side of the body about eighteen inches from the dead man's right hand. The scene had the appearance of a suicide committed by shooting through the mouth.

When the body was examined in more detail at the mortuary a bullet entry wound was found in the middle of the back of the head. This is a most unlikely and awkward place for a person contemplating suicide to choose as a target for self-destruction. Such a wound would be far more consistent with murder and the police were alerted accordingly. Meanwhile, as part of the routine testing, the dead man's hands were tested for powder residues. When a gun is fired, the explosive discharge blows back powder residues onto the hand of the person using the weapon. The presence of such residues on the hand is an indication that a suspect has recently used a firearm. When an automatic pistol is fired, the spent cartridge case is ejected to the right of the gun with the result that powder residues tend to be found on the top of the forefinger (the trigger-finger) and, to a lesser extent, on the middle finger.

The tests on the dead man were negative for the right hand but residues were found on the web between thumb and forefinger of the left hand. This evidence argued strongly that the man had used the gun and also helped to explain how he held the weapon to the back of his head. The natural way to do this would be to hold the gun upside down in the left hand and work the trigger with the right thumb. The effect would be to steady the weapon with the left hand so that powder residues would blow back onto the base of the left thumb and forefinger.

The bullet taken from the dead man's head matched a test bullet fired from the .32 automatic, proving beyond doubt that this gun had fired the fatal shot. Now that the possibility of murder had been eliminated and the manner of the shooting had been explained, it was possible to pursue another mystery. The cartridge case ejected from the pistol had not been traced. Believing that death was due to murder, detectives naturally assumed that the killer stood behind his victim and that the spent cartridge case would have lain to the right of his firing position. It was thought that the failure to find the cartridge case on the sandy soil of the crime scene might have been due to the murderer, or the persons finding the body, treading it underfoot. In light of the new explanation of how the gun had been held upside-down, the search was switched to the left of the body and quickly proved successful.

The death was quite clearly due to suicide but there still remained the mystery of why the man chose to shoot himself in the back of the head, thus necessitating, as I have shown, such an unusual grip on the gun. Who knows what goes on in the mind of a person in such a mental state but my explanation is based on the man's outstanding good looks. I think he took vanity into consideration when deciding how to take his life and elected not to damage his features. The death of this poor down-and-out, which at first looked like a murder, contained all the clues needed to solve the puzzles it presented.

▾▾▾▾▾▾

The motor car is responsible for more violent and sudden deaths than all the other causes put together. Or perhaps one should say not the motor cars themselves, but rather the circumstances in which they are driven. The majority of these, although always tragic, are of little or no technical interest. The exceptions are the hit-and-run cases and other serious accidents where the driver claims that a failure of brakes or steering precipitated the disaster. In some instances, drivers have been known to attempt to fake evidence of failure. The sort of question facing the forensic investigator is, 'Did the tyre burst as a result of the accident or did its bursting cause the accident in the first place?' And again, 'Was the brake hose broken before or after the impact!'. If it was damaged afterwards, was it a result of the accident or was it done deliberately to mitigate the penalty for reckless driving? Hit-and-run cases provide a most fruitful field for forensic investigation.

A road tragedy which killed nine passengers in a bus crash illustrates the kind of problems which can arise. The driver in this incident, which occurred near Sipolilo in June 1974, took a bend in the approach to a river bridge too fast. He lost control and the bus overturned, killing nine and injuring many others. Thinking very quickly, and despite a cut hand, the driver managed to cut one of the rubber brake hoses on the front of the smashed vehicle which had ended up lying on its side. He had been quick to realize that he would be censured for the accident so he tried to avoid blame by making it appear that the crash was due to faulty brakes.

When arrested and charged with culpable homicide the driver still had his knife in his pocket. This found its way to me for examination and the traces of black rubber on it were immediately apparent. There were also characteristic nylon fibres from the hose's reinforcing together with vestiges of brake fluid and greasy soil. This greasy material matched for colour, composition and type that which still clung to the outside of the severed hose. It is possible to estimate the age of grease from the amount of fluorescent material in it. This provided confirmatory evidence as did the smears of human blood on the hose which matched the blood group of the driver. It was obvious to me from the start that the defective hose had been cut deliberately and not broken accidentally.

Time and again the African wrongdoer fails to take elementary precautions to conceal his crime. If the driver had thrown his knife away my job would have been made more difficult and he would have improved his chances of getting away with it.

Most people are unaware of the possibilities of forensic science but for uneducated or semi-educated Africans the whole subject is a complete mystery. It means absolutely nothing to them that it is possible to take a practically invisible fragment of fibre from the edge of a knife and put it under a microscope and determine its colour, shape of cross-section, behaviour with polarized light and ultra-violet light, melting point and reaction to solvents. On several occasions I have tried to convey the power of a microscope by putting a live ant in the field of view and showing it to illustrate the detail of an ant's head, which, under a microscope appears like some monster out of a science fiction film, with its enormous eyes and the antennae waving about. The usual reaction was a startled leap backwards and great difficulty in relating what was seen in the microscope eye piece to the tiny ant on the glass slide.

The driver in this case had only a very vague idea of what I was talking about, but there was no doubt that he had cut the brake hose and he was certainly guilty of trying to mislead the investigation and defeat the ends of justice. While my evidence alone did not prove him guilty, it combined powerfully with the statements of passengers and knowledge of the good state of the road and the skid marks on it to convict him of reckless driving and culpable homicide. This type of accident has to be investigated with great care and thoroughness as large insurance and compensation payments may be involved. The forensic evidence may well tip the balance and determine liability or influence whether any insurance claims are met at all.

I said earlier that every contact leaves a trace. This was the contention of the great French forensic scientist Edmond Locard, and is perhaps something of a generalization. Trace material will naturally only serve a useful purpose if it can be identified. If a man wearing a white cotton suit brushes against a person dressed in a dark suit, a few white cotton fibres will be transferred in the process. If the white suit is new and heavily finished, only one or two fibres will move on contact. As hundreds of alien fibres, including common white cotton ones, are to be found on most suits, an extra one or two mean nothing and looking for them will not benefit an investigation. Conversely, though, fibres from dark suiting material vary tremendously and it is quite feasible to find and identify these on a white suit.

In hit-and-run cases, contact is so violent that a wealth of evidence is usually produced. Even if the victim were wearing a white cotton suit, it is probable that fibres would be unmistakably ground into paintwork of the vehicle by the force of impact. The force of the blow breaks the fibres into small fragments which are so distinctive as to afford clear proof of forcible contact produced in a traffic accident. If the victim had been wearing more identifiable clothing, the evidence would be even stronger.

In most cases the main difficulty lies in finding the evidence. I have known accidents where the vehicle licence disc of a hit-and-run driver was knocked down by the victim's head striking the windscreen, and was found later lying near the body. The name and address of the offending driver thereby provided is not an offering to be ignored—although it doesn't happen very often. A minute and careful search is always made of the scene and any scrap of evidence, however small, is picked up and stored away in a labelled polythene bag. Flakes of paint and fragments of glass are highly identifiable, even where they are retrieved in only tiny pieces, and they can provide striking evidence.

The distinguished British forensic scientist H. J. Walls has said that it would be almost possible to claim that paint keeps the forensic scientist in business. Paint is certainly a commonly encountered trace substance and no more so than in hit-and-run incidents. Paints have a wide range of identifiable characteristics, the most obvious being colour, but also including the number of coats and the type of pigments used. Paint flakes encapsulate a great deal of the history of the object from which they have been separated. Microscopic examination of the edge of a flake will reveal its layered structure made up of several coats and spectrographic analysis yields information about the pigments used in the paint's manufacture. The great variety of colours used by motor manufacturers enables the origin of a coat to be narrowed down to a few possibilities by examining a single paint flake.

When a car is painted, the thickness of any one coat of paint varies widely, quite often being five or six times thicker in some places than in others. Paint detached from a car by the force of an impact usually comes away as a flake with all the various coats stuck together. The importance of this is that fifty flakes of paint may be taken from the same car and, although the colours in the sequence of layers may match, the thicknesses of the individual layers will not correspond unless two pieces are compared which were situated close together on the car surface. If paint from the damaged area of a suspect's car is compared to paint flakes from the scene of the accident and found to match as to the sequence of thickness of the layers, there is no doubt that the suspect car is the vehicle which did the damage. Thus chips of paint, even as small as a pin-head, found at the scene of a hit-and-run incident or on the clothing of the victim can be vital.

Even in a new car there is often a different type of primer paint on the bonnet and wings and in a resprayed car the variation is greater still. In many hit-and-run cases several areas of the vehicle's paint surfaces may be damaged. Each area may have its own specific paint characteristics such that if two or more of a series can be matched the evidence is strengthened. Sizeable paint flakes also offer the possibility of being physically matched to a suspect car by shape.

In the summer of 1979 Earl Mountbatten and other members of his family were murdered while on holiday in Eire when a bomb exploded on their motor boat. Forensic evidence, especially that concerning paint traces, featured prominently in the prosecution case at the murder trial. The clothing of the main suspect bore traces of paint, nitroglycerine and sand of seashore origin. According to press reports the prosecution maintained that the paint was identical to that used on the hull of Earl Mountbatten's boat and the sand was similar to samples taken from the area where the boat was moored. Countering this, the defence produced an eminent forensic expert who declared that the paint was a common type. Despite this opposing view the Court accepted the weight of the prosecution's evidence on the paint but judged the sand evidence as unsatisfactory.

It might have assisted the Court if the forensic paint investigation had included the comparison of say a hundred samples of green paint with the crime sample. Green paint changes colour as it weathers and it is extremely rare to get a good match by chance. It is probable that neither of the two layers of paint in the crime samples would have matched any of the random samples. Microscopic examination of paint samples can also be used to highlight the degree of weathering and the presence of embedded particles of foreign matter and badly ground pigment—all highly identifiable characteristics. This sort of approach to the paint evidence, together with information similarly derived from the sand samples, might have made it easier for the Court to reach a conclusion.

Apart from the paint protection on a car's bodywork, the next most extensively used material on the exterior is glass in the form of light assemblies, windscreen and windows. The glass of car headlamps is frequently broken in hit-and-run incidents and fragments found at the scene are always collected and pieced together. The variations in design of headlamp glasses used by the motor manufacturers provides the possibility of determining a particular car model from the re-assembled pieces of a single glass. Windscreen and window glass are different from that used in headlamps and the use of different types again offers useful identifying characteristics.

The best evidence from glass is a straightforward physical fit. If a piece of glass found at the scene of a hit-and-run incident can be shown to fit the broken headlamp of a suspected vehicle, there is no argument. Sometimes the fit is not sufficiently convincing, particularly if only short, straight edges are involved—it is simply not possible to produce unequivocal court-going evidence where the fit is of two straight edges perhaps only three-eighths of an inch long.

While discussing the forensic study of glass it is perhaps worth mentioning other characteristics of this material in connection with the more general crime scene. When glass is broken, curved lines are formed on the broken surfaces. The curves are at right-angles to one surface and swing round so that they are parallel to the other. By studying these curves, or 'rib lines', it is possible to determine from which side a window has been broken. It might be thought that if a window is broken from the outside all the glass would fall inside, but in the majority of cases this is not so and it is not possible to determine the direction of the blow merely by observing the side to which the broken glass has fallen. This may appear a slightly academic point but it is one which can trap the unwary criminal. For example, the arsonist starting a fire for insurance purposes often breaks a window to make it appear that the fire was caused by a housebreaker. The arsonist does not want to be seen so he usually breaks the window from the inside not knowing that the forensic scientist will be able to tell from the broken glass how the window was broken.

Across the 'rib lines' of broken glass there is formed at right angles another series of fine, short lines known as 'hackle lines'. These are created because when glass breaks it does not fracture with a perfectly smooth surface, but forms a series of tiny, irregular steps, each having one side very much shorter than the other. The short side appears as a line and there are corresponding steps on the two fitting broken surfaces. By comparing the hackle lines on two broken surfaces it is possible to prove conclusively that once they formed one whole piece.

Evidence of this type is viewed on a comparison microscope and photographed for use in court. In 1975, at the Salisbury laboratories, I carried out extensive work on improving the methods available at the time for photographing hackle lines. An example of this work, judged to be the best hackle line photograph taken up to that time, was published in the Interpol magazine, *International Criminal Police Review*. This showed the hackle lines on two pieces of glass about three-eighths of an inch long—one had been found in the trousers turn-up of a suspect in a smash-and-grab raid, the other matching piece was still in the broken shop window. These lines show a wealth of individual features such that, when they are shown to correspond, the evidence is as good as a fingerprint. This procedure for examining glass fragments can be invaluable in the investigation of hit-and-run cases.

Another material which motor vehicles usually carry in abundance, although not by design, is a layer of soil underneath the wings. Pieces of soil may be knocked off these under surfaces in an accident or collision and become part of the debris found at the scene. These soil deposits contain highly identifiable constituents which can be matched to soil samples taken from a suspect vehicle. Apart from the many and varied natural soil elements present, there are other distinctive materials which can help the investigator. For example, if a bottle is dropped and broken on the road as litter, following traffic will grind it to a coarse powder, usually within a few hours. Each small fragment which can be identified to some degree, labels each passing car by lodging in the matrix of soil and mud on its underside. If the road surface is wet, muddy water carrying this material will be splashed over the bottom of the car. In a similar way, soil and mud may be labelled with all manner of identifiable debris, such as plastic, paint, vegetation, plaster, cement, brick dust and coal.

One of the most bizarre materials which I came across as serving to identify a hit-and-run driver was a pound of margarine. A girl with a shopping-basket full of groceries, among which was a pack of margarine, was knocked down and killed by a half-ton truck. This was in Harare, a suburb of Salisbury, and the driver simply made off without stopping. The girl's shopping-basket had been crushed between her knees and the front bumper of the truck and, as a result, the margarine pack had burst open. It was a fair guess that some of the margarine had been transferred to the truck and an appropriate warning was sent out by radio to all police patrol cars in the district. Within ten minutes an observant officer had spotted the truck with what appeared to be margarine smeared on its near-side front bumper. The truck was stopped and the driver questioned. I examined the margarine on the truck which was the same type as that in the dead girl's shopping-basket. A piece of wrapping paper adhered to it and this fitted perfectly into the torn original wrapper. Moreover, the fat on the vehicle contained fibres matching those from the crushed shopping-basket together with fibres from the victim's clothing.

In detective stories the obvious conclusion usually turns out to be wrong and the obvious suspect proves to be innocent. Such is the craft of the story-teller. In real-life detection though, the obvious is more often than not correct but this can never be safely assumed. Police work constantly produces surprises which puts judgment to the test, such as the car accident I was called to early one June morning on the main road to Bulawayo. When I arrived at the scene I saw the burnt-out wreck of a car alongside a fairly straight stretch of road. It appeared as if the car had come off the road at high speed, hit a tree and burst into flames. Most cars burn fiercely once the fire has established a good hold. All that was left of this particular vehicle was an empty shell containing the body of the unfortunate driver which was almost completely burnt away.

There were, however, several pieces of tube-shaped white ash in the wrecked car which it was first suggested might be the charred remains of human bones. It was quickly established that this ash represented the remains of a type of rubber upholstery which contained large amounts of sulphide. I treated a small sample of ash with dilute acid and was immediately rewarded with the characteristic rotten eggs smell of hydrogen sulphide. This confirmed that the origin of the ash was vulcanized rubber and also made it clear that there was only one body involved. The roadside conclusion therefore was that the whole scene added up to an accident where the driver had come off the road at high speed due to fatigue, mechanical failure or alcohol and met a sudden death by striking the tree, both car and driver being consumed in the subsequent blaze. The body was sent to the mortuary as a routine measure and the car ended up at the vehicle Inspection Depot for examination as to possible mechanical defects.

The first discovery which shattered my equilibrium was made by one of the staff examining the car who found in the wreckage a revolver with one spent cartridge in the chamber. The second discovery was made by the pathologist at the post-mortem—he found that the driver had been killed by a shot which had passed clean through his head. The entrance wound was just in front of the right ear and the bullet had emerged at the top of the skull. We found the point in the roof of the car where the bullet had finally struck and thereby established its line of flight. Assuming that the bullet had not been deflected during its passage through the skull, this line was found to meet the ground about nine feet from the car. This assumption was justified in view of the ballistics evidence which showed that the bullet had not become unstable but was travelling point-foremost in the last stages of its flight.

The question we now asked ourselves was where had the gun been fired from? If the shot had been fired by someone outside the car, he would have been within nine feet of it. If the gun was held at arm level its muzzle would have been within three feet or so of the car. At this range and with the car travelling at high speed it would have been impossible to hit the driver. Nowhere on the outside of the car was there any indication of the point of entry of the bullet. If, on the other hand, the car was stationary when the shot was fired it would have been quite possible to put a bullet into the driver's head. But to conform with the evidence of the crash it would have been necessary to start the car with the dead man in the driver's seat and get the car moving at high speed before crashing it. Again an impossible operation; suicide seemed the only explanation despite the strange circumstances.

Once the dead man had been identified it was possible to follow up inquiries about his state of mind prior to the crash. It came out that he had quarrelled violently with his wife and had stormed out of the house at 2.0 a.m. threatening that he was going to commit suicide. In order to make quite sure of success he apparently drove his car at high speed on a quiet stretch of road and then shot himself through the head with the result already described. This explanation was quite consistent with what was known about the line of flight of the bullet and the new evidence regarding the man's threat to take his own life. What started as a possible murder inquiry thus ended up as a suicide case.

Suicides quite often show extraordinary perseverance and doggedness in their efforts to destroy themselves. I have seen several instances where Africans have hanged themselves with their feet on the ground. They simply stood under the branch of a tree carrying the noose, put the noose around the neck and choked themselves by leaning forward into it. By leaning into the noose and tightening it they render themselves unconscious, they sag at the knees and their own weight finishes the job. The most extreme example I have seen of this sort of bizarre suicide was a man who hanged himself from a sitting position on the ground with his buttocks raised to give him a clearance of only four inches.

It is commonly believed that every person who commits suicide is mentally unbalanced to some degree. This may or may not be so, but I am sure that in some instances potential suicides reach a peak of desperation and become frantic in their efforts to achieve self-destruction. I recall one such unfortunate who tried to poison himself but vomited first. He then tried to cut his wrists without success and followed this failure by beating his head against a wall. Finally, he shot himself with a Verey light flare pistol, but the first two shots bounced off his skull and the third, fired into his mouth, burned out the back of his throat. The man was obviously at least temporarily deranged and showed remarkable tenacity of purpose. Such cases, of course, with all their stark horror and subsequent tragedy are part of a policeman's job and experienced officers have a fund of strange stories drawn from their varied experiences.

As a young constable one of my Forensic Science Liaison Officers at Salisbury was stationed in a village in the eastern part of the country. This small community boasted six shops, a railway halt, a garage, a police station, a small hospital and some fifty souls. One wet Sunday night there was a fatal traffic accident in the main street and he was called out to deal with it. There is a great deal of information to be noted on these occasions; witnesses to be interviewed, measurements to be taken and statements to be noted down. All this takes time and cannot be hurried even on a rainy night.

The corpse was put in a 'body box', an aluminium coffin, in readiness to be taken to the mortuary which was attached to the local hospital. The mortuary was rather primitive, consisting of a tiny shed accommodating two concrete slabs and completely lacking in refrigeration facilities. As the police party arrived at the mortuary with its body box it was met by two hospital orderlies wheeling in a man who had died that night in one of the wards. The two slabs in the mortuary were quickly occupied by the two corpses.

By this time it was well past midnight and the constable, tired and wet, was dismayed to find that all his notes on the accident were

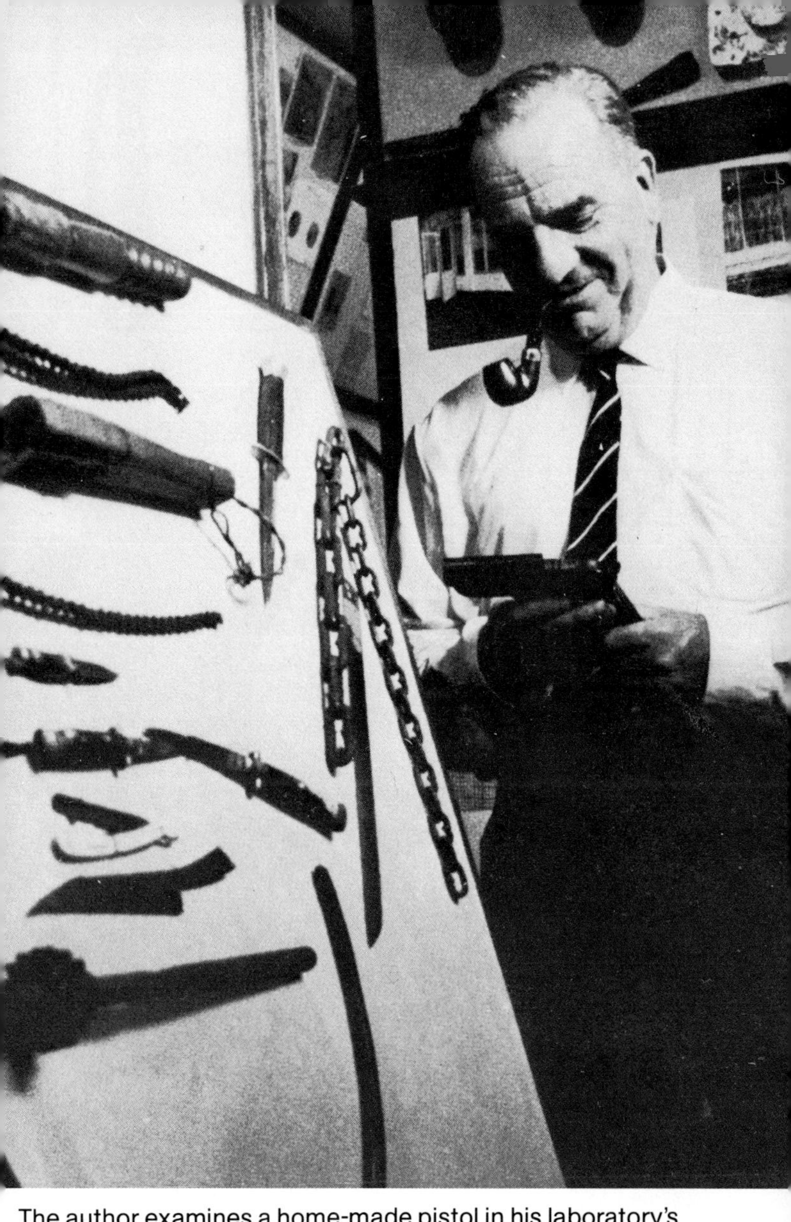

The author examines a home-made pistol in his laboratory's 'Black Museum' (see page 19) *Rhodesia Sunday Mail*

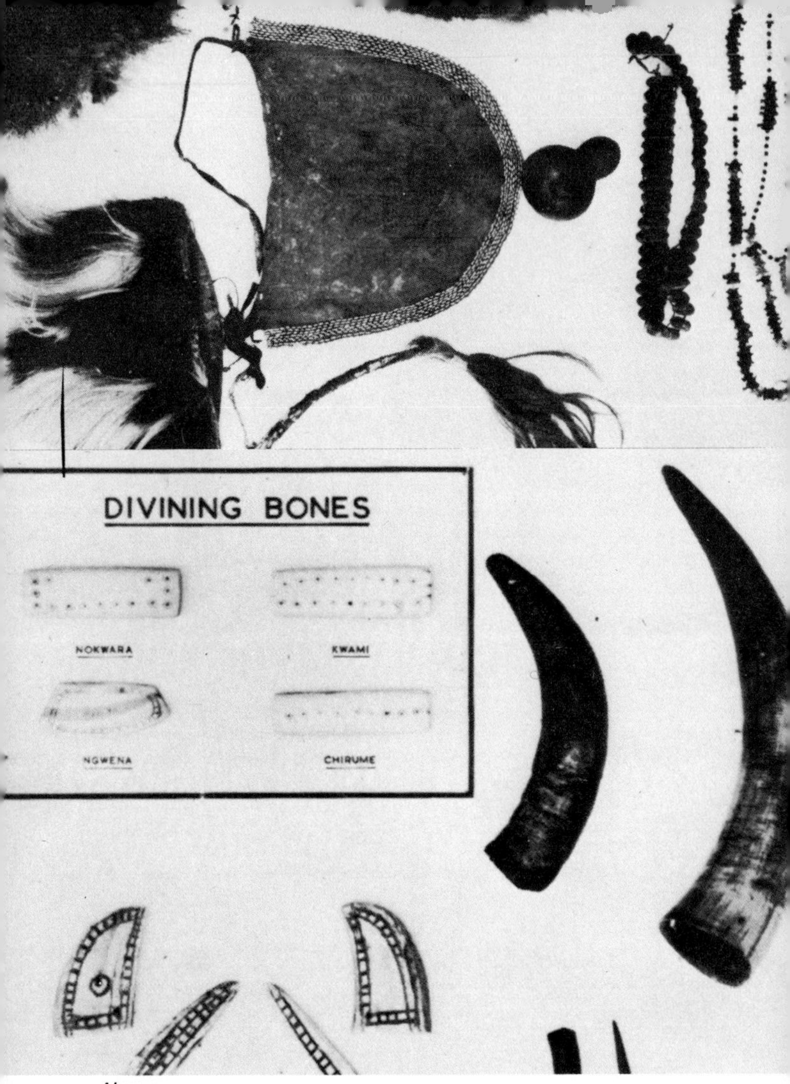

Above
Witch doctor's regalia including two types of fur hat, a leather apron, a calabash gourd, a rattle of groundnut shells and a necklace made of animal and snake bones (see page 25)

Below
Divining bones and animal horns. Each bone has a special name although the patterns on them vary widely. The small buck horns are used to promote healing (see page 25)

Left

Body of a ten-year-old boy killed to obtain his heart for the purpose of making charms (see page 35)

Right

The end of a wire noose used to strangle a pregnant girl. The shape of the broken end proved that the wire had been formed into a loop before breaking (see page 58)

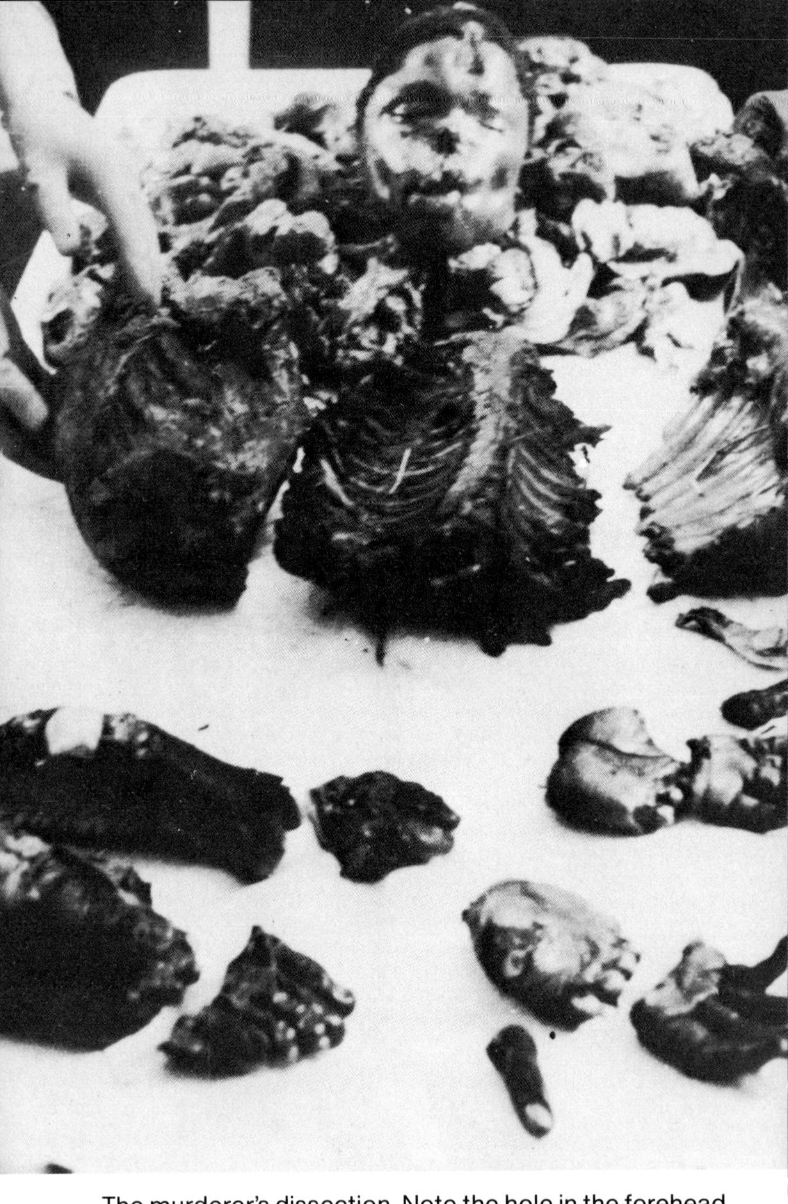

The murderer's dissection. Note the hole in the forehead through which the brain was removed (see page 33)

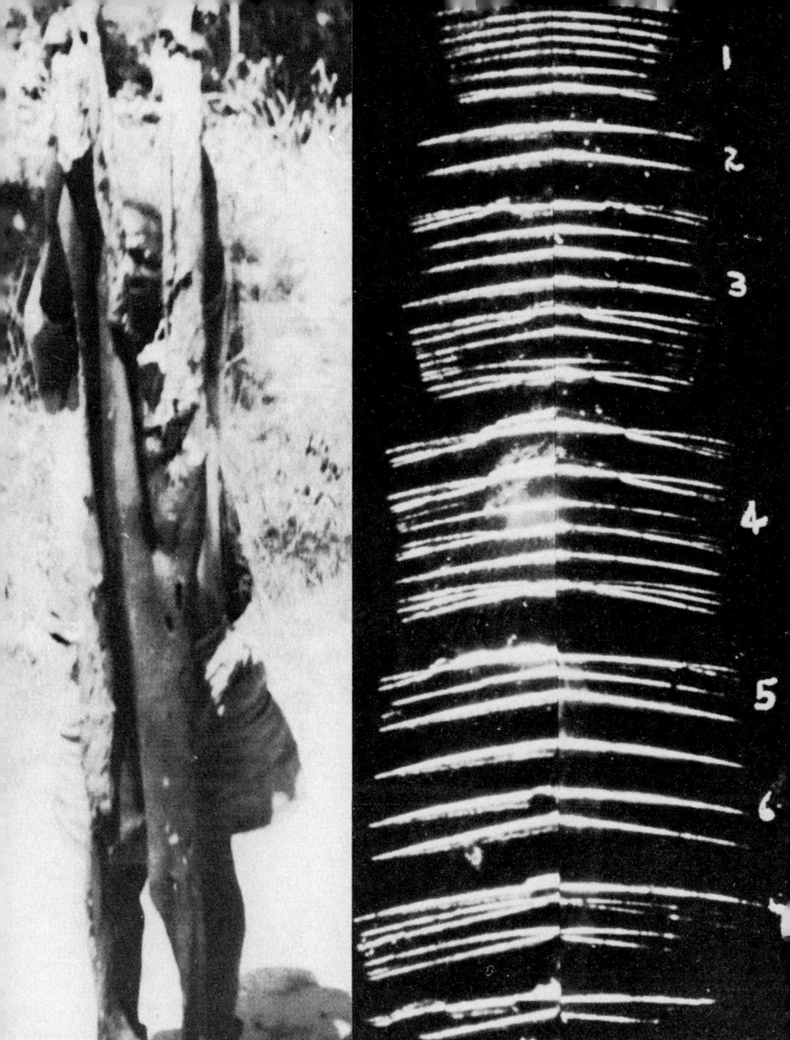

Left

A young herdsman holds the complete human skin which he stripped from his murder victim (see page 33)

Right

Comparison of hackle lines on two broken glass surfaces. The right side of the photograph shows the lines on a piece of glass found in the trouser turn-up of a smash-and-grab suspect. It matches the left side of the picture which shows a piece of glass still in position in the shop window (see page 84)

Above
Skin and hair from the top of the suspect's head showing the pattern of cut hair roots on the underside (see page 119)

Below
Strangulation noose made from tree bark (see pages 37-38)

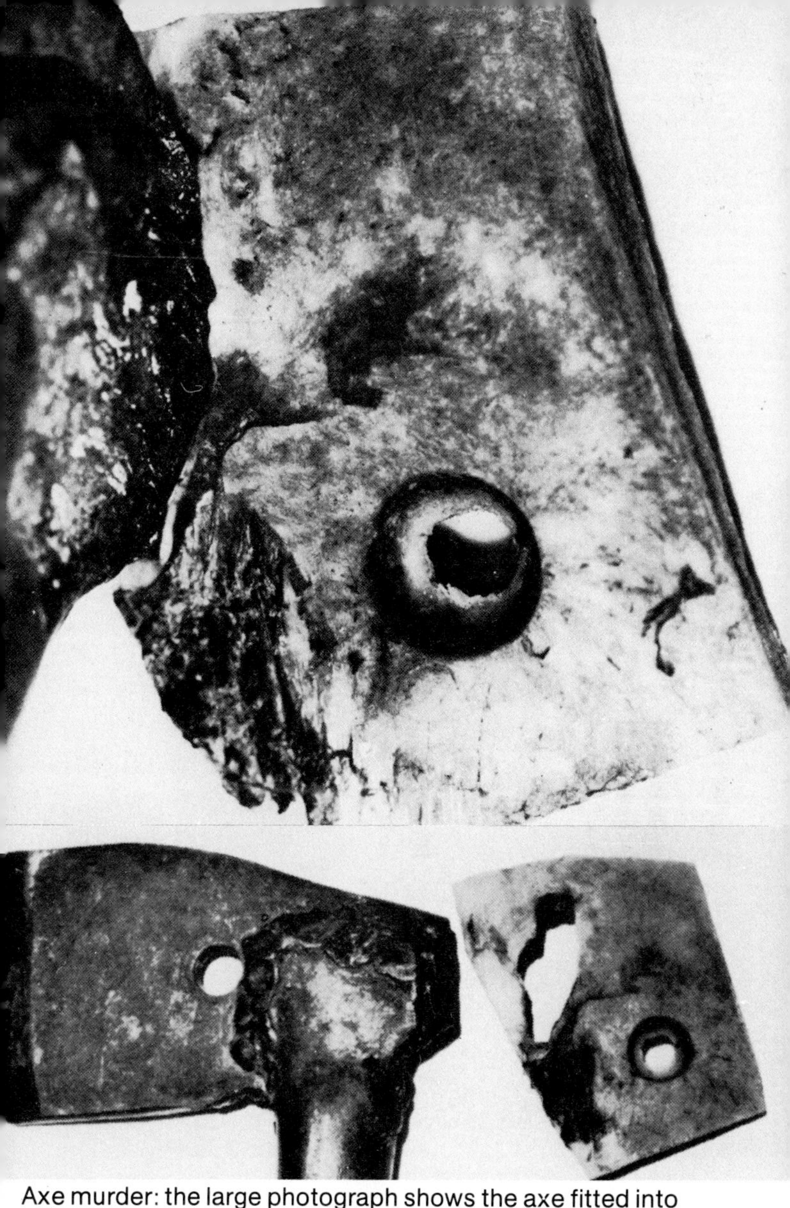

Axe murder: the large photograph shows the axe fitted into the hole in the skull. The small photograph shows the axe together with a portion of the victim's skull. The neat round hole in the skull resulted from surgical trepanning carried out in hospital to relieve internal pressure (see page 101)

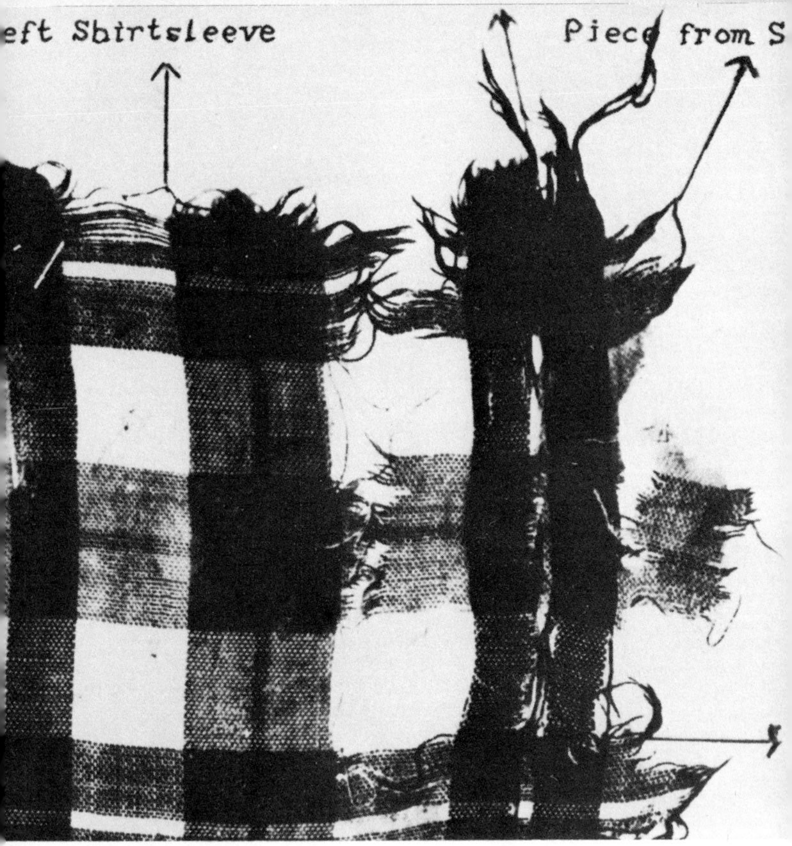

eft Shirtsleeve

Piec from S

Above

The murderer's shoe showing the groove worn by a bicycle pedal (see page 103)

Below

Torn piece of a man's shirt found at the scene of an assault matched to the shirt worn by the suspect (see page 52) rain-soiled. He rejected the easy solution of leaving them until the following day and decided to re-write them there and then while the details were still fresh in his mind. The nearest dry spot was the mortuary itself, so he sat on his haunches between the two concrete slabs bearing their burdens of death. With his back against one of the slabs and by the illumination provided by a solitary candle he began to write.

It must have been an eerie, not to say macabre, scene. The crude and draughty morgue lit by a single flickering candle, the rain drumming on the tin roof, the two dead bodies lying on their concrete slabs and the lonely young constable crouched down, struggling against fatigue, trying to record the details of a fatal traffic accident.

He had been writing for about five minutes when he felt a touch on his shoulder. He slowly turned his head and out of the corner of his eye saw human fingers resting on his shoulder. With one enormous, startled leap, he bounded towards the mortuary door, knocking over and extinguishing the candle in the process. After the initial shock, reason began to take over again and he stopped by the door frantically searching his pockets for matches. He managed to strike a light and saw that the hospital corpse had been placed on the slab with the arms folded across the chest in the customary manner. As the body had not yet stiffened with rigor mortis, one of the arms had slid off the dead man's chest, fallen slowly over the edge of the slab and came gently to rest on the constable's shoulder. The cause was immediately rationalized and the scene was robbed of its terror, but the horror of that moment, as I knew from a similar experience, will always be with him.

▼▼▼▼▼▼

A curious instance of sudden death began with the admission to hospital of a sick African. A man aged about forty-five walked into the small hospital at Fort Victoria late one Saturday night obviously in a bad way and reeking of beer. When he was examined it was seen that part of his small intestine was hanging out of his anus—the intestine had prolapsed through a tear in the rectum. The man denied that he had been the victim of any assault and offered no reason for the injury. Homosexuals sometimes prolapse through the anus but this man's condition was not consistent with that type of injury. It seemed probable that he had been subjected to some sort of violence but he went into shock and died before he could be questioned any further.

Post-mortem examination showed bruising of the intestine and a tear in the rectum. Apart from this there was no other useful information to be gleaned. Of the many strange customs which abound in African tribal life there is a funeral practice which I thought might be relevant to this mysterious case. A tribe in one locality pursued a rather revolting practice whereby, after death, a forked stick is pushed into the anus of the corpse and is then twisted so that some of the entrails are pulled out like so much spaghetti on a dinner fork. These intestines are then cooked in the rice and ceremonially eaten after the funeral—a kind of funeral wake of tripe and rice, or perhaps a cold collation, by courtesy of the deceased!

Doctors assured me that there was no evidence of such a practice having been begun prematurely on our victim of sudden death. Intensive inquiries failed to suggest anyone with either motive or opportunity to murder the man and there the matter rested for the time being. In due course rumours began to mount and after twelve months, by third or fourth hand, gossip reached the police that the dead man had been killed by his wife. The story was that the weapon used was a pole normally employed for stamping and grinding maize into flour. These poles are about four inches in diameter at the bottom, and rumour had it that while her man was lying asleep on his back his wife stamped him heartily in the belly with the pole. After years of daily thumping with such a pole to grind the family's maize, there is no doubt that an African woman could deliver such a blow with tremendous force and accuracy. Such a blow would cause immediate unconsciousness, especially if the victim had been drinking heavily and was asleep at the moment it was delivered. The likelihood is that he would have regained consciousness some time later with no idea at all of the reason for the appalling belly-ache from which he was suffering.

No firm evidence could be found to support this suggestion and no charge was ever brought in connection with this strange death. But about eighteen months after the first man's demise, another similar death occurred in a neighbouring hospital. This man was also positive that he had not been assaulted and the results of the subsequent post-mortem were much the same as in the first case. It began to look as if the story of death meted out by maize grinding pole might have some substance in it after all.

From the standpoint of the potential murderess wishing to do away with her spouse the scheme had outstanding advantages. Most Africans have suffered from malaria and have enlarged spleens as a result. In such cases a fairly moderate blow in that region is likely to burst the spleen, with fatal consequences. It seems probable then that a heavy blow dealt by a maize grinding pole at the right spot would be fatal in most cases. The intestines would rupture, causing peritonitis, and death would follow in a few days. The murder weapon was easily to hand in the guise of a domestic implement. Provided that the blow was well struck (but not immediately fatal) while the victim was sleeping, he would later gain consciousness with absolutely no idea of what had hit him. His murderous wife would be quite safe from suspicion. It seemed that the two men who had died in neighbouring hospitals might have been subjected to this treatment, the blows having been delivered with such enthusiastic vigour as to rupture the intestine and cause a prolapse. A lesser blow would have produced a fatal rupture of the intestine without causing any obvious external sign. Death would occur with practically nothing to show how murder had been committed.

The main objection to this suggestion was that all the doctors consulted considered it unlikely that a blow to the stomach would result in splitting the rectum. Opinions varied from 'very unlikely' to 'practically impossible'. As the area of the diaphragm muscle separating the chest cavity from the abdomen is so much greater than that of the rectum, it seemed far more likely, from a purely mechanical point of view, that the diaphragm rather than the rectum would split. Surgical experience in cases of persons thrown by horses and falling against a fence-post sustaining a blow in the abdomen also indicated the improbability of damage to the rectum.

An obvious possibility to account for this injury was the use of a sharp stick pushed up the anus and tearing the rectum. Any subsequent vomiting would exert sufficient pressure on the abdomen to cause the prolapse. The weakness of this theory was that, however drunk the victim, such interference with his person would be expected to have an immediate sobering effect. Nevertheless, while sensitive to stretching, the rectum is relatively insensitive to cutting. Consequently, with alcohol acting as an effective anaesthetic, the rectal attack still seemed possible. This might well have been a variant of a type of assault practised in Johannesburg where a sharpened spoke from a bicycle wheel is used with deadly effect. Similar practices exist throughout Africa where animals are savaged and killed with a short length of stiff steel wire sharpened at the end. Peritonitis sets in rapidly after the gut is punctured, and death from an indeterminate cause follows swiftly. Such mishaps are accepted as unexplained mysteries and the corpse is often handed over to the African labour force to eat—the object of the operation in the first place.

This lengthy line of inquiry led to a search for a suspect with a grudge against the dead man and with the opportunity to exercise this singular method of attack. Such a man was indeed found and a modified walking stick was his particular instrument of destruction. A convincing case was eventually made against him based on motive, opportunity and the examination of his gruesome stick. He was finally convicted and sentenced to death.

▼▼▼▼▼▼

The strangest story that I have ever heard started when a family returned home late one Friday evening after a seaside holiday. Tired after a long journey, Peter and Sally had a scratch meal and went straight to bed. Their house was one of a number, each on quarter-acre plots, such that the neighbouring houses were only a short distance away. About midnight Sally dug her elbow into her husband's ribs, waking him and said, 'Peter, there is someone digging in the garden next door. It's been going on for the last hour and it's keeping me awake'. Peter grunted in reply: 'So what!' and promptly returned to his slumbers. The noise continued, and a short while later Sally got out of bed, having decided to investigate what was happening behind the garden fence. What she saw made her come running back and she determinedly shook Peter out of his sleep telling him that their neighbour was digging a deep hole which had every appearance of a grave.

Peter, muttering about women's flights of fancy, dragged himself out of bed and made his stumbling way to the garden to look over into his neighbour's plot. To his amazement he saw that his wife's description was perfectly accurate and that the grave was now some four feet deep. As he stood and wondered what if anything to do, his neighbour climbed out of the hole and went into the kitchen of the house. The only lights showing were from the kitchen except for a faint glow emanating through the incompletely drawn curtains of the ground-floor bedroom. Thinking that the digger might be having a break from his toil, Peter decided to risk climbing over the fence and take a peek into the bedroom. Peering through the gap in the curtains he saw his neighbour's wife, whom of course he knew by sight, lying on the bed covered by a sheet except for her head and arms. There were two small tables either side of the bedhead and on each was a lighted candle which provided the sole illumination. The woman's arms lay by her side and a bunch of roses rested on her breast—the lady was obviously dead as the smell filtering through the partly open window amply testified.

Horrified, Peter scrambled back to his own house in a state of alarm and telephoned the police. One can imagine the reaction of the police on being telephoned in the middle of the night and being told such an improbable story. Nevertheless, as in duty bound, officers were despatched to the house to investigate. They quickly established that the lady in question had died of natural causes four days previously and had been buried at the local cemetery. It appeared that, half-crazed with grief, the husband, not liking the thought of his wife lying in a public burial place, decided to inter her body in the rose garden of their home. When it was dark he went to the cemetery, opened the grave and removed the body of his loved one from her coffin. Having refilled the grave to conceal his body-snatching activities, he drove his wife's corpse home in his station-wagon. He was well on the way to completing the re-burial when the noise of his digging woke the neighbours and the police intervened.

The family doctor was located on duty at a nearby nursing home and he confirmed the main points of the story. No next-of-kin could be found so the husband was admitted to nursing care and authority was obtained to re-bury his wife. This was duly carried out before dawn came to relieve a night of macabre activity. The husband's devotion to his late wife was so intense that, despite every possible care, he lost all interest in living and died three weeks later. A clear case of death from a broken heart.

Chapter Five

MURDER FOR MONEY

MURDERS committed for gain constitute the largest category of motive. Yet the stakes are often low and it remains a truism that few swindlers would embezzle the small sums that some men are prepared to murder for. Death and tragedy are frequently visited on individuals and families for pathetically small gains. Usually there are other factors at work, such as jealousy or rage, which magnify trivial incidents to dramatic heights with undreamed of consequences.

A particularly pathetic example which really involved 'murder because of money' concerned the brutal killing of a nine-year old African boy over the loss of one penny. Young Johnny had been given a penny by his uncle with instructions to go to the village store and buy a box of matches. The boy set off happily on his errand with some friends but in the course of their mile-long walk to the shop became side-tracked. They sighted a flock of guinea fowl and the sporting challenge offered by these wily birds proved too good to miss. With the aid of catapults and superlative eyesight Johnny and his young friends went in pursuit, crawling through the bush on their bellies in the approved manner of the stalking hunter. While this diversion was in progress, the errand and the penny payment, not unnaturally, were forgotten. Eventually, tired of game-hunting, and bored by his lack of success, Johnny's mind reverted to the task he had been given by his uncle. Only then did he realize with horror that he could not find the penny. He searched around frantically with his friends' help but to no avail. With justifiable anxiety the youngster returned home and confessed that he had lost the money.

On being confronted with this mild misdemeanour the boy's uncle flew into an uncontrollable rage and with maniacal fury produced a knife and stabbed his nephew. It transpired that the man had a well-deserved reputation for being short-tempered—on this occasion it led to the tragic killing of a child. The fatal incident had been witnessed by several villagers and, in any case, the uncle reported what he had done to the nearest police station. My part in this appalling affair was to provide corroborating evidence concerning the murder weapon. The knife bore traces of blood and fibre fragments which plainly identified it.

I have referred previously to the African's general lack of concealment regarding the commission of crime—it is almost as if the wrongdoer positively invites detection. This he certainly does on numerous occasions simply by confessing in the manner of Johnny's uncle. The same was true in another instance of murder for money—in this case, for sixpence.

Amos and Elijah were inseparable friends living and working together on a farm in the Trelawney area of Rhodesia. Amos's wife was an exceptionally good brewer of beer—a major virtue in any African woman. Beer-brewing requires considerable skill and involves malting the millet, grinding the malt and making a brew from it. This process is repeated to make a brew from maize meal and then the two products are blended and fermented. This procedure takes eight days and, once a month, Mrs Amos set to and made a forty-four gallon drum of beer.

Because of its poor keeping qualities completion of the brew was carefully timed to coincide with the traditional Saturday night party. The guests paid sixpence a quart for this powerful home brew and it was quite common for the weekend carousing to continue for thirty-six hours until the small hours of Monday morning. The drinking was of course accompanied by plenty of noisy conversation and there was non-stop dancing and other diversions to the beat of drums. That 'day after the night before' feeling on Monday morning is well known, but a group of African workmen after a weekend bender exhibit the symptoms of this fragile state with an intensity seldom seen elsewhere.

Towards the end of one of these weekend parties for which Amos and his wife were so famous, Elijah requested a sixpenny refill of beer and tendered a shilling in payment. The shilling was the only money Elijah had left and Amos had no small change. With the two men already well oiled, an argument developed as to whether Amos should hold the shilling and owe his friend the change, or whether Elijah should have his beer on account and owe Amos the money for it. The argument quickly accelerated and, possibly feeling that actions speak louder than words, Elijah picked up a stick and threatened Amos with it. The latter, defending both his person and the six pennyworth of beer, pulled out a knife and, with a quick lunge, stabbed Elijah through the heart.

Appalled at what he had done Amos sat for nearly an hour head in hands, surrounded by the debris of a once happy party. Eventually, he walked to the nearest police station and explained how he struck down his friend in the heat of the moment. In due course he was brought to trial and convicted of grievous assault for which he was sentenced to three years' imprisonment. With the usual one-third remission of sentence for good behaviour he returned home after two years. He was quite unmarked by the whole affair and continued both his work and beer-drinking as if nothing had happened.

▼▼▼▼▼▼

The desire to win is a strong motivating force in human beings and, when it is allied to profit, violence frequently results. The African beer hall all too often provides a third element to this fatal combination.

Mpofu and Sandu, a pair of African labourers, were bosom pals and habitually spent their Saturday evenings drinking in the local beer hall in the Rhodesian township of Sinoia. In addition to their carousing, they played a form of draughts which is common throughout the African continent. Unlike the traditional squared board of draughts, this version of the game uses a series of depressions in the ground. In place of draughts the African uses either small stones or old bottle tops which are moved from hole to hole. Completely at variance with the simple concept of draughts, the African's rules for playing the game are incredibly complicated. This frequently leads to accusations of cheating.

Towards the end of the game being played on this April Saturday evening in 1967, the two friends were at odds with one another and Sandu accused Mpofu of cheating. The pair were seen leaving the beer hall shouting at the top of their voices. This was not in itself unusual for, even without the tongue-loosening effects of beer, many Africans tend to speak in a loud and raucous manner believing it impolite and secretive to talk quietly. The peace of many a European family's Sunday afternoon siesta has been shattered by Africans talking quite happily but noisily as far as two streets away.

Later that night Mpofu was found lying in the road some distance from the beer hall. His hat was on the ground beside him, and as he showed no external signs of damage yet reeked of beer it was assumed that he was dead drunk. When he was examined in the mortuary it was found that only the first adjective applied. Despite a complete lack of visible injury the whole of one side of the top of the skull had been shattered into small pieces. Naturally, Sandu was interviewed by the police but he denied all knowledge of his friend's death. He was subjected to a search and police officers found that he was carrying a railway coupling pin. This was a piece of steel shaped like a nail but measuring some twelve inches in length and weighing about eight pounds. It was quite a formidable weapon and Sandu's reason for carrying it around with him even on his evenings out was 'in case of trouble'. The coupling pin and Mpofu's hat were sent to the laboratory for detailed examination. The hat was a check-patterned golfing cap of good quality. It was made of nylon and had been finished with an inner padding which had prevented any visible surface damage on the victim's head. Check materials, even though they may look subdued in overall appearance, consist of brightly coloured fibres varying in thickness and type. Once again fibre traces were to provide the solution to a crime case and this particular cap proved to be a forensic scientist's dream. It was made from eight different types of nylon in a variety of colours.

Under the microscope the coupling pin revealed fourteen fragments of nylon fibre clinging around the head end. Seven fibres corresponded exactly to the various cap fibres both in colour and thickness. When fibres are rubbed from cloth, those which become detached are usually long ones, but when, as in this case, the fibres are reduced to small fragments, extremely forcible contact is indicated. There seemed little doubt that the coupling pin was the murder weapon. Presumably the argument between the draughts players over an accusation of cheating had become very heated once they left the beer hall and Sandu silenced his erstwhile friend with a savage blow from his steel 'belaying pin'. Perhaps he was unfortunate in that his assault ended in murder, for it seemed that Mpofu had a rather thin skull. At any rate it was Sandu who paid in the end—he spent the following four years in prison.

There is a common belief that the skulls of black people are thicker than those of white people but this is just not true. In fact the reverse is true; on the whole 'white' skulls are slightly thicker than 'black' ones and skulls of females are thicker than those of males. There is however a wide variation in each class and the skull of Mpofu was only about one third of the average thickness. It follows that the class with the thickest skulls are white females. One explanation I have heard is that, as the female brain is smaller than the male brain, the female skull if of normal thickness would result in a head so small as to look ridiculous. In which case an obvious retort is that good packages comes well-wrapped!

The lure of gold has often provided a spur for murder, and the world's gold-mining communities have been cauldrons of greed and violence. The temptation to seize quick riches, not by the hard work of prospecting but by robbing the gold-miner of his spoils, provided an axe murder investigation. This was about the time of my appointment as Director of the Forensic Science Laboratory at Salisbury and was the kind of excitement that I could well have done without at the time.

The victim was a man called Albertson who prospected for gold in a mining area some eighty miles north of Salisbury. He was a small-scale operator employing a few men under a foreman. He lived alone and was looked after by an African 'cook general' named Kerry. Albertson used an extraction process which produced 'sponge gold'. Ore-bearing rock is crushed and washed with water over tables covered with felt which supports a bed of mercury. The gold particles in the crushed rock are held by the mercury and form a semi-solid amalgam which is scraped off the felt. When sufficient amalgam is collected, the mercury is boiled off in a retort leaving a porous mass of 'sponge-gold'.

One May evening, just before eight o'clock, Albertson was about to sit down to dinner with an old friend, Mr McKay, who was staying for the weekend, when he had a visit from his African foreman. The man handed his boss a lump of gold amalgam which represented the mine's output for that day. Albertson pocketed the amalgam and joined his friend for dinner.

After the meal McKay retired for the night leaving his host dosing in front of a log fire. The time was approximately nine fifteen. At ten o'clock McKay was awakened by the dogs barking and, as the animals persisted with their noise, he left his bed to investigate. He found Albertson lying on the living-room floor bleeding profusely from head wounds. Having rendered first-aid to the best of his ability, he got his friend into bed and then went in search of Kerry whom he dispatched to find help. On his return Kerry helped McKay to clean up the gold-miner's wounds while they waited for neighbours to arrive with a car to take the injured man to hospital. Albertson died a few hours after being admitted.

Post-mortem examination showed two wounds on the top of the head, one of which had penetrated the skull. There were also wounds on the left cheek. It seemed that the wounds had probably been made by an axe of the type traditionally used by Africans. Such axes were in use long before the Europeans arrived in the continent and consist of pieces of steel shaped into an elongated 'V'. The cutting edge is usually between two and three inches wide and the handle is fashioned from a piece of wood about two feet long which is bulbous at one end. Quite often, a young tree is felled for the purpose of making a handle, the bulb or swollen end being the part of the tree which is at ground level. The steel axe head is heated until it is red-hot, the point being used to burn a hole in the thick end of the handle, so fixing the blade in place. Traditional methods have to some extent been modified and broken car leaf springs often provide raw material which the African can fashion into a serviceable axe with the aid of a hammer, cold chisel and a suitable rock to serve as an anvil.

When he was summoned to answer routine questions Kerry proved evasive. He was asked to produce the axe which he used in connection with his daily chores. He replied that he had burnt the handle and thrown away the blade. According to his statement Kerry had also burnt his trousers because they were blood-stained. Destroying the trousers was perhaps understandable as they had no doubt been soiled when he helped to clean up Albertson's wounds. None of his actions seemed very bright in the circumstances; his reason for disposing of the axe was that he had seen other Africans busily throwing away theirs, so he followed suit.

There were generally three axes in use in the house for the purpose of chopping wood. On further questioning, Kerry provided the useful information that he had thrown away not one but two axes. The third axe was the property of the gardener, a fellow called Sabuteni. His axe was normally kept in his own quarters about half a mile from the main house. He maintained that this was where his axe had been for several days. Although he had chopped wood at Albertson's house on the day of the murder, he stated emphatically that he had used one of Kerry's axes which he left on top of the pile of chopped wood near the house when he had finished.

This chopped wood obviously deserved attention, especially the striation lines made on the pieces by the axe used to split them. From this examination it was determined that two axes had been used. Experimental cuts confirmed that one of them was Sabuteni's. Striation lines had been made in the dead man's skull by the weapon used to kill him. These lines did not match the marks made by Sabuteni's axe on the chopped wood but they did correspond with the marks made by the second, as yet unidentified axe. It was possible to determine the length of the cutting edge of the axes in question. This made it clear that Sabuteni's axe had not been used to inflict the fatal injuries.

Suspicion re-focused on Kerry when blood was found on his shoes. Unfortunately the quantity was not sufficient for the blood group to be determined and his explanation of how it got onto his shoes was not satisfactory. He maintained that the blood must have dropped on his shoes when he was helping to clean Mr Albertson's wounds. It was shown, however, that although Kerry was wearing shoes when he served dinner, he was barefoot when he returned to the house in response to McKay's call for help. Moreover, one of the mine-workers during routine questioning claimed to have seen Kerry surreptitiously hiding an axe in the woodshed on the night of the murder.

Kerry was sent for trial and a powerful prosecution case was presented to the court. It was shown that the axe used to kill Albertson was the same one as that employed to chop some of the firewood piled outside the house, the remainder having been split by the axe belonging to Sabuteni, the gardener. As Kerry admitted splitting some of the wood with his axe, the obvious conclusion was that the murder had been committed with his axe. The evidence strongly suggested that on the evening in question Kerry had taken the axe from the woodpile and hidden it in the woodshed. Consequently he was almost certainly the only person who knew the exact whereabouts of that particular axe. He admitted destroying the axe and burning his blood-stained trousers and there was no doubt that human blood had been found on his shoes.

Although the evidence against Kerry was weighty, there were no witnesses to confirm his presence at the crime scene at the time of the attack. Motive was obscure too and none was ever proved. The obvious thought was that Albertson had been murdered for the gold amalgam which he was known to have in his pocket. The gold was still on his person after the murderous assault, which tended to rule out robbery—although I suppose the murderer might have panicked. Despite the lack of motive Kerry was found guilty with no extenuating circumstances and received sentence of death.

The technical evidence clearly demonstrated which axe had been used—even though it was never found. I am thankful I was not responsible for the verdict, for no satisfactory explanation was offered by the prosecution why Kerry chose to attack his master at a time when he was entertaining a guest in his house. It seemed far more likely that he would have chosen one of the many evenings when his employer was alone.

If the motive was unclear in the case of the gold-miner, it was blindingly obvious in another axe murder in which I identified the murder weapon. An African woman aged about 32 was found lying unconscious on the floor of her home in Harare a Salisbury suburb. She had been savagely attacked and suffered severe head injuries as a result. Despite being rushed to hospital and undergoing immediate surgery she died within hours of being found. Police inquiries revealed that two men had been seen in the neighbourhood and it was known that they had been collecting money for a political party. It was well known that such activities were frequently accompanied by forceful, intimidating approaches. It was quite likely therefore that the victim of this assault had been resolute in her refusal to contribute funds and was attacked in consequence.

The African tendency not to part with incriminating evidence made the solution of this crime easy. The pair of money-collectors was rounded up and one of them had an axe in his possession. This had been made by welding the head on to a piece of three-quarter-inch steel piping which acted as a handle. The welding was lacking in skill for the metal had bubbled; this had left a pitted surface ideal for picking up hairs and fibres. Indeed fragments of hair on the axe matched perfectly the head hair of the victim. Moreover, the victim had worn a printed, cotton headscarf at the time she was attacked and fibres from this were also found on the axe. Thus, evidence provided by hairs and fibres once again played a crucial role in identifying the murder weapon. And the African's disregard for concealment clinched the case, for one of the two accused men admitted ownership of the axe and helpfully contributed the information that it had been in his possession for some time.

Despite an attempt to intimidate witnesses in this case by smashing the windows of their houses, the pair of political fund-raisers were brought to court where they were duly found guilty and convicted of murder without extenuating circumstances. The courage of the witnesses was commendable in the circumstances and was the kind of steadfast attitude which helps to defeat wrongful political pressure and the violence which all too often accompanies it.

Sadly, however, violence also flares up in African political activities when the members of the same political organization set on one another. Sometimes money is at the root of such violence, but the overriding and universal desire for power comes a close second. This happened in Kenya when the great majority of Mau Mau victims turned out to be Africans and also proved to be the case in a particularly savage murder in Rhodesia in 1964.

A small, sub-branch of one of the emergent African political parties, consisting of only sixteen members, engaged in discussion as to the appointment of its chairman. The group split with nine on one side and seven on the other. In order to resolve their differences it was agreed to take the matter for arbitration to the branch chairman. The members made their separate ways to the arbitrator's house and on arrival began the argument all over again. Heated exchanges deteriorated into violence and the leading candidate of one of the factions was struck savagely on the head with a blunt instrument. He died as a result of a depressed fracture of the skull.

The weapon turned out to be the stub axle of a car—a more or less mushroom-shaped piece of steel with an irregular shaped head, weighing about six pounds. The owner and user of this remarkable offensive weapon fled the scene of the crime and returned the weapon to the boot of his car where it was carried as a spare part. It was not difficult to trace the attacker for there were many eye witnesses to his assault. In common with many African criminals, and most unlike the wily politician he no doubt aspired to become, he left the incriminating evidence in his car. The axle stub was found and on it were tell-tale hairs from the victim's head. The heavy end of this unusual weapon also neatly fitted into the depression made in the dead man's skull.

In this sort of case the evidence of eye witnesses tends to be heavily biased and can only be relied on if some independent evidence is provided. The murder weapon in this case provided the necessary confirmation and a conviction for murder resulted.

▼▼▼▼▼▼

The disturbed robber all too frequently turns to violence and ends up committing murder. This fate overtook an elderly European lady who disturbed a burglar who was ransacking her house. The African robber had taken a short iron bar with him presumably to meet such a contingency as being confronted by the owner. Without hesitation he beat the poor woman savagely over the head, knocking her to the floor. As she lay dying in a pool of blood the murderer walked past her body and fled from the house. In his haste he trod in his victim's blood and left a perfectly detailed footprint on the floor.

Examination of the footprint showed that the murderer had been wearing an unusual type of golf shoe with a groove worn in the middle of the sole. This distinctive mark had almost certainly been worn into the shoe as the result of riding a bicycle. It was the kind of highly individual clue that crime investigators dream about, but I could not have imagined the way in which it was to lead to the murderer.

There was no difficulty in finding a shoe of the same type from the local manufacturer and a groove was cut in the sole to simulate the worn area visible in the footprint. Every African constable and detective in the district was then shown the shoe and a photograph of the footprint. Eight days later a perceptive African constable recognized an impression left by the suspect's shoe. Incredibly he had spotted it in the dust collected on the pavement outside an African beer hall in one of the townships. The constable closed in on his prey, whom he observed sitting at ease, conveniently displaying his distinctive footwear and drinking beer with his feet propped upon a bench.

The shoes in question were very quickly brought to my laboratory. Even though a week had passed since the crime was committed traces of blood were found on the shoes which matched the victim's blood group. The suspect's house was searched and several items were retrieved which were identified as having belonged to the dead woman. Among these was part of a table-cloth, the other half of which had been left at the crime scene. It was assumed that the robber, determined to take his spoils with him, but lacking a suitable receptacle in which to carry them, grabbed at the table-cloth and, tearing it in two, used one piece to wrap up the stolen goods. In the peace and quiet of the laboratory we painstakingly matched the two halves, thread by thread. There was no doubting that the two pieces had originally been one.

The dead woman's daughter, who had identified the stolen items, also told police that her mother had two fifty-dollar American notes in her possession at the time of her death. These were missing from the house and did not come to light during a thorough search of the suspect's home. Inquiries at banks and exchange agencies in the area eventually resulted in a bank-teller identifying the suspect as the person for whom he had changed two fifty-dollar notes into Rhodesian currency. The circle of evidence was thus complete and the suspect was eventually brought to trial and convicted of murder.

The most remarkable facet of this otherwise routine case was the part played by the constable in recognizing the suspect footprint. Few Europeans could so easily aspire to this type of extraordinary visual feat. It is well known that Africans have great visual ability, as I mentioned earlier in connection with distinguishing between shades of colour. For that reason Rhodesian Africans have been trained as emerald-cutters, a highly skilled and well-rewarded profession. An accomplished gem-cutter can cut facets the size of a pinhead on an emerald simply by eye and without any optical aids.

There are many other illustrations of this ability, but it is not merely a matter of the African being able to 'see' better than others. In most police forces detectives are trained in the arts of observation by playing 'Kims' game. A tray holding an assortment of some twenty objects is looked at for a few minutes and then removed. The participants are required to write down the names of as many objects as they can remember. Some television programmes have been able to exploit this game as glamorized family entertainment.

One would anticipate that the African with his undoubted visual powers would excel at this sort of test. But, in practice, European trainee detectives fare rather better than their African counterparts. The reason for this apparent anomaly is that the African tends to see things as a whole and not analytically in a manner which involves breaking down the overall picture into its related parts. A good example of this was demonstrated in an arson case in which the African owner of a burned-down house claimed to recognize footprints made by the suspect in the earth outside. When asked why he was so sure, he replied simply that he knew he was right. He was pressed to point out the particular features, an extra large big toe, possibly, on which he based his identification. He failed completely in this exercise but when confronted with twenty-four prints of different foot impressions, including the suspect's, immediately homed-in on it. He was still not aware of any individual peculiarities in the print until they were pointed out to him—he simply saw the print as a whole.

▼▼▼▼▼▼

In contrast to other parts of Africa armed robbery is relatively rare in Rhodesia. Up to 1977, when I retired, no armed robbery of any of the country's institutions had been successfully carried through, but that is not to say that no attempts are made. I was asked to give evidence in a case in 1974 which had led to the killing of an innocent member of the public.

A pair of robbers, one of whom was armed, held up a restaurant-owner in Salisbury as he was closing his premises and preparing to bank the day's takings. When threatened by the gunman he reluctantly parted with the money. Despite the lateness of the hour the attention of a number of passers-by was attracted to the scene of robbery. Several of these bystanders, who were mainly Africans, decided to give chase as the gunman and his accomplice made off. Among the attributes of most Africans is a natural gift for running and quite a high proportion of them run with style and speed.

After a chase of some three hundred yards, the man leading the pursuit was beginning to close on the fleeing gunman. Realizing that he would soon be overtaken, the gunman turned and fired at the man who crumpled and fell with a bullet in the stomach. The pistol used fired only a small-calibre bullet which ordinarily need not have been fatal. By a twist of fate, however, this brave citizen was struck down by a bullet which cut a major artery and he died shortly after reaching hospital. The gunman and his accomplice escaped in the confusion as the pursuers stopped to look after the injured man.

Descriptions of the robbers were given to the police by several eye-witnesses and, with information provided by other leads, the pair was arrested within two days. Some of the money stolen from the restaurant-owner was still in their possession and useful confirmatory evidence was provided by a leather belt. In the course of his flight the gunman lost the belt fastening his trousers, an event seen by several witnesses. Most belts pick up a liberal quantity of fibres from the clothes they support and this one was no exception. The gunman's trousers were made of cloth containing five different types of fibre, all of which were present on the belt. This armed robber who cruelly murdered an innocent man was sent for trial. He was convicted of murder and sentenced to death while his accomplice received a six-year sentence of imprisonment.

European murders in Rhodesia are also relatively rare, but when one is committed it tends to inspire others so that murders of this sort occur in cycles. In the midlands district of Rhodesia in 1958 there were five entirely unrelated murders of Europeans within the space of two months. There were none during the next eight years, but then in 1966 a series of five murders, all unrelated, was committed in less than six months. The same phenomenon seems to have happened in the Salisbury area where groups of three European murders tend to occur every two years. The odds against these events being simple coincidence are easily calculated. The probability of murder happening five times by chance in a short period in successive eight-year periods is one in six million times six million. Can a reason be deduced for this phenomenon?

Some murders seem to incite others to violence. For example, it is well known that Jack the Ripper had his imitators. But the same sort of thing has also happened in more recent times. Charles Whitman, the mass murderer who shot dead sixteen people at the University of Texas in 1966, had his coypists. It seems that unusual murders tend to be infectious and trigger off copy killings.

In any large community there must be quite a few individuals with secret leanings towards violence and murder. Perhaps they are excited by news of sensational killings and resolve to do likewise. It has always seemed to me that there is a reasonable argument to be made out in favour of suppressing details of murder cases at least until the investigation has been completed. Repetition of killings might thus be avoided and innocent lives saved.

Against this, however, it is fair to set the view that publicity often helps to apprehend the criminal. I think this advantage need not be lost and publicity is acceptable within limits. Current trends in the press and on television, however, tend to provide a feast of morbid details for the sensationally inclined. The good that this achieves for the forces of law is to my mind greatly in danger of being offset by triggering latent psychopaths to murder.

Disputes over money are among the main causes of European murders in Rhodesia. On occasions the outcome can be singularly bloody as in the case of a triple murder which I was called to in May 1968. This came after a particularly busy period when I had travelled some 500 miles in two days to the scene of an explosion and an attempted murder. I had just arrived home in the early evening thinking of little more than a cool drink and a chance to relax when Mollie greeted me with the news that police headquarters had telephoned asking me to contact them immediately.

I learned that a triple murder had occurred in a fairly remote farming area some 120 miles north of Salisbury. 'Would I visit the scene to join the murder investigation team?' Within half an hour I had bathed and shaved and, with a sandwich in my mouth, was in a car being driven north.

The murders had taken place on a large farm which included several houses accommodating the farm manager and a number of assistants—all Europeans. Tragedy had struck the home of the farm manager who, with his wife and mother-in-law, lay dead inside. All three had received a heavy blow on the back of the head. The mother-in-law lay face downward just inside the door of her bedroom. Evidently she had come from the bathroom because she had a spongebag in her hand and except for her dress—which she was also carrying—was clothed under her dressing gown.

Lying in a similar position in the next bedroom, except that she was fully clothed, was the wife. Her husband was found in the kitchen also fully clothed and wearing his boots. He too was lying face downward. It was obvious even when blighted with death that this was a tidy and methodically run household—everything was in apple-pie order. There was not the slightest sign of a struggle having occurred and not a rug or carpet out of place. It was clear though that the mother-in-law's body had been dragged to the room she was found in.

By now it was quite late and experience told me that tired men searching a scene such as this by artificial light were not at their best. More harm than good can result in these circumstances, with the possible loss of vital evidence. Having taken a careful look around to ensure that nothing requiring immediate attention had been missed, we retired for the night in the temporary quarters put at our disposal. We would resume at first light.

There was a strange feeling of unreality about the place when I walked into the kitchen next morning and looked at the table meticulously laid for the previous day's breakfast—which had never been eaten. Two eggs lay partly cooked in the poacher, slices of bread were on the grill ready for toasting and the teapot, with tea leaves in it, stood beside the kettle. It was like the *Marie Celeste* except that we knew where the bodies were!

Our inquiries began in earnest and we set about establishing some times for the morning routine of this methodical but now dead household. John Due went off to work on the farm each day at 6.00 a.m., returning for breakfast at about 8.00 a.m. His wife, Elsie, rose at around 7.00 a.m. to prepare breakfast, and his mother-in-law, Mrs Viljoen, took a bath at about 7.45 a.m. ready to join the others at breakfast. The state of preparation for breakfast which was evident in the kitchen suggested that the murderer must have entered the house just before 8.00 a.m. A likely scenario was that, silently and with ruthless efficiency, he first killed Elsie Due where she stood in her bedroom. He then waited for Mrs Viljoen to emerge from the bathroom when he killed her and dragged her body into her bedroom and out of sight. The murderer then lay in wait for John Due who, as usual, entered by the back door of the house leading into the kitchen. As he walked into the kitchen to wash his hands at the sink he was felled by a single blow to the head and dropped dead to the floor.

The method of killing was a most unusual form of attack and I had already discussed this with my fellow-investigators. We observed that in the African ritual sacrifice of cattle it is customary to strike the animal a death-dealing blow above the neck, usually with an axe. When this is skilfully carried out it is a merciful method of dispatching the animal, which drops dead without fuss. Each of the three persons murdered on the farm had been killed in a similar manner. In the great majority of murders committed by Africans the murderer runs wild, striking many blows to ensure his purpose. Consequently, the single, neat killing blow with a heavy, blunt instrument seemed un-African in manner—save for the similarity with the ritual killing of animals.

Motive for the murders was not immediately obvious. A dressing-table drawer had been forced open suggesting robbery, although it still contained some money and passports. It was known that two commercial travellers had called at the house during the day of the murders but routine inquiries eliminated them as suspects. The murder took place on the house servant's day off and his claim not to have been near the house all day was substantiated by witnesses.

As the inquiry progressed, news began to filter through the grape-vine that an African house servant had been spending considerable sums of money in the local village. The man in question proved to be George, who worked for Mr and Mrs Due and who had obligingly served tea at regular intervals during our investigations. He looked harmless enough, but then it is not possible to distinguish a murderer simply by looking at him. We began to view George with more suspicion, however, as evidence about him accumulated. What began as a trickle finished up as a torrent. The African woman who shared George's bed stated that on the afternoon of the murder her paramour had shown her three five-pound notes. A male acquaintance identified the watch George was wearing as belonging to the murdered Mr Due, and so the evidence mounted.

Asked to explain these matters, George finally admitted having a disagreement with Mr Due over pay. A dispute arose over his leave entitlement. He claimed that while the family was on holiday he took some leave, part of which was due to him with part being unpaid. He said this disagreement took place with his employer before he left for work at 6.00 a.m. George claimed that Mr Due became angry and hit him with a stick. After a good deal of close questioning George eventually admitted that he went on the rampage with a length of one-and-a-half inch steel piping and felled his employer and the other two occupants of the house. The sequence of events which he related hardly varied from our reconstruction. He also admitted breaking into the dressing-table drawer with a screwdriver and taking a sum of money consistent with his ideas of what he was owed.

George said he threw the piece of piping and the screwdriver into two different places in the long grass beyond the house. In police terminology, he agreed 'to make indications' and we were soon in possession of the two implements. Together with the drawer from the dressing-table they were whisked away to the laboratory. We were able to establish quite conclusively that the piping was the murder weapon and that the screwdriver had been used to force open the drawer containing the money.

Not only did the piece of pipe fit the shape of the head wounds of the three victims, but hairs found adhering to blood smears on it matched the head hair of Mrs Viljoen. Marks made by the screwdriver when used to force open the dressing-table drawer were matched to experimental marks made with the tool. The screwdriver also bore appreciable traces of the rather unusual varnish with which the piece of furniture had been painted. Moreover, there had been a transfer in the other direction. The screwdriver had at some stage been used to stir green paint, traces of which were still caked on its blade—some slivers of this paint had been transferred to the drawer. As the screwdriver was normally kept in a special place in Due's garage, its use indicated knowledge of the house.

It had taken three days at the scene of the triple murder to piece together the events of that fateful breakfast-time. All the evidence pointed at George who was eventually brought to trial and convicted of murder. For my part I was pleased to return to Salisbury and to sanity at the end of an extraordinary week which had begun with an attempted murder case, gone on to include investigations of explosion and arson and finished with a triple murder. As if that was not sufficient, the fates had also contrived to squeeze in the case of the missing gardeners.

While driving back to Salisbury at mid-week with my Forensic Science Liaison Officer we had received a call on the car radio requesting us to attend a crime scene at a suburban house in Wankie. The household was of the type which employed a cook and a gardener in the accepted Rhodesian manner. It seemed that some time previously the family gardener went missing. When he failed to re-appear after two weeks he was replaced by a second gardener. He also disappeared after only a week. Following a decent interval a third gardener was taken on and after starting to dig the garden he rushed up to the house to report an unusual discovery to his employer—he had unearthed a human arm. Further digging exposed a body which proved to be that of the missing second gardener. When we arrived on the scene the body was moved out of its grave to reveal another corpse underneath, that of the first gardener. All the evidence pointed at the cook, who turned out to be mentally unbalanced and apparently harbouring a pathological dislike of gardeners. At least he was not out for gain—his motive was pure hatred.

▼▼▼▼▼▼

Murder in a locked room has been the basis of many detective stories but the puzzle occurs only rarely in real life. Most detectives serve the whole of their career without meeting this phenomenon so I suppose I can count myself fortunate that my career as a forensic scientist encompassed such a case. Fictional accounts have included explanations ranging from the absurd to the intriguingly possible. One extravagant flight of fancy had the body being discovered in the locked room of a bungalow and the murderer escaping through a gap made by hoisting up the roof with a car jack. After making his exit he lowers the roof and of course there is no trace of evidence to show how he managed it! A more sober suggestion was contained in a story wherein the door was locked from the outside by using a special pair of pliers pushed through the keyhole to turn the key on the inside. Another version of this idea had the key turned from the outside by a piece of string passing under the door and pulling on a pencil inserted through the hole in the end of the key. A further, less subtle, suggestion has the murderer remaining in the locked room until the door is broken down by the police. As the officers rush headlong into the room, their attention riveted to the gruesome sight of the dead body, the murderer slips quietly away unnoticed.

On the only occasion I encountered a murder in a locked room the solution proved so simple that it remains a source of shame and irritation that I spent several sleepless nights trying to work it out. This was in 1969 and the phenomenon occurred in a well-appointed bungalow standing in an acre of ground in one of Salisbury's classy residential suburbs. This was the home of Mrs Whitworth, a fairly wealthy widow aged fifty-eight. She was a healthy, well-preserved woman of vigorous pursuits such as gardening, polo and swimming. Although she employed two African gardeners it was quite commonplace for her to spend several hours cracking up stones with a seven-pound hammer to decorate her rockery. Everything about her suggested a remarkably fit and energetic woman.

The story began when her small dog, which usually slept in the bedroom with her, disturbed the neighbours by its incessant barking throughout the night. That was unusual in itself but about sunrise, one of the neighbours, a retired naval officer, realized that the dog was out in the garden barking its head off. With rising curiosity the neighbour telephoned Mrs Whitworth intending to tell her that her dog was loose. Receiving no answer he decided to investigate and walked over to the bungalow, knocking on the door and calling the owner's name. There was no response so he moved to the bedroom window and peered through the curtains. He could see the end of the bed and the edge of the bedside carpet on which rested a pair of feet. The rest of the body was hidden from his view, but deciding that something was wrong he called the police.

A police inspector arrived within minutes and together with the neighbour entered the house through an unlocked outside garden door. They proceeded to the bedroom only to find that it was locked. The door was of wooden construction and without too much hesitation the two hefty men put their shoulders to it and broke it open. As the door burst open both men distinctly remembered hearing the key drop to the floor on the inside. The widow was found lying, face upwards, on the carpet in the gap between the bed and the wall. She had injuries on the face but no other apparent wounds apart from some slight bruising on the throat.

Careful examination revealed that the bridge of her nose was badly bruised and there were further bruises about an inch apart under her left eye. The right nostril was torn and the right side of the upper lip was split through to the teeth. There were no indications that a struggle had occurred in the room except that the dressing-table had been displaced by a foot or two. A pinhead-sized piece of human skin was found on a corner of the dressing-table top. Post-mortem examination showed that the poor woman had bitten her tongue, making it bleed so profusely that she choked on her own blood. Tongue-biting of this sort is a characteristic of an epileptic fit which is usually accompanied by convulsions. The obvious suggestion was that the unfortunate woman had suffered an epileptic fit and struck her face on the dressing-table while gripped by convulsions. As a result she bit her tongue badly.

Mrs Whitworth had resided in Rhodesia for two years, having previously lived in Kenya. So far as could be ascertained from friends and neighbours she had consulted a doctor on only one occasion during that time and then only for a minor ailment. No one knew the name of the doctor and her previous medical history could not be traced. She had in her possession a small bottle containing sleeping tablets—the label bore the solitary word, 'Mogadon'. No medical preparations could be found suggesting that she was being treated for epilepsy. That did not necessarily rule out the possibility of her suffering from the disease, for the stigma attached to it is such that sufferers are often driven to concealment for social reasons. Avoiding the cancellation of a driving licence is one such reason. Furthermore, I learned from the medical examiner that cases were known of epileptics wishing to conceal their affliction who made a point of locking themselves away in the privacy of their own room when they thought an attack was imminent. The fact that Mrs Whitworth's dog had been left outside tended to support this viewpoint.

As to the locked room itself, the critical evidence—the key—was found about eighteen inches inside the door. It lay there with wooden debris from the broken door and frame together with the metal latch-plate normally fixed to the door jamb which receives the door catch and tongue of the lock. All the windows of the room, except one, were tightly shut with the catches, which were stiff, firmly closed. The catches were of the type incorporating two notches, one position to close the window completely, the other to allow a narrow opening of about half an inch. One window had been left slightly open on its second catch. Although it was theoretically possible to close this from the outside with an implement such as a table knife the catch was about seven feet above the level of the ground outside the house. The exterior of the house had been freshly whitewashed and it seemed inconceivable to me that anyone could have climbed out of that window, closing it from outside, without leaving some trace on the whitened surface. There were no such tell-tale traces apart from some muddy paw marks on the window ledge. These were traced to Mrs Whitworth's cat which was known by the neighbours to use this window as a means of entering the house. Thus I found it difficult to imagine that any person had used that window as an exit on the night of Mrs Whitworth's death.

The locked bedroom was puzzle enough but the lounge also revealed some curious features. On the mantelpiece was an empty beer bottle and in the fireplace, in the burnt-out remains in the grate, was a small, empty corned beef tin. This had been hacked open, possibly with a penknife, and lay alongside a charred and almost completely burnt sponge. All this was quite out of character with the otherwise spotlessly clean and well-ordered domestic scene. According to friends Mrs Whitworth seldom drank beer and, if she did, it would not be in her nature to leave an empty bottle on the mantelpiece. It seemed equally improbable that she would crudely hack open a tin of meat, eat the contents and throw the empty container into the fireplace. Doubts began to creep in!

While the experts theorized on the evidence to date, routine inquiries went ahead. Were there any fingerprints in the house which were not accounted for? Were there any signs of forcible entry or hasty searching? Was anything missing? Had any strangers been seen hanging around the house or neighbourhood? Had there been any visitors to the house? Did the dead woman have any men friends? These and many other questions formed the basis of the police investigation and represented the kind of laborious and painstaking work with which police forces around the world solve their murder cases.

As a result of these inquiries two interesting facts emerged. Mrs Whitworth had employed two gardeners, one permanently and the other on a temporary basis. The fingerprints of the second man,

Mpani, were found in the house, in the kitchen, in the lounge and on a box in which it was the dead woman's custom to put her small change. Police records revealed that he had previous convictions for violent assault. When Mpani was questioned it was noticed that there were two spots of blood on his shirt front. He protested that he had cut himself while shaving. We took the shirt away for testing and established that the blood on it was of the same group as the dead woman. Unfortunately, this did not help us, for Mpani belonged to that group also.

I turned my attention again to the epilepsy theory and had an uneasy feeling that there was really remarkably little evidence of the dead woman having suffered convulsions. One would have expected greater signs of disorder if she had been so afflicted and the wounds to her face were worrying. I would certainly have expected to find more than a single tiny piece of skin on the corner of the dressing-table to account for the facial injuries sustained by falling against it. The state of the facial wounds seemed worthy of more detailed examination. Although the nostril and upper lip had been split right through, there was no blood on the wounds when we first saw the body. A possible explanation, following the epilepsy line of thought, was that as convulsions often came in series she might have cleaned up her injuries between spasms. She might then have locked herself in the bedroom to close herself off from the outside world. Apart from the natural feminine desire not to be seen when she was in a mess, there was also the need to keep her illness secret for fear of social consequences such as losing her driving licence. She was known to be a keen motorist.

If this was indeed the sequence of events it was possible that she experienced a further convulsion in that locked bedroom as a result of which she bit her tongue. It seemed to me that if the bitten tongue could possibly produce enough blood to choke her, the split lip would certainly have bled profusely. Yet it was remarkable how little blood there was on her face. I suddenly realized the implication was that someone must have cleaned her up after she was dead. If this were so it was clearly a case of murder, and Mpani, the gardener, led the field of suspects.

Mpani's fingerprints had been found in the house and while this was not necessarily suspicious—he was after all a servant—he was questioned intensively on his movements. He admitted having knocked at the door of the house on the evening before Mrs Whitworth was found dead and asking his employer for an advance on his pay or, failing that, for a loan. Police officers now pressed Mpani with questions and he began to go to pieces. He said that a friend had accompanied him to the house and this companion assaulted Mrs Whitworth. He claimed that his own action was to run away while this violence was being enacted. Somewhat treacherously Mpani named his friend but unfortunately his story fell in ruins when the friend in question furnished the police with a cast-iron alibi supported by numerous reliable witnesses.

Confronted with this news Mpani changed his story completely and confessed to murdering Mrs Whitworth. He had gone alone to the house to ask his employer to lend him money. He claimed that she refused and brandished a big steel poker at him. Outraged, he pushed his way into the house where he knocked her down in the lounge and throttled her. As she fell her face struck the fireguard. He went into the bathroom and, taking a soapy sponge, thoroughly cleaned the blood off the fireguard. Next, he cleaned up the wounds on Mrs Whitworth's face and carried her through into the bedroom where he laid her on the carpet. He closed all the windows save one which remained slightly open, left the room and locked the door from the outside. Using a piece of newspaper he then slid the key under the door and inside the bedroom. His work completed Mpani treated himself to a bottle of beer and a tin of meat in the lounge.

The mystery of the locked room was thus solved, but what of the key which the two men who broke into the room believed so firmly they heard fall to the floor? They had simply misinterpreted what they heard and had unwittingly misled the investigation. What they thought was the noise made by the key dropping to the floor was actually caused by the latch-plate shaken out of the door-frame by their assault on the door. It joined the key which, of course, was already on the floor. I well remember mentally noting the positions of the key and latch-plate on the floor when I first entered the room. I accepted, perhaps too readily, the account of the two men who were first on the scene. What puzzled me at the time was that while the key lay on the wooden floor, the latch-plate had ended up further inside the room on the carpet. It must have first hit the wooden floor then bounced onto the carpet. A clear example of the perils of taking things for granted in a forensic investigation!

I was now able to build up a more precise picture of what had taken place in Mrs Whitworth's house and to find substantiating evidence. The burnt sponge found in the fireplace rewarded the minute attention given it by my laboratory staff when they found hairs on it matching the head hair of the victim. Most of these hairs also bore traces of bloody water. Clearly, this was the sponge discarded by Mpani after he had mopped up the injuries on Mrs Whitworth's face. The carpet in front of the fireplace in the lounge was made of a wool fibre mixture comprising six colour shades—two blue and one shade each of green, yellow, red and brown. Microscopical examination of the knees of Mpani's trousers produced a rich harvest of woollen fibres. All six colour shades were represented, leaving little doubt that Mpani had knelt on that particular carpet. If two lots of wool or two woollen fibres are taken at random it is unlikely that they will match in colour by pure chance. If a sample of wool containing six different shades is taken, the chance of finding another sample containing all six matching colours is so remote as to be negligible. As further proof of Mpani's presence in the house there were of course his fingerprints and his independent knowledge of the beer bottle and corned beef tin.

By this time the pathologist's report on the post-mortem was available. This showed that while Mrs Whitworth had indeed died by choking on her own blood, the bitten tongue has resulted from her being strangled and not, as we had thought earlier, by having an epileptic fit. There was also bruising of the throat which was not apparent at the original medical examination. Epilepsy was thus firmly ruled out and, as falling against the fireguard did not in my view satisfactorily explain the facial injuries, we began to search for a weapon. Thinking along the right lines now, we did not take long to pin-point a pair of old-fashioned, heavy steel tongs which were kept beside the fireplace in the lounge. These were about thirty inches long and had been as vigorously cleaned by Mpani as the fireguard. Nevertheless, microscopical examination picked up traces of blood and skin. There is nothing like 'showing the tool to the job', so I took the tongs to the mortuary and found that they fitted perfectly to the bruises under the victim's eyes and to the damage on the nose. The match was so striking that there could be little doubt that this was the weapon which had been used to assault Mrs Whitworth. It was also evident from this new interpretation of the injuries that she had been lying on the floor when the brutal blows landed on her face.

Mpani was eventually brought to trial and found guilty of murder. Before sentence was passed, he was asked in the age old manner if he had anything to say. He replied simply, 'I did not mean to kill her but a devil got into me'. In retrospect I suppose this tragedy ran along almost classical lines where luck is with the villain to begin with but later everything turns against him. The manner of the victim's death showed a remarkable resemblance to epilepsy which combined with the confusion over the bedroom door key to mislead the early investigation. This was all extraordinarily good fortune for the murderer. If he had destroyed his shirt and with it the tell-tale spots of blood it is questionable whether he would have been caught. Our finding of his fingerprints on the cash box in the house was sufficient to suggest his motive and from that moment his luck deserted him. Recalling that evidence concerning the coloured fibres in the lounge carpet contributed to Mpani's guilt, it is worth noting that the ability to distinguish fine shades of colour is not a product of intelligence. In fact the opposite is true. There is a pronounced tendency for those considered not particularly bright to be the best judges of differences between colours. It is also true that, on the whole, women have better perception in these matters than men.

▼▼▼▼▼▼

That most murders for money involve remarkably small gain has been demonstrated by the cases I have referred to. It is also evident that in Africa disputes over wages can lead to violent consequences. Non-payment of African wages is an almost certain prescription for disaster and I recall a tragic incident in which a European living in Salisbury unwittingly caused his wife's death by failing to pay his house-boy. The man was called away on business and overlooked this essential chore. In his master's absence, the house-boy took up the matter of his unpaid wages with the wife. An argument ensued which ended dramatically with the complaining employee stabbing the young wife to death. The house-boy walked to the police station to give himself up taking with him the dead woman's two-year old child whom he carried gently in his arms.

He was later convicted of murder and sentenced to twelve years imprisonment.

Non-payment of his wages on due date is a humiliating experience for the African employee. By any judgment this is understandable, for a trust is broken and offence is given. To rural Africans, and many suburban dwellers also, who enjoy little in the way of material possessions, there is also an element of cheating. Consequently, what they have and what they are due must be protected—with violence if necessary.

Chapter Six
ROBBERY

ROBBERY is one of the leading categories of crime and comes in numerous forms, ranging from simple burglary to the organized robbing of banks. House-breaking is frequently a solo operation whereas most of the grander schemes involve two or more criminals. Sophisticated and violent robbers, like other felons, are outwitted and caught by an alert public and by determined and well-trained police-officers.

Robbery is almost always associated with violence if only of the kind that causes damage to property and, occasionally, violence is used against the person. As in every criminal enterprise, the wrong-doer invariably leaves behind traces of his presence and his activity which help the investigator. Robbery ranks next to 'hit-and-run' cases as a source of forensic material.

The nature of trace evidence is often unusual and I'm certain that the African shop thief who left behind a tiny piece of his scalp never imagined in his wildest dreams that he would be caught because of it. This man had developed a routine with a European racketeer who 'fenced' the camera equipment which he stole from retail photographic shops. The African thief's technique was simply to smash a hole in the window of his selected shop and grab two or three expensive cameras and any other photographic accessories conveniently in reach and flee into the night. He later met with his fence who disposed of the stolen property. Several shops had been 'done over' in this manner and a lucrative racket had developed.

On what proved to be his last venture the thief broke the window of a photographic dealer's shop and, while leaning through the aperture grabbing at cameras, he touched his head on a razor-sharp piece of broken glass. He left behind a small piece of his scalp about one-third of an inch long consisting of both skin and hair. By the time it arrived at the laboratory this piece of skin was rolled into a tightly curled ball. With careful handling I managed to straighten it out and photograph it. This showed that the piece of skin was evenly tapered on both sides, a shape which helped me to decide the part of the head it had come from. If the man had caught the front part of his scalp on the broken glass I would have expected a wedge-shaped piece of skin to have been lost. The fact that it was evenly tapered, front and back, suggested to me that he had only just touched the glass and that therefore he had just sliced off a sliver of skin at the top of the head towards the back. I made this observation to the police and suggested that they look for a man with a dressing or a plaster in that position on his head.

In the course of rounding-up likely suspects for questioning, the police found a man with such a plaster on his head. But was he the right man? Fortunately, the broken window glass had cut through the hair roots which appeared as an irregular pattern of black dots on the under surface of the sliver of skin. It seemed quite possible therefore that a corresponding pattern would be left on the cut surface of the man's scalp. The only way we could verify this was to photograph the wound on the top of the suspect's head.

Now it is quite an awkward task to take a close-up photograph of the top of a person's head. The camera must be rigidly fixed on a tripod as it is impossible to hold it steadily enough in the hand for close-up work. The camera must also be within a few inches of the surface to be photographed and two spotlights are normally required to give adequate illumination. There were two possible ways to tackle this problem. The man could either lie flat and face downward on a table so that the camera and spotlights were horizontal, or he could sit on the ground with the camera and lights in a vertical plane. We decided that the second arrangement was best both from the technical point of view and also out of consideration for the man's comfort.

The photograph was successfully taken and the print compared with that of the piece of skin found at the crime scene. A striking match was immediately evident between the hair root patterns in the two photographs. Our delight in this technical achievement was somewhat dampened when the suspect, puzzled and terrified by the whole procedure, blurted out a confession. He told the police where he had dumped stolen goods which proved difficult to fence. This turned out to be a reservoir, and a skin-diving squad spent a morning bringing up a sunken treasure of cameras and photographic equipment. All the items recovered were identified and formed impressive exhibits at the trial at which a conviction for theft was obtained.

The pitfalls waiting to trap even the wariest of thieves are unlimited and utterly damning evidence can be provided by the most insignificant trifle. A good illustration of this was afforded by a case involving the theft of motor tyres which was solved by evidence gleaned from a scrap of paper. Two juvenile delinquents in the Salisbury district occupied themselves in 1964 by stealing tyres from lorries and trucks; they also made a tolerable living by selling these valuable articles.

Many criminals—and thieves are no exception—develop a *modus operandi* which becomes the hallmark of their speciality. They repeat the same sort of crime in much the same way, frequently to the extent that they might as well leave their name and address at the scene of the crime. This tendency probably results from the criminal's innate laziness and inefficiency which prevent him from making the effort to earn his living and blind him with thoughts of easy pickings from crime. Being basically lazy he establishes a successful routine and is too idle to change it. Fortunately, he thus ensures his own downfall by repeating the pattern and making his activities known to the police.

This happened to the two tyre thieves. They stole three almost new tyres from a parked truck and attempted to sell them to a regular scrap dealer who was under surveillance. The police swooped on the scrap yard, taking in the two young delinquents for questioning and impounding the stolen tyres. The first thing we noticed was that the numbers on the tyres had been obliterated by rubbing with coarse sandpaper. What we had to do was to establish that those particular tyres had indeed at one time been on the truck from which it was alleged they had been stolen. With this objective in view the tyres and the wheel rims from the truck were sent to my laboratory.

The first essential in any trial proceedings is to prove that a crime has been committed. It was no use the prosecution in this case going into court and arguing that the articles were stolen because the two accused were in possession of three tyres from which the marks had been carefully erased and for which they could give no reasonable account. In the eyes of the law this would not constitute theft—it would be necessary to prove that the tyres were stolen and to show where and from whom. Hence the appeals on television showing stolen goods and asking the owners to identify them. The police are aiming at a conviction for theft as well as trying to return the goods to their lawful owners. Fortunately, the juvenile tyre thieves were out of luck due to a small piece of seemingly inconsequential paper. A piece of waterproof baling paper, formed from two sheets of brown paper stuck together with a layer of tar or bitumen, had been caught between one of the tyres and the rim to which it was fitted. A small piece of such paper, about one inch long and a quarter of an inch wide, had separated when the tyre was taken off the wheel rim leaving one piece adhering to the rim and the other stuck to the tyre.

We proved that the two pieces of paper were mirror images of each other. In matching materials such as this it is not expected that the two pieces will be identical—one piece will bear the same relation to the other as a person's two hands, which are not identical. It is not possible to put a left-hand glove on a right hand unless the inside is put on the outside, as the left hand is the mirror image of the right. In the same way, the two pieces of paper were not identical but were exact mirror images, clearly proving that the tyre about to be sold by the two youngsters had come from the wheel rim on which the piece of paper was found.

With what to me seemed wisdom and insight, the magistrate trying the case gave the delinquents a fairly stiff prison sentence which was suspended for three years on condition that they were not involved in another crime during that period. This brush with the law was sufficient to jerk these two youngsters off their seemingly inevitable path of crime and back to the 'straight and narrow' again. Their subsequent behaviour was commendable and they turned out to be responsible citizens in worthwhile jobs. This was another example of an immensely significant sequence of events being put into motion by a trifle—in this case, a small piece of baling paper.

As I have shown many times in this narrative, trifles are very much part of the forensic scientist's lot. Time and again we came back to those fateful hairs and fibres which link criminal and crime. Few things in life appear of less worth than a ball of fluff, yet they have their place in the world of criminalistics. Loosely woven cloth and woollen materials tend to form prills or fluff balls on worn surfaces of garments and they drop off during the wearing-out process of the article of clothing. At times they can provide highly significant evidence, especially if the cloth is made from a variety of unusual fibres—which is quite often the case owing to the use of a tremendous range of commercially produced fibres. Small clumps of fibre, smaller than a pin head, will contain scores of fibres often of different and unusual kinds.

Balls of fluff containing unique mixtures of fibres appear in all sorts of places, one of the more fertile grounds being the pockets of garments which have been washed or dry-cleaned. In the cleaning process the clothes are jumbled together and fibres are transferred from one garment to another and lodge in pockets and trouser turn-ups. I can recall an incident in which a housebreaker was trapped by identifiable balls of fluff adhering to his handkerchief. The burglar, having broken in, was disturbed by the woman occupant of the house whom he savagely attacked. He struggled with her and inflicted a deep stab wound in her chest. In the course of the scuffle the intruder dropped his handkerchief which was left at the scene as he made good his escape. As he had been suffering from a cold, his handkerchief was well-moistened from continuous use. Not surprisingly it had picked up several balls of fluff from his pocket which could be clearly seen adhering to it. When the suspected burglar was apprehended it was shown that the handkerchief belonged to him as the fluff balls on it matched perfectly with eight different types of fluff in his pockets. It was even possible to tell precisely which pocket the handkerchief had been kept in as there were appreciable differences between the fluff from various pockets.

An unpretentious ball of fluff also played an important part in the prosecution of a gang of cattle thieves in 1975. This gang, using a well-organized routine, had been highly active for several months and used the town of Hartley as a base. The first step in the rustlers' operations was to contact the herdsman of a farm within a sixty-mile radius of their base. For a suitable bribe, or under threat of violence, the herdsman would arrange for some of the cattle in his care to be at a particular spot at an agreed time. Factors which might help or hinder the success of the proposed raid, such as the absence of the farm-owner or overseer and dates of forthcoming communal beer-drinking parties, were taken into consideration. This information-gathering part of the exercise was carried out by messengers or bully-boys who travelled about by bus or bicycle. The informants must have been effectively terrorized for in the whole series of thefts there was not one betrayal.

On the night fixed for the raid a group of five men would visit the designated farm and kill sufficient cattle to make a full load for their one-ton truck. The carrasses were skinned and dressed on the spot and then loaded up for transportation. The rustlers had contacts with unscrupulous butchers who were prepared to buy meat at cut-prices without asking too many questions regarding the source of supply. Before completing the night's business the gang invariably tidied up their truck and thoroughly washed it.

Two pieces of evidence were instrumental in terminating this series of cattle thefts—a ball of fluff and traces of bovine blood and hair. During the scene of crime investigation at the latest farm to fall victim to the gang, a young policeman only recently out of training was sharp enough to spot a small ball of fluff caught in the grass of the pasture from which the rustled cattle had been removed. It appeared to be a fairly common type of dark blue wool. Nevertheless, it was carefully collected, sealed in a polythene bag and labelled. Two days later the inevitable rumour reached the CID in Hartley naming the men alleged to be members of the cattle-thieving gang. A truck used by these men was located by investigating officers and, although it showed signs of having recently been cleaned, traces of blood and hair were found in it. Laboratory tests showed both blood and hair to be bovine in origin. This was interesting but not sufficient proof of guilt.

In the hope of finding cattle hairs on the clothing of the suspected men, various working clothes were sent to me at the laboratory. The bundles of clothing were accompanied by several wooden-handled, home-made knives belonging to the men. These implements had been made by riveting slats of wood onto a strip of steel to form a primitive but effective handle. In the joint between the wood and the steel we found numerous cut fragments of cow hair adhering to caked bovine blood. Some of these hairs were matched to samples taken from the slaughtered cattle but again this was inconclusive evidence.

A number of cow hairs was also found on the clothing of four of the men but the garment which captured my attention was a dark blue jersey. This garment was well worn and had frayed badly on both arms and between elbow and wrist. Its owner obviously had an attentive and homely girl-friend, for the worn sleeves of the jersey had been patched with carefully knitted strips, about three inches wide. It was a commendably neat job but, unfortunately from the owner's point of view, wool was used which had been given to the girl by the woman who employed her as a nursemaid. The history of this wool, as we later discovered, was that it had been sent as a gift from America and was one of the occasional small lots of wool made up from leavings and surplus fibres from other jobs. Thread and yarn makers are careful and economical people who waste nothing. Surplus fibre is used either to make knitting yarn or to form the selvedge of woven cloth which frequently contains all manner of odd fibres bearing no relation to the main run of cloth.

In this case the blue wool of the jersey patch was such a mixture. It contained three types of wool, four of rayon and two of orlon. This highly individual mixture was, for all practical purposes, unique and would not be repeated again by chance. When the tiny ball of fluff picked up at the crime scene was examined in the laboratory its composition was found to be far from commonplace. It contained some eighty fibres consisting of the nine types found in the jersey wool. Each corresponding type matched exactly, leaving no doubt that the jersey had been worn by someone present at the farm where the cattle were slaughtered. As this was a quiet, secluded spot, well off the beaten track, the inference was clear that the wearer of the patched jersey had played a part in the cattle theft. We discovered that the remainder of the gift parcel of wool sent from America had been used to knit a pullover for a twelve-year-old boy who was away at boarding school throughout the period of cattle rustling.

Another unusual link with the crime scene turned up in one of the suspect's rooms. This was a piece of tree bark which had been used as string. This is a common practice in Africa and dates back to the earliest times when cloth was made from bast fibres which come from the inner bark of many plants and trees. The ancient Egyptians produced fine linen from the bast fibre of flax, and other plants such as sisal, hemp, ramie and coir are widely used today. The piece of bark which had done service as string on this occasion had probably been used to tie up a bag containing meat as it had on it blood-stained hemp fibres from a sack. The likelihood was that the piece of bark had been stripped off a handy tree at the crime scene. This was indeed the case, for we found a small tree at the scene of the raid into the surface of which we were able to fit the piece of bark string. Thus a further link was demonstrated between the five suspects and the cattle thieving.

Not surprisingly, with the likely thieves in custody, the cattle raids suddenly stopped. Two of the men had been prosecuted just over a year previously for the same offence, although they had been acquitted. Several of the herdsmen who had been threatened by the gang members came forward to identify them. They had been so thoroughly terrorized that while they were willing to give evidence of identity to the police, they steadfastly refused to appear in court. Threats of subpoenas and penalties for contempt of court had no effect on them—they were more frightened of witchcraft than they were of confinement in prison for contempt. It appeared that one of the five suspects was the son of a well-known witch-doctor and was widely believed to have inherited much of his father's craft. Fortunately for the forces of law and order, a bit of forensic magic with a tiny ball of fluff and a few other trifles helped to secure the conviction of four of the thieves, the fifth man being acquitted.

▼▼▼▼▼▼

The best emeralds in the world are found in Africa and, weight for weight, some of these stones are more expensive than diamonds. These gorgeous green gems are characterized by the presence of fine needle-like structures known as tremolites. It is these needles, which can only be seen with a good microscope and correct illumination, that give emeralds their beautifully rich appearance. They also offer a means of identifying the particular area from which the stone originated.

In 1965, following the opening of a new emerald mine in the Fort Victoria district, £100,000 worth of uncut gems disappeared. A consignment of stones, thought to be the missing gems, later found their way onto the Paris market by irregular means. It was easy enough to prove the presence of tremolite needles in the stones, but to prove conclusively in a court of law that they came from a particular mine it would be necessary to show that nowhere else in the world was it possible to find emeralds with those characteristic needles. This was, and is, an impossible undertaking. Consequently, the mining company spent a great deal of money buying back their own emeralds. They finally reached the laboratory, accompanied by a request for my opinion as to how they might have been stolen. Naturally, the company wanted to tighten their security arrangements to prevent any future thefts.

The emeralds were still in the rough, uncut state with traces of the original matrix rock clinging to them. Some of this debris contained brown biotite mica, which powdered rather easily and, in view of my next discovery, tended to confuse the issue. I came to the conclusion that half of the Paris consignment of stones bore traces of faecal matter while the remainder were clear of this foreign material. As the presence of the brown mica made the position uncertain, I asked the investigating officer if he could arrange for me to have, for the purposes of comparison, an emerald which had been swallowed and recovered. Being a conscientious and helpful man, he replied, 'I'll be back in two days' time'.

When he returned he produced such an emerald, having performed the necessary duty himself. It must have been a worrying time for him with thoughts of the emerald causing damage inside his body. However, the real concern was of losing the valuable gem, for it is remarkable what a human being can swallow without causing serious harm. Examination of this 'recycled' stone confirmed the manner in which half of the Paris consignment became soiled with faecal matter. It was also clear that, owing to the presence of tiny cracks in the surface of the uncut emeralds, it was extremely difficult to remove entirely the traces of faecal material.

If all the Paris emeralds had been swallowed and recovered all of them would have been contaminated. As only half of them were contaminated it appeared that half the emeralds had been swallowed and the remaining half had been stolen by some other means. Another possible explanation for the half and half condition was that each thief had secreted an emerald in his anus so producing a less thorough contamination. When I put these possibilities to the investigation officer he arranged for a snap inspection at the mine. Thirty-five African mine-workers were found attempting to leave their company's premises with stolen emeralds hidden in their anuses. I was never told how the inspection was carried out nor did I inquire. Suffice it to say that we had established the smugglers' *modus operandi*! The agent with whom the smugglers were dealing represented a gang operating in an organized crime network a thousand miles away in Johannesburg. Being outside the orbit of terror of the parent gang, he was persuaded to talk freely. The information he provided enabled the police to wind up the smuggling operation successfully.

This emerald theft was my only encounter with organized crime. It illustrated that provided the organized crime syndicates are reasonably careful, the odds in the battle for law and order are in their favour. While some of the lesser fry in the crime underworld are sacrificed to the law from time to time, the top operators are rarely convicted. Al Capone, who ruled the Chicago crime world in the 1920s, amply demonstrated this. When the law finally caught up with him it was not for crimes of violence but for income tax evasion.

Large-scale crime is invariably the product of large towns with huge populations. The criminal has a better chance of preserving his anonymity and he has ready access to all the weaponry, equipment and other resources which he needs in the furtherance of crime. The development of scientific detection methods has been spurred on by the growing sophistication of criminal methods. Paris, London, Berlin and New York have featured as the focal points for criminological studies, for the need has been greatest in those cities. In Rhodesia, with its more sparse population, a few large towns and many rural communities, the odds against the criminal are greater.

In a small town or sparsely populated community the number of individuals capable of committing a large-scale robbery, for example, is very low. Moreover, without the cover provided by a teeming city, the criminal has fewer places to hide. He is more open to suspicion by casual observers and passers-by and, in Africa, may fall victim to the power of rumour. Every police force in the world depends on 'information received', an important factor in crime detection. Against this, of course, must be set the bribing and intimidation of witnesses often with the all-powerful connivance of witchcraft.

The professional operating in the small community is also more detectable by his method. Once a *modus operandi* has been established and is recognized by the police, crime investigators are able to limit the field of suspects considerably. Police officers in Rhodesian towns have their list of 'potentials' for any particular category of crime. When one of the criminal fraternity decides to 'make it with the bigtime' by trying large-scale robbery, he is usually quickly rounded-up as one of the 'potentials'. It is for reasons such as this that the spectacular robbery, fairly commonplace in the world's great cities, is virtually unknown in Rhodesia.

▼▼▼▼▼▼

The extent of resourcefulness and ingenuity displayed by some petty thieves is occasionally quite extraordinary. Magongo, a thirty-four year old African, decided to take up a life of crime and started on armed robbery. His first task was to obtain a gun and some ammunition which he did by the simple expedient of theft. When he examined his acquisitions at home, he found he had a .45 revolver and some rounds of .303 rifle ammunition. He quickly made the unfortunate discovery that the cartridges would not fit the gun. Many aspiring gunmen would have been put off at this stage, but Magongo was made of sterner stuff.

He cut the rifle rounds down to the length of a .45 cartridge and made slugs or cylinders of solder which he fitted into the cut end of the case to push as much as possible of the original cordite down into the shortened case. These lead slugs also served as bullets. He then hammered the lip of the case inwards so that the slug of solder, or bullet, was gripped tightly. Rather surprisingly, the base of a .303 rifle cartridge more or less fits a .45 revolver and can be fired from it.

From a ballistics point of view this was all hideously amateurish. In any gun the propellant charge or cordite burns in layers from the outside to the centre, like a piece of coke only much more rapidly. The thicker the cordite, the longer it takes to burn, and its size is so arranged that it is all burnt just before the shot leaves the muzzle of the weapon. When coarse cordite is used in a gun with a short barrel most of it will be unburnt at the moment the shot leaves the barrel. Consequently, the discharge is ineffective and the bullet will have only a low velocity. Conversely, when very fine cordite is used in a gun with a long barrel, the propellant will be completely burnt by the time the shot has moved a few inches and the tremendously high pressure that is developed may burst the barrel and cause injury to the firer. In the case under consideration, involving rifle cordite in a revolver, and with all other things being equal, it would be expected that much less than 20 per cent of the cordite would burn usefully. The remainder would burn after the bullet had left the weapon and would in no way contribute energy to the velocity of the bullet.

From a purely theoretical point of view, Magongo's revolver with its modified ammunition should have performed little better than an air gun. However, it had one special feature which redeemed its efficiency. This was the manner in which the bullets were fixed into the cartridges. In place of the normal crimping which holds the bullet in the cartridge case, Magongo's modified ammunition had a special fixing. The bullet was pushed well down into the brass case so that only its tip was showing. The lip of the case was then hammered over the edge of the bullet giving a much firmer grip than the normal crimping. The effect of this arrangement was that on firing, the bullet was held in the cartridge case until a high pressure was developed by the burning cordite. An extraordinarily high shot start pressure thus built up which expelled the bullet from the weapon with a fairly high velocity.

Probably by sheer luck rather than from any technical understanding of what he was doing, Magongo had made some usable ammunition for his .45 revolver. His next stop was to fire a practice shot into a tree and then he was armed ready to begin his career as a robber. For his first exploit he enlisted the help of his younger cousin and the pair staged an armed hold-up at a large garage. They bound and gagged the two attendants and made off with all the available cash.

With the proceeds of this first robbery Magongo and his accomplice bought an old, half-ton truck. Now that they had transport they were able to step up their activities and embarked on a series of shop raids. Their technique was to hold up the night-watchman, threaten him with the revolver and, when he was subdued, bound and gag him. They also occasionally clubbed their victims for good measure. Valuable, portable goods were loaded into their truck and taken to a house in the African part of Umtali, where they rented a room in which to store their stolen property. As part of their own security arrangements they paid two neighbours to act as look-outs during unloading and to take note of any undue interest in the storeroom. Samples of the stolen goods were shown to shady shopkeepers who were offered them at prices well below the wholesale rate. As an added protection, no direct contact was made with any shopkeeper until he had committed himself to buying. Initial approaches were made through an intermediary who was usually a stranger to both parties. This unusually astute operation lasted for about four months with robberies being carried out at fortnightly intervals.

Suddenly, during one of their sorties, disaster struck the robbers. They encountered a night-watchman who was more valiant than any security man they had met thus far. He would not easily be subdued but struggled with the intruders, broke free and started to run for help. Magongo raised his revolver and fired a single shot, felling the escaping night-watchman with a bullet lodged under his shoulder blade. Fortunately, the power of the weapon was not sufficient to kill the man; but the shooting of one African by another is no light matter and, when the gunman was thought to be of the same tribe as his victim, local sensibilities were outraged. In no time at all information was received naming the gunman. Magongo was duly arrested and four reliable witnesses told police they had seen him throw a revolver into a septic tank near his lodgings. The weapon was recovered and little imagination is required to visualize what a filthy and disgusting job its retrieval was. It was a .45 revolver and its chamber was loaded with six rounds of home-made ammunition.

The number on it identified the gun as one which had been stolen from Magongo's last place of employment while he was still working there. There seemed little doubt as to its ownership.

The bullet extracted from the night-watchman was cylindrical with a diameter of 0.4 inches and about the same in length. The normal procedure in a case of this sort is to fire a test shot from the weapon in question and compare the marks on the test bullet with those of the bullet recovered from the victim. Scratches and striation marks are normally made on the soft metal of the bullets by the rifled barrel of the weapon which fires them. On this occasion the home-made bullets did not fit tightly enough in the revolver's barrel and consequently no striation lines were made on them.

Now and again in forensic science investigations normal methods are found inadequate for dealing with the problem at hand. This was certainly the case with the home-made bullets and I had to find an effective alternative. This is part of the challenge of forensic work and is what fascinates its practitioners. Fortunately, the resources of forensic science are so wide that, given patience and determination, a solution can be found to most problems and this case was no exception. A possibly fruitful approach seemed to be by using spectrographic analysis to identify and measure the various impurities in the solder of the home-made ammunition.

The spectrograph is widely regarded as 'The Queen of Scientific Instruments' and I had used it extensively during my days in agricultural research. Its working principles are quite straightforward. Any element heated in the form of a gas or vapour produces its own identifying colour or mixture of colours—the blue light emitted by mercury vapour lamps and the yellow glare of sodium street lighting are well known. The spectrograph analyses light passed into it by separating it into its component parts and a positive identification is given in a flame or electric arc of the elements present. The great advantage of this method for forensic work is that it will cope with tiny samples of material and register all the elements and impurities present which appear as lines on a photographic plate.

From a spectrographic point of view solder is a delightful alloy which contains a wide variety of easily identified impurities. On this basis then we put the home-made bullets to the test and found that there were two groups of three in the six rounds of ammunition in the loaded revolver recovered from the septic tank. The bullets in one group were made from printer's metal and those in the other group from solder which corresponded eactly in composition with the bullet removed from the night-watchman. The method used clearly distinguished the crime solder from all other available samples of solder unrelated to the crime. The crime bullet, although distorted by impact, showed sufficient of its original shape and dimension to confirm the spectrographic identification.

The evidence against Magongo and his companion was complete. The revolver with the home-made bullets in its chamber was firmly associated with the robbers, and witnesses claimed to have seen Magongo furtively casting pieces of lead. Finally, various items of stolen property were found in his possession. He was duly convicted of robbery with violence and escaped a charge of murder only because his revolver performed so poorly with its home-made ammunition. If he had hammered the lip of the cartridge case a little more firmly round the top of the bullet, he would have created a missile which would have been expelled from the gun with greater velocity and which would probably have killed the night-watchman. Thus, for the want of a few taps with a hammer, one man doing his duty escaped with his life and another bent on robbery escaped execution for murder.

A case with similar ballistics interest occurred in London in 1940 when an Indian, Udham Singh, went berserk with a .45 revolver at a public meeting. His intended victims were all men of distinction in Indian affairs, Sir Michael O'Dwyer, Lord Zetland, Lord Lamington and Sir Louis Dane. The would-be assassin fired six shots at close range, all of which hit their targets. Sir Michael O'Dwyer was shot dead and his three companions although hit were surprised to find that the bullets just bounced off them. Udham Singh used a perfectly serviceable .45 revolver but fired .40 ammunition from it. The cartridges were such a loose fit in the barrel of the gun that they did not even engage with the rifling grooves and literally just fell out of the muzzle. Unfortunately, the first two shots were powerful enough to take the life of Sir Michael O'Dwyer, an act for which Udham Singh was subsequently hanged.

▼▼▼▼▼▼

It is well known that on many occasions the police know who committed a particular crime but prosecution is not possible due to lack of evidence or because some facts are inadmissible. This can be frustrating to those intimately involved in the investigation of crime. They well understand that guilt must be independently established beyond reasonable doubt but sometimes the gap separating guilt and innocence is tantalisingly close.

In 1968 I provided evidence in a case of assault in the course of robbery which fell into this category. An African housebreaker forced an entrance to the house of a European couple in Bulawayo. The intruder made his way to the bedroom but was insufficiently stealthy, for the woman woke up and challenged him. He assaulted her savagely with a brass candlestick breaking it over her head. She fell back stunned and her husband, awakened by the commotion, tackled the intruder who jumped out of a window and made his escape through a rose garden trampling down some of the bushes in the process.

The police investigating officer was impressed by the extraordinary savagery of the attack. The victim fortunately survived the crushing blow she received but might well have been killed or permanently disabled. The police short-listed three African 'potentials' who lived in the locality and who might have been capable of such brutal violence. A call went out for these men to be brought in for questioning. Within two weeks the search had been narrowed to one man who was regarded as the most likely suspect.

When he was found this man was wearing shoes with thick crepe rubber soles of the type popularly known in the 1950s as 'brothel creepers'. When I examined this footwear, I was delighted to find several thorn points embedded in the thick rubber soles. I discovered five aloe thorns and seven rose thorns and my mind was working on the possibility that these had been picked up by the escaping housebreaker's flight through his victim's rose garden.

When pruned, rose trees produce new growth with thorns which are clear shades of red and brown. Thorns on the old wood are a dull, buff colour often spotted with minute dots of black fungus. The thorns of most rose varieties are of the same shape although a different shape is produced by a few unusual varieties or by abnormal growing conditions. The rose bushes trampled down at the crime-scene had thorns of the common shape on both old and new wood. The thorn tips embedded in the soles of the suspect's shoes were from both old and new wood. The old thorns showed black fungus spots similar to those at the crime-scene.

The aloe thorns were rather more identifiable. The aloe plant grows in many different varieties which bear thorns along the edges of the leaves. The particular aloe growing in this garden had thorns which, on the basis of shape and colour alone, were distinguishable clearly from fifteen other varieties which were all we could find for comparison. While aloe thorns superficially look similar to rose thorns they are quite different internally as we confirmed by examining cross-sections under the microscope.

The position we had reached was that the thorns in the shoes represented strong evidence that the owner of the footwear was guilty—that he had been present at the scene of the crime. Against this, however, it could be argued that another person might conceivably be found with similar thorns embedded in his shoes. I thought it highly unlikely that the same type of rose and aloe thorns would turn up in this way. What looked like decisive evidence was provided by the suspect's previous history—he had just completed a ten-year prison sentence for robbery with violence.

Criminal proceedings have their own logic and established criteria of fairness. Any mention of a defendant's previous convictions are scrupulously avoided during the main part of a trial, although such factors are taken into account after a verdict has been reached and when sentence is being imposed. In this case the evidence provided by the thorns was not thought to be sufficiently substantial by itself and, as evidence of previous convictions was inadmissible, no prosecution was brought. After a severe warning that he would be picked up immediately if another similar crime occurred, the man we viewed as a suspect was released.

In cases like this the crime investigators are left with a certain feeling of having been cheated. In this affair, as in every other that I was involved in, I performed my duty according to the accepted standards and reported exactly what I had found. I could not help feeling that the necessity to adhere to a strict set of rules had allowed a guilty man to go free. There was a strong probability too, bearing in mind the man's record, that he would at some time in the future endanger the life of an innocent person, and this is what actually happened. Two years later he committed a particularly brutal murder, stabbing the victim four times in her stomach and then cutting her head off with a small axe with a blade two inches long. He was barefoot and left a print in blood beside the body. This print showed lines like a thumb print and was an absolute identification.

There seems to have been a tendency throughout history for men to stick to the letter of the law rather than to its spirit. Until the end of the eighteenth century confession was rigidly held as the best form of evidence. Consequently, even after he was found guilty by due process, an accused man was tortured in order to produce a confession. A classic demonstration of this was perpetrated in 1720 by the Chief Justice of Malta, Lord Crambo. This distinguished gentleman observed two men fighting in the street beneath his dressing-room window one morning. He saw one of the combatants stab the other, and leave the stiletto blade in the dying man's body. As he ran away the attacker dropped the sheath of the stiletto in the street.

The learned judge also observed the sequel to this incident when, shortly afterwards, a baker walking along the street noticed the body lying there and ran over to it. He also saw the sheath lying nearby and, foolishly but quite naturally perhaps, picked it up and examined it closely. At that moment several other people appeared on the scene and, seeing the baker kneeling beside the body, assumed he was the attacker and charged at him. The baker quickly realized his plight and fled with the mob baying at his heels. Unfortunately, he was too well fed to summon the speed that his predicament demanded and he was soon caught.

Protesting his innocence, the baker was tried for murder before Lord Crambo. It was proved that the sheath found in the baker's possession fitted the stiletto used to stab the victim. Several witnesses testified that they had seen the baker standing over the body holding the sheath. The jury found the accused man guilty and the judge ordered him to be tortured in order to extract a confession. The poor baker groaned out an admission of guilt and Judge Crambo, with an unclouded conscience, sentenced him to death and he was duly hanged.

Some time later the real murderer was found and brought before the courts. In his defence he stated that during the scuffle in the street he had seen Judge Crambo at the window observing the incident. He called on the judge to testify that the killing resulted from a fair fight. The judge admitted witnessing the incident and in answering criticism of his conduct, indignantly asserted that he could not possibly use private knowledge in deciding the case. In his view this had to be settled on the basis of the evidence presented in court and he contended that he had tried the case faithfully and truly according to the law. He was dismissed from his post for this extraordinary behaviour, although he was later reinstated to the bench. This kind of thinking deserves Mr Bumble's observation, 'If the law supposes that, the law is a ass'.

The rules have, of course, altered in modern times and I feel not necessarily for the better. In some of the advanced democratic countries there is a tendency for the legal system to protect accused persons to such an extent that a majority of crimes are not punished at all and only minimal sentences are given for major offences. In Britain this has reached the point where relatives of a murder victim have sought to appeal against the lenient sentence given to the murderer. Justice is pictured blindfolded and holding a pair of scales, representing the balance between the individual accused and the community. It is appropriate in a civilized society that the rights of accused persons are recognized and upheld; Judge Crambo reminds us what prejudice can do. But there are those who feel that the scales have tipped too far in favour of the criminal.

It is certainly a duty of society to be fair and objective in its treatment of wrongdoers but it also has a duty to protect itself. And it is the duty of the courts to provide effective deterrent punishment such that the community can pursue a normal, peaceful and secure existence. I do not underestimate the difficulties and the law is rightly concerned about the dangers of wrongful conviction; but I do think the proposition that it is better that ninety-nine murderers should go free rather than one innocent man should be hanged is perhaps overrated. It is inherently difficult in any human activity to arrive at absolutely sure decisions but we expect the courts to give definite answers, either 'guilty' or 'not guilty'. Moreover, we expect these decisions to be derived from verbal evidence, a notoriously unreliable material.

Absolute certainty is not a commodity given to ordinary mortals and it is in recognition of this that the term 'Guilty beyond reasonable doubt' is used. Errors are possible, even inevitable, yet if the courts set the standards of proof too high in an attempt to ensure against mistakes, such a high proportion of guilty individuals will be acquitted that deterrents against crime will disappear altogether. An American Supreme Court Judge remarked: 'To maintain its health, a society may have to run the risk that the innocent are mistakenly punished; if it is impossible to cut out the bad without destroying something that is good, the good has to be sacrificed . . .'

Judge Crambo was in office at the time the American Constitution was drawn up. That great document included a paragraph forbidding a man being forced to give evidence against himself. This was an obvious reference to the use of torture to obtain confessions and was a sensible and humane provision. It also assisted the courts to arrive at the truth without being misled by false confessions. However, this principle, subjected to 200 years of interpretation by lawyers, had been converted into a major obstacle in the path of reaching the truth. There is no doubt that an accused person's previous history has a bearing on any alleged crime, especially as there is a strong tendency for criminals to repeat their *modus operandi*. Yet the evidence of previous convictions is avoided in court proceedings on the grounds that the court might be prejudiced against the accused. This is where I think the scales have tipped too far in favour of the criminal. Moreover, I believe this tendency defies logic. Certainly as a scientist my aim in life is to bring every conceivable resource to bear on a problem—the idea of deliberately ignoring relevant information in deciding any serious question is just absurd.

Like Judge Crambo's extraordinary behaviour, this philosophy shows an exaggerated respect for the letter of the law which demeans its status. The welcome effect on professional criminals may be imagined but the demoralization of those engaged in the fight against crime should not be discounted. The policing of the world's cities is a tough job and, if the men and women who risk their lives doing it have a diminishing respect for the legal apparatus to which they submit prosecutions, social disintegration cannot be far away.

In Rhodesia a criminal is usually tried by a judge along with two assessors. These are often ex-District Commissioners with a thorough knowledge of African life and thought. A white man, however, has the option of trial by jury if the charge is a serious one but a black has no option. This difference is mainly due to the difficulty of finding a black jury capable of understanding the proceedings. With the emergence of an educated class of African this arrangement is now out of date and will almost certainly be eliminated.

As far as the death penalty is concerned the simple basic logic lies in the question whether it has a deterrent effect. If it has, sacrificing the murderer's life has the effect of saving innocent lives and is therefore justified.

No deterrent effect has been shown for the majority of cases but in special cases such as the shooting of a policeman in the course of an armed robbery there is good evidence to support the deterrent nature of hanging. After all, a bank robber caught red-handed will get much the same sentence whether or not he shoots and kills a policeman, so he has not got much to lose by killing a policeman. It is obviously grossly unfair to ask unarmed policemen to tackle an armed robber under these circumstances, and if I were a policeman going to the scene of a robbery I would not hurry there and the siren would be sounded loudly as I approached the scene to make sure that I did not become a target. It is no wonder that violent [illegible] on the increase.

A great deal has been said and written about the brutalizing effect on the people concerned with carrying out the sentence. I have never seen a hanging but I have seen the place where it was carried out. The condemned cell was on the first floor of the prison. The door on the other side of the corridor was the execution chamber. At the appointed time the prisoner's hands were handcuffed behind him, the door of his cell was opened and, with the hangman following close behind, he took his last four steps across the corridor into the death chamber. Here his feet were strapped together, a hood put over his head, the noose placed around his neck and the trap door on which he was standing opened. All over in twenty seconds or so. I have had drinks with the hangman who regarded the whole business as a reasonably well-paid sideline and as simply a job to be done. He struck me as a singularly well adjusted and cheerful individual, who had my own ability to divorce a job from his personal feelings.

Chapter Seven

FRAUD AND FORGERY

THE great American showman, Phineas T. Barnum, is remembered among other things for his remark that 'There is one sucker born every minute'. Even though he made the remark a hundred years ago when American society was a lot less sophisticated than it is today, the remark still holds true. Normally rational and intelligent people can be extremely gullible and no more so than when it comes to parting with money. When a swindler of the city-slicker mentality is let loose among simple African tribesmen he is like a fox let loose in a hen roost. The sad aspect of this type of crime is the ruthless exploitation by the African of his brother who is defenceless against his trickery.

In Rhodesia a popular target for fraud is the African returning home after a two-year spell in South Africa's diamond mines. Young men with ambitions of working hard and saving money to pay for a wife travel south by train to the Republic's mining towns. After a long stint of back-breaking labour, these young men return to their home villages. With two year's savings in their pockets and with hearts full of joyful anticipation at their homecoming they set out on the long rail journey to Salisbury or Bulawayo. From the rail station they complete the journey by bus, travelling up to 200 miles into the interior and finally walking as much as forty or fifty miles through the bush to a triumphant village welcome.

It is at the rail stations in Salisbury and Bulawayo that the returning miners are most vulnerable. Their simple-mindedness is no protection against the rapacious cunning of the human vultures who lie in wait outside the station exits. One of the commonest forms of swindle is the 'envelope switch'. Two men approach the intended victim and tell him they are CID officers. They inform him he is wanted for theft of money from his employer and subject him to a search. Finding money in his pocket they declare that this must have been stolen. One of the men produces a check list of the numbers of the stolen notes and, moving off to one side, pretends to compare the numbers on the victim's notes with those on the list. When he returns he says that one of the numbers on the list corresponds with one of the man's bank notes. He will therefore have to take the money to the police station for proper examination. The money is put in an envelope and sealed. One of the 'CID officers' writes his signature across the flap to guarantee the security of the envelope's contents. The sealed and signed envelope is shown to the victim and then the pseudo-detective puts it in his pocket.

Torn between fear of the law and anguish at the prospect of losing his money the homecoming miner protests loudly that this money represents his hard-earned wages and is rightfully his. The 'CID men' reply that it is their duty to see that the money is properly examined to rule out the possibility that it is stolen. The argument goes back and forth for a long while and finally the 'detectives' agree to let the man have his money back on condition that he reports next morning to the police station with the envelope intact. The envelope is produced complete with the signature across the sealed flap and handed to its relieved owner. He pockets it and resumes his homeward journey, relief giving way to horror when he opens the packet to find it contains nothing but cut-up pieces of worthless newspaper.

The 'envelope switch', and variations of it, has been worked on countless occasions at Rhodesia's railway stations. In spite of the increasing sophistication of the tribal African he still falls prey to the unscrupulous practitioners of this fraud who, for their part, make an easy living. They mercilessly fleece their fellow-countrymen of savings accumulated from years of grinding toil and deprivation.

Another, less common, form of swindle is the 'money-making machine'. This is where two ordinary-sized envelopes are stuck together on their plain sides, the side on which the address is usually written. There is no gum on either of the flaps so that each side may be opened. The trick may be played with coins but a note is preferred. A one-dollar Rhodesian banknote is placed in one side of the dual envelope. This side is kept facing downward when the trick is presented to the victim who therefore is unaware of the presence of the note. The sucker is invited to place a piece of newspaper about the size of a dollar note into the envelope which is offered to him. Once this is done the envelope is wrapped in a piece of cloth and some suitable mumbo-jumbo is performed. Occasionally, at this point, the envelope is put in the victim's pocket with the explanation that the 'money machine' only works for a few people and he has been picked out as one of the lucky ones.

Once the ritual is completed, the swindlers carefully open the envelope and reveal that, wonder of wonders, the piece of newspaper has changed into a one-dollar banknote. The victim, convinced that he has acquired money-making powers, exchanges his wages for the miraculous 'machine' and its wrapping cloth.

Apart from the usual police procedures of running to earth known swindlers and seeking identification by victim's descriptions, there is also the forensic evidence. Fortunately, the envelopes for working these tricks are carried about in the swindlers' pockets where they inhabit the world of fluff and fibres—two forensic faithfuls. In the course of use a jacket, for example, picks up an assortment of fibres, hair and other debris, and this forms a grey-looking fluff which lies at the bottom of its pockets. Although this fluff appears to be generally grey in appearance, it is made up of hundreds of different fibres, many of them coloured, from the garment itself and also from numerous other sources. Each garment, therefore, has its own characteristic assortment of highly identifiable fluff.

In the case of one 'money-making machine' swindle where the perpetrator was picked up by the police from the victim's identification I was able to provide corroborating evidence. The envelope had been carried by the swindler in one of his pockets where the still damp glue holding the pair of envelopes together had picked up some fibres. These proved to be easily identifiable and matched precisely fibres retrieved from a pocket in the suspect's jacket. The wrapping-cloth which forms part of this trick and ends up in the possession of the luckless victim also carries useful identification. In this same case the swindlers had used a piece of cloth made from a rather uncommon type of acrylic fibre with a printed pattern on it. The implication of this was that it had probably shed some identifiable fibres in the pocket of the person carrying it. An examination of the suspect's jacket pockets revealed fourteen matching acrylic fibres; this clearly indicated that he had carried the cloth. These fibres are particularly identifiable as the pattern is printed on the surface of the cloth and does not penetrate completely—so many of the fibres show two colours.

To round off the forensic story in this case we also found two hand hairs on the wrapping-cloth. Individual hairs are held in the skin pores by a root which shrivels when the hair dies. With nothing to anchor it in the skin the hair falls out, a process which is helped in the case of hand hairs when the hand is put into a pocket. Invariably the hand rubs against the edge of the pocket and any loose hairs are detached and fall into it. Hand hairs are consequently commonly found in their owner's coat and trouser pockets. Although these hairs cannot be wholly identified with a particular individual, there is a sufficiently wide variation in the thickness, colour and shape to make a useful comparison possible. The evidence against the two swindlers was regarded as conclusive and each was sentenced to three year's imprisonment. The news of their punishment was sufficient to stop this particular form of fraud for several years but, inevitably, the practice resumed as greed overcame caution among the members of the criminal fringe.

▼▼▼▼▼▼

As I mentioned earlier in connection with witchcraft and murder, most Africans believe that the spirits of their dead parents and grandparents have a great influence in their daily lives. Misfortunes are put down to the displeasure of one of the spirits and, conversely, the spirits can be relied on for help in times of need. A cunning trickster I came across convinced a wealthy African shop-owner that he could double his money with the assistance of his dead father. The idea was that the shopkeeper should put some money in a tin and bury it just below the surface of his father's grave as the sun was setting. His benefactor would then make suitable invocations over the grave and when the tin was opened the next morning the money would be doubled.

A strong streak of greed runs through most human beings, yet it never ceases to surprise one how easily caution and logic fall victim to the lure of a quick return. The shop-owner was sufficiently convinced to risk the equivalent of five pounds which was solemnly committed to the ground to the accompaniment of diverse incantations. Sure enough, by the following morning, the money had doubled. The shop-owner was now on the slippery slope of disaster—he raised all the money he could lay his hands on, which totalled the equivalent of eight thousands pounds. This too was committed to burial, only this time the resurrection produced only an empty tin and a benefactor who was conspicuous by his absence.

This particular shark turned out to be a wide-boy from Johannesburg who fled that city to avoid the heat generated by a previous crime. He returned to South Africa with the generous proceeds of his short spell of swindling in Rhodesia. He was arrested by the South African Police and ended up in prison for such a long term that the statute of limitations came into effect thus making him not liable for prosecution in Rhodesia. It seems incredible that an intelligent shopkeeper could be so gullible as to part with such a large sum of money and participate in a ploy which had swindle written all over it. But that was the swindler's art—to sniff out greed and drive away caution by introducing the idea of a helping hand from the spirits.

▼▼▼▼▼▼

Swindlers in Rhodesia, of course, are by no means always Africans. Although the majority of accountants are honest and highly professional in their business dealings, there are a few who succumb to temptation. In the early 1970s there was a spate of accountancy swindles in Rhodesia probably caused by one case bringing to light many others. Difficulties in arranging extradition meant that if the villain could leave the country before he was found out the authorities could not touch him. In turn, this caused auditors to be particularly on the look-out for discrepancies, and a number of swindles were thus brought to light which might otherwise have gone unnoticed.

Some of the methods used by the swindlers were highly effective. One accountant developed several techniques which brought him in the equivalent of three hundred thousand pounds over a period of about seven years. He exploited the auditors' own methods. When his company's books were scrutinized, the auditors sent girls along to his office to check the totals on each page. A day or so later the auditors themselves looked at the books to check each individual item but they accepted as correct the totals previously initialed on each page by their girl assistants. The accountant regularly drew cash to pay the wages of his African staff. If he required a sum of one hundred and fifty Rhodesian dollars he would draw seven hundred and fifty. When the first phase of the audit began the girl assistants checked the totals which were shown as seven hundred and fifty dollars. Before the auditors arrived to carry out the second phase of the audit the accountant altered the figure seven to the figure one so that the individual entries would be found correct.

Impressions made by some ball-point pens are easily obliterated using ordinary ink eradicator. Thus, alterations can be made which are quite invisible in ordinary light. Seen under ultra-violet light, however, ink eradicator gives off a brilliant fluorescence. This, of course, is a dead give-away unless the paper has been treated with optical bleach which itself fluoresces. Many types of paper, particularly writing paper, are treated in this way and consequently any fluorescence due to the presence of ink eradicator tends to be masked.

This particular accountant was undone, not by the application of scientific methods but by the unforeseen. The day the auditors and their assistants arrived together to check the accounts was the day his scheme was exposed. Perhaps the most astonishing aspect of this case was that the whole of the three hundred thousand pounds had been dissipated in gambling. The embezzling accountant was in the habit of buying 600 national sweepstake tickets at a dollar each but he never won a single prize. Needless to say, the town's bookmakers went into deep mourning when the gambling career of their best-ever client was finished.

Another accountant, during this hey-day of fraud, made over a hundred thousand pounds by faking worksheets for African labourers. When these men were paid they signified receipt of their money by putting their thumb-print on a form. The swindle was accomplished by the accountant making out fictitious worksheets and putting his own thumb-print on the forms. He, of course, drew the extra money and perpetuated the fraud for three years. Eventually, an unusually alert auditor noticed that the thumb-prints on many of the forms was the same for ostensibly different individuals.

A short investigation pieced together the facts of this lucrative swindle and the case had an unusual conclusion. The accountant had adopted the habit of only spending the notes out of the wages he embezzled and, in consequence, accumulated considerable amounts of copper and silver coinage. He kept this at home in two suitcases hidden away in the attic. He readily admitted the whereabouts of this loot to the police officer investigating the case who went up to the attic to see for himself. He spotted the two cases and bent down to pick one up so that he could open it. The suitcase filled with metal money was such a massive, dead weight that the unfortunate officer slipped a disc. I doubt that the imagined hazards of police work include such dangers as this.

▼▼▼▼▼▼

Some types of fraud are almost provoked by the totally unreal and inflated values placed on some classes of rare but inherently valueless objects. Postage stamps have long been objects of temptation for the forger. Perhaps the collector who pays several hundred pounds for a single stamp with a rare fault in its printing is enticing the forger to exercise his skill.

When postage stamps are printed they are carefully inspected for faults. Several independent checks are normally carried out but, inevitably, when millions of items are being printed, the occasional imperfect stamp slips through. Post Office clerks are best placed to spot such faults when they handle stamps for sale to the public. If they are unscrupulous they can buy such stamps themselves, and are assured of a handsome profit, many times the stamps' face value, by reselling to a dealer.

The person who ultimately buys the stamp with its singular imperfection is looking for some egotistical satisfaction out of owning something unique. This desire for the unusual and the unique unwittingly opens the door to a certain amount of crime. Rigid precautions are taken at the security printing firms, many of them in London, which specialize in the production of stamps, bonds and certificates. Some of these firms have generations of experience of printing postage stamps for countries around the world and enjoy the highest reputation for quality. They are also well versed in the wiles and craftsmanship of the world's most expert forgers, and security measures are virtually foolproof. There are loopholes, however, and occasionally even the best security is breached—overprinting of postage stamps is a weak spot in the armour.

In 1965 the Rhodesian government overprinted some of its existing postage stamps to commemorate the Unilateral Declaration of Independence. There was no experience in Rhodesia of printing postage stamps so it was decided to overprint on stocks originally manufactured in London. Stamps of all values up to and including One Pound were overprinted in black with the words 'INDEPENDENCE, 11th NOVEMBER 1965'. The one exception was the stamp with a value of One Shilling and Three Pence bearing a portrait of Sir Winston Churchill. This handsome stamp was treated differently being overprinted in red with the independence date. The figure 1*s*. 3*d*. was deleted with two cancelling bars and the value of the stamp raised to five shillings.

I came into the affair when a senior Post Office official, together with two security advisers, visited me at my laboratory in 1966. He produced two Churchill five shilling overprinted stamps and told me that there was doubt about their authenticity. Apparently they had been examined by two independent stamp experts who believed them to be genuine. However, the intending buyer was unhappy about the stamp and so too was the Post Office. I am not a philatelist and have no pretensions to being a stamp expert but my first impressions led me to disagree with the opinions of the experts and to side with the doubters. I compared the questioned stamps with a series of genuine stamps supplied and guaranteed by the Post Office—I thought there were clear and obvious differences.

It is common practice in the printing trade to adjust the thickness of ink by adding thinners, usually light oil. When this is properly done the resultant printed matter is crisp with no in-filling of the spaces in individual letters and no ragged edges to the characters. It seemed to me when looking at the suspect stamps that the ink had been thinned too much, with the result that the overprinted characters were pale and lacking in solidity. Excess ink had also been squeezed out around individual letters giving them a ragged appearance.

The two experts who considered the stamps genuine were well-known and reliable men in their field and it was with some trepidation that I felt I had to disagree with their opinion. My verdict was that the questioned stamps were forgeries. The police decided to act on my judgment and they traced the suspected forgeries to a man who was found to have a large number of similar stamps in his possession. These were impounded and forwarded to me for examination.

At this stage there was no information regarding the origin of the overprinting. There was no shortage of theories, however, for the man who owned a number of the suspected forgeries had recently returned to Rhodesia from a journey during which he had visited South Africa, Zambia and Great Britain—the forged overprinting could have been carried out in any of those countries. I had a strong feeling in my bones that clues about the origin of the forgery would be gleaned by examining the stamps themselves. I was chastened by the knowledge that even the strongest hunch is not proof without supporting evidence, and after four days of intensive effort I failed to turn up a single, useful fact. There seemed to be no difference between the suspected and genuine stamps as regards the type of ink used for the overprinting; though the ink on the suspect stamps appeared to be thinner it had the same chemical composition as the genuine stamps. This did not concern me greatly, for I was aware that with relatively few printing inks on the market the forgers could well have used the correct ink, even by accident.

A long time was spent searching for identifiable differences or faults in the individual characters of the overprinted words. This was a slow process involving the microscopic examination of each letter on each stamp, looking for possible faults which were repeated in each genuine stamp, and then checking if the fault was repeated in the suspected stamps. The same process was repeated but this time I looked for faults which were repeated in the doubtful stamps in the hope of finding something by which they could be identified. Knowing that the edges of individual letters were ragged due to excessive inking, I felt this was a lost cause. My apprehensions were fully realized and the exercise proved to be a waste of effort.

But then the penny dropped. There were sixty stamps in each sheet and, as the whole sheet is printed at once, the block for the overprinting is made up of sixty sub-blocks arranged to make an impression on each stamp. It followed that each impression, while appearing the same as the rest, must have individual characteristics, some of which were likely to be faithfully reproduced in the stamps. The most obvious variations in the suspected stamps were the relative positions of the first 'D' of INDEPENDENCE and the second figure 1 in 11th NOVEMBER. By designating each of the six rows of stamps on each sheet with the letters A,B,C etc. and by numbering the stamp in each row of ten with the numbers 1,2,3 etc, each stamp was given an identity. Thus the top left-hand stamp in each sheet was A1 and the bottom right-hand stamp was F10. I found that for stamp A1 on the genuine sheets, the D of INDEPENDENCE was slightly to the left of the second figure of 11th NOVEMBER (lining up on the upright stroke of the D). For A2, they were exactly in line and for A3, they were slightly to the right. Examination of the sheets of suspected stamps showed the same variations in the same positions. This correspondence was maintained throughout the whole sheet of sixty stamps. Each of the sixty stamps was compared but the work on the last fifty-six was simply a formality as the first four had settled the question. This was clear proof that the forged stamps had been overprinted with the block used to print the genuine stamps.

Thus, all the theories favouring a foreign origin for the forgeries were undermined and it was certain that the work had been carried out by a person who had access to the original block. This narrowed the field considerably and it did not take long for the whole story to emerge. The culprit did not work for the official printer but his contacts at the works were sufficient to allow him free access. He claimed to have been approached by a man called Frederick Noble who wanted his help. His story was that Noble had attempted to overprint some stamps with the aid of the owner of a small printing shop at Marandellas some forty miles from Salisbury. Some preliminary overprints were made but these proved unsatisfactory as the wrong type face had been used. Noble then learned of the man with contacts at the official printer and persuaded him to 'borrow' the genuine blocks. These were temporarily purloined one evening when the printer was at full stretch working on a rush order. The blocks were taken away, used for the illegal overprinting, and returned without the knowledge of the official printer.

The taker of the blocks was convicted of theft and served several months in prison. In 1967 Noble was charged with organizing the affair but, as the only evidence against him was that of an accomplice, he was found 'not guilty'. He was an endearing man with a delightful personality who, like a character in *My Fair Lady*, 'oozed charm from every pore'. He was, nevertheless, found guilty of possessing and selling clandestine stamps, although the Appeal Court subsequently quashed the conviction.

▼▼▼▼▼▼

Counterfeiting coinage is an old-established criminal pastime. The sophisticated counterfeiter knows that coins made by melting base metal in a mould or by electro-plating to simulate precious metal are readily detected as forgeries. This, of course, does not inhibit the small-time criminal from counterfeiting coins and passing or offering them for a quick return.

A large quantity of counterfeit coins, mostly Rhodesian half-crowns, came into circulation in Salisbury in 1963. These had been passed in shops and stores in which the lighting was bad in exchange for goods and small change. They were only recognized as worthless when daily takings were cashed-up. The counterfeits were handed in to the police, who had little difficulty in tracing their origin to Mrewa village where crude coin-making implements were found.

Two Africans, called Mafait and George, who hailed from Malawi, owned these tools and they were quickly arrested.

After their complaints of being assaulted by the police were dismissed, this pair confessed to a counterfeiting operation using moulds for 1948 and 1951 half-crowns. The moulds, together with nearly two hundred coins made of plumber's solder and some chunks of solder, were produced as exhibits in court when they were charged with counterfeiting and uttering.

I examined the counterfeit coins and demonstrated to the court that they contained a number of faults which proved they had been produced in the two illegal moulds. Several of the figures and letters on the coins were doubled and these blemishes took on dramatic proportions when shown in photographic enlargement. In any event, the coins on close inspection had what dealers call 'a wrong feel', but they certainly passed a cursory examination as Mafait and George had proved. The two counterfeiters were convicted and received sentences of three months imprisonment.

Because they are generally more remote from their victims, counterfeiters are possibly regarded more leniently than swindlers. It has been suggested also that counterfeiters have the excusable vice of taking great pride in their workmanship. Certainly, the American counterfeiter Melvin G. Parsons, who made ten-dollar bills, lavished such time and devotion to his work that he hardly covered his expenses. He told US Treasury Officials that the urge to counterfeit was in his blood. In the majority of cases, however, I suspect that those who 'make' money do so with the profit motive clearly in view.

Counterfeiting of coins is no longer a productive occupation for most of the world's forgers. Inflation means that the expense of making a plausible imitation is greater than the face value of the coin. Antique coins and medals with rarity value still offer a return to the counterfeiter and the unusual coin is worth a try. The introduction of the seven-sided English fifty-pence piece inspired one London gang to manufacture effective counterfeits using melted metal from soda siphon tops. Money remains the most obvious target for criminal enterprise and forgery; it avoids the risks of confrontation involved in robbery and can pay off handsomely. High denomination bank notes, travellers cheques and passports are lucrative fields for the forger's art. The world's banking organizations are constantly stretched to ensure the security of their printing and minting techniques in an attempt to outwit the counterfeiter. For the forger, the challenge is to heighten his own skills to outwit the system. Forensic science plays its part in identifying forgeries but by then it is usually too late to protect the victim, for the crime has been committed.

One form of swindle is based on a technique known to many children. The easiest way to copy a signature is to start with a sample of the genuine signature and then cover the back of the paper under the signature with pencil lines. This acts as a sort of carbon paper and the signature can be traced on to another document giving a faint pencil copy of the signature which can then be inked over.

Some ingenious gentlemen have been signing cheques or hire purchase agreements by writing faintly in pencil and then signing slowly. In due course they claim that the signature is forged and microscopic examination shows the traces of pencil mark and the slight wave on the lines due to slow writing, so the expert reports that the signature shows all signs of forgery. If a hire-purchase agreement is involved the swindler gets the goods having paid only the original deposit.

The one case that came my way was a disaster for the swindler because he left a beautiful thumb-print on the paper. Ninhydrin will bring up fingerprints on paper months after they have been placed in position, even though ninhydrin reacts with the aminoacids in the thumb-print and these are quite volatile materials. The paper in question had prints on it from ten different people but the best and clearest prints belonged to the swindler. Perhaps the concentrated effort involved made him sweat more than usual.

All this bears out the remark made by Harry Söderman, the distinguished Swedish criminologist, that one of the greatest appeals of crime is the hope of easy money.

Chapter Eight

MURDER, ACCIDENT OR SUICIDE?

PRESS advertisements announcing job vacancies for forensic scientists are always soberly worded, as befits a professional appointment. If they were allowed to follow modern trends for advertising job vacancies and career opportunities in other fields, they might take on a different character. What used to be called hard work but is now euphemistically known as 'unsocial hours' would be one of the less advantageous aspects but the scope for variety might be viewed with enthusiasm. A knowledge of occult practices, the ability to make important judgments and an adventurous spirit might also be considered desirable attributes.

What makes forensic work challenging is the balance between what is obvious and what is unexpected and unusual. As the late Professor Francis Camps said of forensic pathology, it is '. . . only too easy to find what one expects . . .' even at the expense of missing the obvious. The dangers of forming pre-conceived ideas are ever present and the best safeguards are experience, skilled hands and observant eyes. These are the characteristics needed to separate proof from suspicion and to distinguish between accident, murder or suicide.

One pathologist I know uses a very unusual case to emphasize the point in his lectures.

A young man about twenty years old became involved with a woman nearly sixty years old. In the end they quarrelled and he strangled her and buried her body in the sandy bed of a dried up stream which was shaded by trees. The body was found by a man who was hunting along the stream bed for semi-precious stones and in the course of his search he noticed the dead woman's toes protruding from the sand. As it was winter time the conditions preserved the body so effectively that when found six weeks after death it looked as if it had been kept under refrigeration—as the pathologist remarked, she was fresh as a daisy!

The young man, with the idea of ensuring that the body received a proper burial, carefully wrote in block letters the name and address of his victim on the skin on the side of her chest.

For his lecture the pathologist has slides showing both sides of the body. He first shows the 'unwritten' side and then asks the students how they would set about identifying the body. Having received various suggestions along the lines of—take fingerprints and search the records hoping that she has had a criminal conviction; record the state of the teeth and inquire amongst dentists, and so on—he now says that the first step is to examine thoroughly the surface of the body and he then shows the slide of the other side of the body giving the name and address!

One of the classic cases in which the immediately obvious clouded professional judgment was that of a thirty-three-year-old British Army Sergeant. He was serving with the occupation forces in Germany in 1953 when a fellow-soldier was found hanging from the stairs in one of the barrack blocks—obviously a suicide. It was only after an army court had accepted this verdict that evidence emerged of antagonism between the two soldiers. The case was re-opened eighteen months later when it was proved that the Sergeant had killed his colleague with a karate blow to the throat and then suspended his body to feign suicide. The dead man therefore had been murdered. There is a premium on judgment and experience in any job but perhaps none more so than in forensic work where justice is at stake.

▼▼▼▼▼▼

In most walks of life there are persons who stick to rigid ideas and conventions regardless of common sense or the possible consequences of 'going by the book'. For such individuals convention and precedent are the main considerations in deciding how to deal with any situation or problem. In western society this kind of rigid outlook is often a bulwark against thinking for oneself. It may be rooted in basic personality traits or emerge as the product of an over-disciplined childhood.

In tribal African life, conservatism is virtually endemic and this is readily observed. There is a rigid order of seniority, for example, in which every individual knows his or her place. This extends into all areas of village life including the degree of deference shown in greeting another person and in the order of eating from the communal food pots. The times for ploughing, sowing and reaping are laid down and most actions are governed by some convention or other. This respect for precedent is often reinforced in Africans living and working in a European-dominated environment where they take on inferior roles. If they are given responsibility they frequently lack confidence and prefer to have their judgment backed by some external authority. There is a marked tendency to follow rules to the letter, occasionally with disastrous results which test the judicial process.

An African who attempted to commit suicide by hanging himself was helped on his way to oblivion by a well-meaning bystander. The scene was the Colonial Mutual Building in Salisbury, a pleasantly designed office block built around a large, open courtyard. There was an open-air tea garden with well-kept rockeries and a fountain on the ground floor. Access to the offices on the four floors of the building was by a series of open-air stairways and balconies skirting the courtyard. Some of the offices were used by doctors, solicitors and accountants and by mid-morning the tea-garden was usually crowded with people waiting for, or relaxing after, appointments with their professional advisers. The air of this little haven was filled with the buzz of conversation and the clatter of crockery. Suddenly the tranquil scene was rent with commotion and drama. An African man had jumped from the fourth floor and he hung suspended in mid-air from his belt which he had tied around his neck, having tightly secured the other end to the balcony rail. In the pandemonium which ensued, a voice from the third floor shouted out, 'Quick get him down, he's still alive'. An African messenger watching this drama heard the command and took prompt action. Rushing along to the fourth-floor balcony, he pulled out a knife and cut through the belt by which the man was suspended. The would-be suicide, still just alive, plunged four floors to his death on the rockery below. Strictly speaking, the messenger could have been charged with culpable homicide. He obviously intended no harm, acting impulsively and not thinking out the consequences of his action. No charge was made against him and, despite the victim's clear intention to commit suicide, a verdict of accidental death was brought in.

I felt particularly sad at this loss of a useful life. The victim had a good job as a sales representative for a cigarette manufacturer, a position he had obtained on merit. His parents had made tremendous sacrifices to see him through school where he finally gained four creditable 'A'-levels which qualified him for the sought-after post which he held at the time of his death. His job entailed handling considerable sums of money for his company which he did with distinction until the day a friend who worked in a horse-racing stable offered him a few betting tips. He placed a few minor bets and won. Then, in the nature of gambling, he suffered a few set-backs and was tempted to recoup his losses by placing heavier bets. He did this using company funds and before long he had misappropriated large sums of money. Faced with disgrace, loss of employment and poverty, he gambled with the only asset left to him—his life. And he lost, not because of his own action but by that of a brother African. For me, the tragedy was compounded by the loss of a much-needed educated African life when it might conceivably have been saved but for a well-meaning though ill-judged act of intervention.

Another illustration of well-intended but disastrous intervention involved the rendering of first aid. Late on a wet November evening in 1972 an African was knocked down in a Salisbury street by a car. Despite the heavy tropical rain drenching the scene, the usual crowd of onlookers gathered round the victim. Fortunately, someone had used his wits and the police and ambulance had been sent for.

The victim of the road accident appeared to have a broken arm and he had sustained a severe cut over the right ear which was bleeding profusely. There was a delay of an hour or more before the ambulance arrived and in the meantime comfort and first-aid were given to the injured man. When he was eventually taken to hospital and examined he was found to be dead, or, in the parlance of casualty departments, DOA (dead on arrival). The reason for the man's demise was not connected with his injuries but with the method used to stop the bleeding—a tourniquet had been applied tightly around his neck. This certainly stopped the bleeding but also his breathing. It was never established who had applied the tourniquet and we presumed it was a well-intentioned but poorly trained first-aider—possibly even one of the ambulance attendants! What started as a non-fatal accident ended in disaster and, in the circumstances, it could only be described as death by misadventure.

▼▼▼▼▼▼

Open-mindedness is the greatest virtue for those engaged in forensic work. It is fatal to jump to hasty conclusions without first seeing and pondering over every single piece of evidence. What seems obvious on first impression may be contradicted by other evidence and the most complex and bewildering maze of evidence may mask a simple yet elusive solution. Deciding whether a particular death was due to suicide, accident or murder can pose some awkward problems and none more so than when there is a contradiction between different aspects of the evidence.

A case which teased my judgment in this way occurred in Bulawayo in 1967. The police were called to a rather poor boarding-house by the landlady after she heard a shot fired in one of her tenants' rooms on the ground floor. She had hammered on the door but got no reply and when the police arrived they had to break into the room which was locked with the key on the inside. The door was burst open with the aid of tyre levers and a man's body was seen lying on the floor near the foot of the bed—he had been shot through the mouth, shattering the back of his head. Blood and brain matter were spattered on the wall above the bedhead and also on the ceiling, door and a chest of drawers. A 12-bore shot-gun lay on the floor near the corpse. As is usual in such cases the police photographer recorded the scene through the door of the small room before anything was touched. Then he entered the room to photograph the corpse lying on the floor. This proved difficult because of the furniture crowding the small space. However, he completed his work and then made way for the detectives to go in.

The deadman's landlady told police that her tenant had been depressed for several weeks. He changed his job frequently, having had as many as five different employers in two years, and he had recently been dismissed from his latest job. His girl friend had deserted him, no doubt deciding that he offered no real prospects of a steady relationship. To add to his problems he had been involved in a motor accident which resulted in his car being written off. He was in deep trouble for he was drunk at the time and had only third party insurance cover for his car. In desperation he tried to borrow money from friends, acquaintances and members of his family. His affairs gathered pace down the slippery slope to disaster and ended with him taking his life.

It looked then as if we were confronted with a straightforward case of suicide—or was it? The fact that both barrels of the shot-gun had been fired, with the two shots entering the head by way of the mouth, gave rise to suspicion. The first discharge would have taken the back of his head off and even if he had a finger on both triggers it would be impossible to fire both barrels as the recoil of the initial shot would have taken the pressure off the second trigger. The gun was fitted with a black rubber shoulder guard and this provided a possible answer. If this rubber guard had been resting on the floor, the recoil from the first shot would have made the gun bounce upwards so allowing the second barrel to be discharged if a finger was on the trigger. A black scuff mark was found on the floor of the bedroom which microscopic examination showed to have been caused by impact with a rubber object. Moreover, the shoulder guard of the shot-gun bore traces of varnish and polish which clearly indicated that it had made forcible contact with the floor. Once again, the evidence pointed to suicide.

At about this time in the examination of the death room, the landlady brought in a large tray bearing tea, biscuits and buttered scones. The investigating team tucked into these welcome refreshments and then began packing equipment and exhibits in readiness to leave. The senior detective, like all good police-officers, took a final look around and in so doing opened the drawers of the chest which stood just inside the door. These had been closed throughout the investigation and his horror can only be imagined when he found a portion of the dead man's skull in one of them. The obvious inference was that someone had closed the drawer after the shooting. And further, that the person had left the room in a manner allowing it to be locked from the inside.

The whole investigation was gone into again. There were no signs of interference with the lock or the key. The bars fitted to the windows of the ground-floor room to keep burglars out showed no indication of having been forced and there were no signs of exit by unusual means. The usual locked-room devices such as long-nosed pliers, and rods and cords were all ruled out. The door fitted so well at floor level that it would have been impossible to pass anything underneath it. Was this a genuine case of a murder in a locked room, that much-loved situation of detective fiction?

When we thought about our arrival at the scene and went through every action step-by-step, we realized that the solution to our problem probably lay with the police photographer. After he had taken his photographs through the open doorway, he moved into that tiny room, flattening himself against the furniture and walls to take pictures of the corpse. It seemed possible that while concentrating on the difficulties of getting the camera angles he needed and hampered by the smallness of the room, he accidentally pushed against an open drawer in the chest. Thus, the drawer with its unseen contents was closed without his being aware of it. Our next thought was that this possibility might be confirmed in his films. These were rushed off for processing and anxious inspection of the negatives provided the answer in the first frame—the drawer had been open before the photographer entered the room. Once again, then, we were back with suicide.

The point about a suicide firing more than one shot into his head is not as clear cut as is commonly believed. Cases have occurred where quite horrifying injuries have been sustained without causing immediate death. A suicide case is on record where a man locked himself into his room and fired two shots into his head from a single barrel 12-bore shot-gun. One shot had been fired upwards and against the left lower jaw. Most of the left side of the face was shot away including the left upper and lower jaws, the left cheek bone, the left eye and part of the bone over the forehead. For the second shot, the gun muzzle was placed in the mouth, blowing away the back of the head and most of the brain. The gun was a single shot weapon, and it was difficult to believe that after the hideous damage caused by the first shot the suicide victim could have reloaded the gun and fired the second and fatal shot. That he did so was beyond dispute for his fingerprints in blood were on the cartridge case remaining in the gun's breech. His bloody fingerprints were also found on the room's door handle. This suggested that he might have thought of seeking help but then changed his mind, reloaded the gun and finished himself off.

In the end we were satisfied that in his depressed state of mind the victim in our on-off suicide did indeed fire two shots from his shot-gun and that there was no question of foul play. Although this case had some strange and unexpected turns, the questions it raised were solved by straightforward observation. Thus the truth finally emerged and earlier doubts were irrevocably dispelled.

▼▼▼▼▼▼

A dead python giving rise to a series of arson cases hardly seems a plausible scenario but it certainly taxed my patience. Most European-owned farms in Rhodesia have a village or compound in the grounds where the farmer's African employees live with their families. The labourers' wives usually have a plot of ground on which they grow mealies and beans for consumption by their families. Basic rations are normally supplied by the farmers and the womenfolk merely cultivate their patch of ground to provide a few extras. These families can, of course, survive at a minimum level without these extras and in consequence many of the women spend their lives in comparative idleness. All too often they degenerate into dull, listless, poverty-stricken creatures, totally lacking in intelligence and energy. They are the victims of an environment which, in addition to the ravages caused by such diseases as bilharzia, hookworm and malaria, condemns them to being inferior all their lives. Tribal law forbids them to own property, any money they may earn becomes the legal property of their husbands, and if a husband dies his wife is pushed off on to another member of his family. In consequence, these villages on European farms are as much strongholds of ignorance and superstition as the African villages in the tribal trust areas.

The houses in most of these villages are built with wooden poles with mud walls and roofed with thick thatch. One family will own several huts, using different ones for sleeping, cooking and storage. The cooking hut usually houses an open wood fire in the centre of the floor. This arrangement under a low, bone-dry thatched roof, suggests the possibility of a fire hazard although I had never heard of a single case of an accidental fire in a cooking hut. That is until 1975 when there was a spate of hut fires in a farm village near Sinoia. Five huts went up in smoke in one week and a further hut caught fire within yards of an African police sergeant who was questioning witnesses in response to an official call by the farmer. The conflagrations all occurred at about midday and for no readily apparent reason.

The villagers, however, were unanimous in declaring the reason for the fires. They were caused as a result of the farmer shooting and killing a python. These large snakes are often credited with magical powers, including the ability to control rainfall. A farmer friend told me that after he had shot a python his African workmen told him the coming season would be bad for him due to lack of rainfall. The prophecy was borne out for he suffered an extraordinarily dry season compared to his neighbours. Local variations in rainfall in Africa can have this effect but my friend vowed that he would never again kill a python.

In the matter of the burning huts, local African opinion was that the spirit of the python was causing the fires and it would be necessary to appease it. A square yard each of black and white cloth would have to be bought and given to the nearby witch-doctor together with a fee of ten pounds. He would then go to the home of the snake on a local hill top and burn the pieces of cloth in a ceremony which would appease the spirit of the python. This course of action was advised by the African police although neither their European colleagues nor the farmer were greatly impressed. When the ninth hut fire occurred, the matter took a serious turn, for a child was burnt to death in the blaze. The labour force was edgy and many began to panic and leave the farm. This exodus built up to the point where the farm was in danger of having to be closed down. At this stage the farmer gave in, producing the witch-doctor's fee and allowing the ceremony to proceed. Despite the witch-doctor's incantations and the presence of a number of village elders, the python's spirit seemed not to have been appeased because a further hut fire occurred the next day.

The witch-doctor having failed, I was called in to see if I could offer any useful suggestions. I spent a morning in the village looking for possible causes. The fact that the fires always occurred about midday suggested that the hot noon sun was associated in some way with their cause. Broken bottles and bottles partly full of liquid will sometimes act as burning glasses, focusing the sun's rays on any suitable combustible material and igniting it. I could find no evidence of this type of ignition, however, in any of the huts.

Another line of thought was that haystacks will occasionally catch fire spontaneously if the stack is made up when the grass is still damp, although this does not apply to wheat straw. The thatched roofs of the huts did not seem thick enough to start spontaneous ignition and there were no apparent signs of this type of ignition beginning in any of the remaining unburnt huts. In any case the thatching grass used in the huts was more like wheat straw than hay and did not seem a likely material for spontaneous combustion. Oxidizable oils such as linseed or tung oil can start fires under certain conditions but again there was no evidence of such a cause.

As I discounted the python theory, there remained for me only one possibility and that was fires caused by human agency. This suggestion had already been thoroughly investigated by the police who established that there was a complete absence of any ill-feeling between the African families which made up the farm village. This was supported by the evidence of one of the huts catching fire within yards of the police sergeant when he was questioning three women and some children who were the sole occupants of the village at that time. The police were satisfied that the rest of the villagers were away working in the fields when this particular blaze erupted.

Inquiries from various sources elicited the suggestion that an African delayed-action arson device was known which consisted of a ball of cattle manure wrapped with damp potter's clay. When the clay dried out, the dung acted like compost, heated up and finally burst into flames. If such a device were placed in the bone dry thatch of a hut roof, the results could be well imagined. Despite its improbability, I decided to put the theory to the test and tried various experiments with samples of cattle dung. When the dung was made up into six-inch balls, the maximum temperature rise obtained was only 15°C: nothing like that needed to start a fire.

In the meantime more huts went up in flames, which at least tended to disprove the effectiveness of the python spirit appeasement theory. The blazing hut mystery was solved with incident number fifteen when the cause was clearly identified in the shape of an eight-year-old mentally retarded boy armed with a box of matches. I suppose, like the postman in one of G. K. Chesterton's detective stories, he was unnoticed because everyone naturally expected him to be there. Not surprisingly perhaps, both Africans and Europeans immediately said, 'I told you so'. The Europeans claimed that events showed a perfectly understandable, if unexpected, outcome which required no supernatural explanation. On the other hand, the Africans accused us of lack of comprehension and put forward a different interpretation of the same events. They maintained that the spirit of the python motivated the child and when that spirit was appeased the child was seen causing the fires. If the spirit had not been appeased the child would not have been seen and the fires would have continued.

I might have been entitled to shout out 'Great balls of fire' or some equivalent verbal demonstration of exasperation but, in Africa, one is reminded that logic is not everything when it comes to solving problems. It also had to be borne in mind that a child lost its life in one of the earlier fires. Where on the scale of culpability should one place the action of a child arsonist? Was it murder or accident? It is on such fine points that the balance of justice is decided in Africa.

▾▾▾▾▾▾

Probably the most upsetting type of case is that in which a perfectly acceptable conclusion is reached only to be undermined by later evidence. A case in this category, involving death by firearm, came to my attention in 1964. This was a time when building construction in Rhodesia was booming and there were fortunes to be made in the building trades. Naturally, this boom tempted people from far and wide and Jim Fennell, a Canadian, decided to establish a building business in Salisbury. He installed his attractive wife in a rented house in one of the city's suburbs and set about his building enterprise.

Having heard stories of the pitfalls and tragedies caused by the excessive use of Rhodesia's credit facilities, Fennell instructed his wife, Martine, to use cash, not credit, for all her purchases. After three weeks Martine grew tired of these restrictions and succumbed to the temptation to buy a dress and coat on credit terms. Her husband was furious and insisted that she accompanied him to the shop to return the clothes. He added insult to injury by giving his wife a stern dressing-down in front of the shop assistants. After this public disagreement the couple returned home at about 5.0 p.m. One hour later Fennell telephoned the police to report that his wife had committed suicide by shooting herself.

When the wife's body was examined it was found that she had a gunshot wound in the head, the bullet entering just inside the hair line level with the top of her right ear and travelling in a slightly downward direction. It is possible to gain a firm indication of the distance at which close range shots are fired from the appearance of scorched hair. Where the range is very short, half an inch or so, there will be intense scorching over a small area while a shot fired from four or five inches will result in less intense scorching covering a wider area. If the range is increased by a few more inches, scorching is negligible or non-existent. In this case the scorching of the hair was severe, indicating that the range was between a half and one inch.

The weapon used was a .32 automatic pistol which lay near the body. It bore the dead woman's fingerprints and a paraffin test for cordite residues on her hands was positive. This test, though not conclusive, is evidence of having fired a weapon. It seemed to be an open-and-shut case of suicide and that was the verdict returned at the inquest.

Several weeks later, police inquiries about Fennell in Canada produced some intriguing information. It appeared that he had been a suspect in a small-town murder case there a year previously. His car was known to have been parked near the murder scene and a witness had written down the registration number. The suspect was given an alibi by a woman who claimed that he had been in her company at all the key times. This was the woman whom he took to Rhodesia as his wife and who was now dead. No action was taken against him in Canada in view of the conflict of evidence but, had his previous history been known at the time, the investigation in Rhodesia might have taken a different turn. As I have mentioned previously, a suspect's record plays no part in a trial, but every police-officer knows that one crime follows another. We were left then with an uncertain feeling about the suicide verdict.

Occasionally, a case produces gratifying results with no loose ends or uncomfortable feelings about the inadequacies of the law. The incident I remember most vividly for these reasons concerned a wealthy European businessman who was suffering marital problems. His wife, a thoroughly pleasant woman with three grown-up children, was so distressed by the break up of her marriage that she decided to kill herself. Her plan, in order to achieve maximum effect, was to wait until her husband returned home and then to shoot herself as he walked into the room.

Come the moment of decision, however, the plan went wrong and her husband ended up dead, shot in the stomach with a .32 automatic fired from close range. The wife's story was that she remembered him opening the door and walking into the room—after that she could remember nothing. She was obviously a strong suspect for the murder of her husband.

I was called in to carry out tests for the presence of cordite residues on the wife's hands. When an atuomatic pistol is fired, the spent cartridge case is ejected to the right of the pistol and is followed by a puff of cordite residues which are deposited on the lower joint of the forefinger and, to a lesser extent, on the lower joint of the middle finger. These residues are detectable by various methods but the oldest technique is known as the paraffin wax test. The suspect's firing hand is dipped for a second or so in melted paraffin wax which is allowed to dry and set like a glove. The wax glove is removed in two pieces and any residues on the skin will have been transferred to its surfaces. Chemical reagents are then applied to the wax and the presence of cordite residues is signalled by the appearance of coloured patches. This test has been the subject of considerable technical criticism over the years, but with modifications it can provide reliable results.

In this particular case the suspect's hands were completely clear of cordite residues on the fingers but there was a slight deposit on the palm of her right hand. I next applied the test to the hands of the dead man with rather more spectacular results. Heavy deposits were found in two places, on the palm at the base of the right thumb and a separate patch on the palm at the base of the fore and middle fingers. When the hand is closed, a fold of skin forms between these areas of the palm and it appeared, therefore, that at the moment of firing, the husband was holding the top of the gun. It was also evident that when the gun was fired there was a space between the butt of the pistol and the palm of the suspect because some residues had blown back onto her hand. In spite of her lack of memory regarding the incident, there was no doubt that her husband had tried to take the pistol from her, and in the course of this tussle the gun fired as it was torn from her grasp. Under the circumstances the death was clearly accidental and no blame could be attached to the wife.

The wife was deeply shocked at the turn of events and was too ill to attend the inquest which cleared her. After all, she had been prepared to kill herself only for fate to take a hand and remove her philandering husband, the source of her distress. What started out as the intended suicide of one party ended with the accidental death of the other. I like to think that the one-time murder suspect found happiness in her later relationships.

Chapter Nine
REFLECTIONS

FORENSIC science is frequently introduced into detective stories and crime fiction but explanations of its use are often wildly inaccurate or incomplete. This might be because it is considered contrary to the public interest to give detailed instructions on how to commit murder or, perhaps more frequently, because ideas are simply not checked for accuracy. A case which illustrates the vulnerability of public interest arose as a result of a crime writer's story involving murder by an overdose of insulin.

In May 1957 a doctor was called to a house in Bradford where Kenneth Barlow, a male nurse, reported finding his wife drowned in the bath. Barlow said his wife had been unwell and after vomiting in bed had decided to take a bath. He had dozed off to sleep and when he woke found her lying dead in the bath. He said he tried to revive her by artificial respiration, but to no avail. Suspicion was aroused by the lack of splashing in the bathroom and by Barlow's pyjamas which were quite dry. This was not consistent with his account of applying resuscitation but what hardened suspicion was the presence of water trapped in the inner folds of the dead woman's elbows. When she was found her arms were folded across her chest and the tell-tale water in the crooks of the elbows made it clear that her arms had never been straightened for the purpose of applying artificial respiration.

Careful examination of the body eventually revealed two injection marks under the buttocks. Extracts made of the tissues around the injection sites were analysed and traces of insulin were found. Forensic testimony played a vital role at Barlow's trial for murder and he was convicted on unassailable evidence that he had killed his wife with a large dose of insulin. He was sentenced to life imprisonment for a crime which echoed a fictional story. One is tempted to conclude that 'Murder will out', but a feeling lingers that perhaps others have had the same idea and got away with it. It is estimated that one murder in three in England is reported and that convictions are obtained in one out of three reported murders. That means that eight out of nine murderers get away with it.

One reason why the 'facts' in some detective stories are inaccurate is that writers in fiction tend to borrow an idea from one of their predecessors and then adapt and dramatize it to suit their immediate purpose. After this process has been repeated a few times, any resemblance to fact is purely coincidental. There is also a tendency to romanticize death or to dress it up with drama. For example, some very odd notions have popular currency regarding death by shooting. On films and television, the unfortunate victim who is shot either falls in a heap or goes into a sudden spin like a startled ballet dancer before dropping down dead. Small boys at play delight in 'dropping dead' giving many highly imaginative embellishments to the portrayal of death by shooting which they see nightly on television.

It is exceptional for a person to drop dead instantly from a gunshot wound. There are numerous cases in my own experience in which an injured man has put up a strong fight. In one such incident following a house break-in, two intruders were rushed by the owner who was fired at four times with a .38 revolver. Although hit in the stomach by one of the shots, the owner continued to defend his property, felling the gunman to the floor with a determined rush. The second intruder put him out of action by hitting him over the head with a chair. All ended well with the recovery of the wounded man and the conviction of his assailants. Another demonstration that a gunshot wound in the stomach does not necessarily incapacitate the victim was provided by an eternal triangle shooting. A jealous young man burst in on his fiancée who was entertaining a rival in her flat. Brandishing a .32 automatic, he shot his rival in the stomach but the injured man's retaliation was so fierce as to put the gunman in hospital for ten days. Of course, the ability of a person wounded in the stomach to fight back depends on the bullet not striking a vital part. If the femoral artery, for example, is severed, collapse occurs within seconds.

Survival from gunshot wounds in the head can be equally remarkable, and I recall a shooting which posed a dilemma as to whether it was murder or suicide. Police were called late at night to the home of a woman who had telephoned, saying 'Please, my husband has been shot!' A young constable arrived at the house to find the woman's husband sitting in an armchair in the front room. He had a bullet hole in the head just inside the hair line, level with the top of his ear, yet he was completely conscious. He seemed to resent the appearance of the policeman whom he told to go away—he spoke in a forthright manner spiced with invective. Senior police-officers were called but by the time of their arrival the wounded man was unconscious and died two days later in hospital. A high velocity .22 rifle lay near the armchair and the most pressing question was to establish whether he had killed himself or had been murdered. One of the first things I wanted to establish was the range at which the shot had been fired. All forensic science text books describe how cordite residues can be detected on clothing and the skin and explain how the distribution of residues can help determine the distance at which the shot was fired. Unfortunately, these cordite residues are soluble in water, and when the victim was taken into hospital his head wound was washed and the evidence literally went down the drain.

A wound caused by a gun discharged with its muzzle pressing against the skin is known as a contact wound. Such wounds are characterized by ballooning of the tissues around the bullet entry hole which produces splits in the skin radiating from the entry. Contact wounds are quite rare in suicide since intending victims do not like the feel of the gun on the skin and tend to pull the muzzle back an inch or two. The wound under consideration was not of the contact type so I had to think of another approach. Again, the text books usually deal with scorching of clothing when considering the range at which a shot was fired, but I have not seen mention of the fact that hair scorches rather better than clothing. It is a curious phenomenon that scorched hair falls into two distinct classes. The hair of some individuals when scorched forms little blobs at the end of each hair; in others, the scorched end forms a twisted, tapered point like a short plant root. I think the difference may be attributed to the amount of grease in the hair, which varies between individuals.

I arranged for a few tufts of the dead man's hair to be fixed at one-inch intervals in an old blanket so that I could carry out some scorching experiments. Shots were fired at the tuffs of hair from different distances in order to simulate the degree of scorching and hence the range at which the fatal shot was fired. This method effectively demonstrated that the range was only half-an-inch. It also helped to establish suicide as the mode of death and the position of the wound and sitting posture of the victim were consistent with the rifle being placed with the butt on the floor and the trigger operated with the thumb. It seemed unlikely that the man would have sat quietly in his chair while his wife approached him with a loaded gun saying, 'Shut your eyes, darling. I have a surprise for you.' The point is, that even a head wound caused by a high-velocity rifle did not cause instantaneous death.

Wounds in the heart like those in the head do not always kill immediately and so they often leave room for doubt at the scene of death. I was called to an apparent suicide in which a man had shot himself through the heart. His body was found lying on the bed but the gun was on a table some eight feet away. The murder investigation process was started but a suicide note was found which was proved beyond doubt to be in the dead man's handwriting. Some of the investigating team found it difficult to reconcile the position of the gun with that of the corpse but it is a fact that even though a person is shot through the heart, he is conscious and able for five to ten seconds. In this case the suicide victim must have stood by the table to shoot himself, placed the gun on the table and then taken a couple of steps to the bed where he collapsed and died. Cordite residues found on his right hand in places, consistent with using the gun himself, put the matter beyond doubt.

The most striking illustration of the fact that a man does not drop dead when hit by a bullet occurred in New York where an elderly man was living in the same house as his daughter and her husband. He decided to commit suicide and went to his bedroom and locked the door. Using a .38 revolver he shot himself twice in the chest wounding either side of his heart. He then shot himself one inch below the left eye and again through the left eye. By this time the family had broken down the door and he was seen sitting on the edge of the bed trying to reload the gun. An ambulance was called and he died on the way to hospital.

The reality of such matters is far removed from the mystique of the wild west gun fight depicted in innumerable films. Here, the contestants stand a few feet away from each other in a bar and the man who gets the first shot off is the victor. This is quite dramatic but in reality would be a sure-fire method of committing double suicide. The wild west gun fight is one of the great myths of the twentieth century and has as much basis in fact as a fairy story.

The idea probably arose from the earlier practice of duelling where un-rifled, inaccurate weapons firing a heavy, relatively slow bullet were used at fairly long range. Officers and gentlemen protected their honour in this way but it was considered unsporting to take deliberate aim before firing. Under these circumstances there was a good chance of one of the contestants surviving although the loss of officers through duelling was sufficiently high for the Duke of Wellington to forbid the practice in the British Army during the Peninsular War. In the less aristocratic environment of America's wild west, survival came before chivalry and the more realistic accounts of gun-fights show the Sheriff or US Marshal sensibly taking cover and challenging his man from a relatively advantageous position. By this time, of course, the cumbersome duelling pistol had given way to the .45 revolver, the supremacy of which was not to be challenged lightly.

It is a common occurrence in film shows for a man to be knocked out by a blow on the head with a cudgel or baton. The victim is shown recovering a few minutes later and few people realize that death results from about one in five of such attacks. Death is due to the formation of a subdural haematoma which is a small bruise or area of broken blood vessels on the surface of the brain. Sometimes these are no bigger than a large pea. The combination of such film violence shown to millions of viewers and large-scale violence such as happens in football crowds, picket lines and political demonstrations will inevitably produce unnecessary deaths. The point is illustrated by all too numerous incidents in which persons are killed as the result of violence which erupts in the course of public demonstrations. It cannot be argued too forcibly that an individual who strikes another on the head with a cudgel or similar weapon with sufficient force to knock him unconscious, is open to a serious charge, even though the defence would undoubtedly argue that the assailant had no intention of killing and had every reason to believe that the blow would not be fatal.

It would seem, however, that violence generally as portrayed in the media has been carried to such absurd lengths that credibility has suffered considerably, but some of the thug elements are likely to be incited to further violence.

Another device which has been used time after time in crime fiction is the Mickey Finn. In the form dramatized for home entertainment, the villain puts a few drops of powder or liquid into the good guy's drink and seconds later he passes out. This legend has arisen because when a man has three or four drinks his sense of taste is dulled, which is not surprising as the imbibed alcohol comes into direct contact with the taste buds. After a few drinks very few persons can tell the difference between drinking whisky or brandy. This, of course, is the basis of the well-known night club swindle in which, late in the evening's proceedings, patrons are served cider in champagne glasses and charged champagne prices.

In the days when seamen were shanghaied for service in sailing ships, the press gangs would wait until their victims were good and drunk and then slip a spoonful of chloral hydrate into their drinks. By the time the cheerful imbibers awoke they would be far from home on the high seas. The old custom is still honoured. I believe, in tough bars in seaports and elsewhere where the proprietor keeps a bottle of chloral hydrate behind the bar. If one of his well-oiled customers becomes aggressive and looks likely to start a fight which will wreck the premises, the bartender slips a spoonful of chloral hydrate into his next drink. A few minutes later the would be trouble-maker passes out and his friends gather round shaking their heads and saying, 'Poor old George! He isn't the man he used to be'. Then they wheel him away to sleep it off and the bar proprietor has saved himself a great deal of trouble and expense. The only after effects are felt by George who has a gigantic hangover.

There is no effective substance which can be put into the first drink and have the effect of a Mickey Finn and yet be unnoticed. The advantage of chloral hydrate is that there is a wide margin between effective and lethal doses and it is safe to use compared with barbiturates—for example, where the margin is slender. I have heard of experiments using two-thirds of a lethal dose of cyanide as 'knock-out drops'. While cyanide is almost tasteless, it suffers from severe practical disadvantages as susceptibility to it varies widely. About one person in four is unaffected, two out of four pass out according to plan but one in four drops dead which rather defeats the object of the exercise. Many detective stories mention the bitter almonds smell of cyanide not realizing that about twenty-five per cent of individuals cannot smell cyanide at all. Perhaps the day will come when a crime fiction story will hinge on a plot in which one character resistant to cyanide shares a doctored drink with a susceptible individual so that one dies and the other lives.

Air injected into a vein to cause death as a result of embolism or blockage of the blood supply to the heart or brain is a popular basis for crime fiction. Air introduced into a vein in the arm travels along the blood stream to the heart where it forms a froth which prevents the valves of the heart working properly. This volume of air may also reach the pulmonary artery and travel through the lungs to the brain. The amount of air needed to stop the heart varies according to the individual and his state of health but is usually between 50 and 70 ccs. Air injection is a favoured method for mercy killing in patients with terminal illness. In a sick person 40 cc of air might be sufficient to cause death. The amount of air in an ordinary 5 or 10 cc hypodermic syringe injected into a vein in a healthy person would merely annoy the victim and cause local pains. As some air will stay in the veins, the amount of air which must be injected is considerable. Dr Milton Helpern, who for twenty years was Chief Medical Examiner for New York City, discussed the medical controversy over air embolism in his memoirs. Some doctors spoke of 200 to 300 cc of air being needed to kill a human being and one medical colleague disbelieving that 40 cc might kill rolled up his sleeve and said 'Come on, Milt, I'll take forty cc right now'. There is no doubt that it takes a lot of air to kill a person and lethal results might best be obtained by fitting a hypodermic needle to a bicycle pump.

Dabbling with undetectable poisons is a favourite pastime of detective story writers. Pre-war authors were rather addicted to the idea of rare and deadly poisons which emanated from the jungles of South America. Curare was popular along with other potent compounds in which the natives dipped their poison darts before directing them via blow pipes to their unfortunate targets. Writers of the post-war generation, having been brought up in a world where the wonders of science featured daily in the news media, poured scorn on the concept of undetectable poisons. There is a great deal to be said for this view. After all, modern methods of analysis, such as gas chromatography, enable one picogram of an insecticide to be detected. A microgram is one millionth part of a gram and a picogram is one millionth part of a microgram. Thus, one microgram of insecticide distributed throughout the human body can be detected and identified in a one-gram sample from that body.

With such methods as this available it would seem that any poison could be readily detected. It is not as straightforward as that, however, for not all poisonous substances can be detected by such methods and some of the poisons are unstable substances. As if that were not complication enough, there is the added difficulty that the human body has some extraordinarily effective mechanisms for decomposing chemicals which gain access to it. Common Epsom

Salts or magnesium sulphate, for example, is a sulphur compound which involves heating with charcoal at white heat in the laboratory in order to free the sulphur. The human body manages to perform this reaction at bloodheat, producing sulphuretted hydrogen which is easily recognized by its unpleasant smell.

Some of the unstable poisons are so elusive that it is difficult to separate them from natural sources. The procedure for isolating the active principle from a natural source such as a fungus is to shake up the material with a series of solvents, concentrate the extract, and then determine whether the active agent is in the extract or the solid material. Many of the factors which influence these procedures can be varied—the degree of acidity or alkalinity, the temperature, the method of concentrating the extract, use of a nitrogen atmosphere to prevent oxidation or anything else which the ingenuity of the analyst suggests. In some cases the active principle just breaks down and is not to be found in either the solid or the extract. It is clearly a difficult task to detect these substances in their natural form. Once they have entered the human body and been subjected to dilution and the workings of body chemistry their detection becomes a more remote possibility. Other approaches to detection have been tried, such as identifying fragments of the original fungus from its microscopic botanical features. The difficulties have been emphasized in studies of plant materials which have been used, like LSD, to produce hallucinations. Four out of fifteen examined had an unknown active principle, which means that if somebody is poisoned with one of these materials the analyst does not know what he is looking for, let alone finding it.

Some poisonous substances break down rapidly in the body and produce compounds already present in the system. They are thereby conveniently disguised and the analyst's task is virtually impossible. I have been told by my friends in the police that the professional hit men in the world's organized crime capitals now use these poisons in preference to firearms. Among the hundreds of commercially available insecticides is one which is lethal to humans and which is easily absorbed through the skin. Only a small dose is required to kill and a frighteningly simple and subtle means of murder is thus provided. The possibility of sprinkling a couple of drops of such a poison on a person's underclothing in order to procure his speedy death must fuel the imagination of the crime writer.

Poisons of the more sophisticated kind have recently been in the headlines. It came out during the post-Watergate congressional inquiry into the US security services, that FBI laboratories had isolated the poisonous principle of botulism, the anaerobic growth in tinned food and shell food which causes severe food poisoning. The lethal dose of this toxin was reported to be about 0.2 milligram. Public unease was created by the knowledge that 11 grams of this material had been prepared—a quantity sufficient to kill 55,000 persons.

Another poison bound up with a great deal of secrecy and alleged intelligence activities is ricin. Although this poisonous derivative of the castor oil plant has been known for many years, it made the headlines in September 1978 with the murder of Bulgarian broadcaster Georgi Markov. This was the widely publicized umbrella case. While standing in a London bus queue Markov had a poisonous pellet fired into his thigh by means of an umbrella. He died from the lethal effects of one of the most toxic materials known. Ricin is almost impossible to detect in the body but its effect on the blood, causing strong agglutination of the red corpuscles, sets up antibodies which denote its activity.

In Markov's case the vehicle for the poison was a tiny platinoid pellet which his killer fired into his body before melting away into a London crowd. This pellet measuring only one and a half millimetres in diameter contained two small holes which probably carried the deadly ricin. The manufacture of such a device required specialized knowledge and equipment available at only one or two organizations within Britain and at a small number of centres worldwide. If the poison had been introduced by some means which left no trace, the cause of death would probably have remained a mystery.

Ricin ranks with botulinus among the most toxic materials known. One gram would be sufficient to kill 36,000 people and its powers are well known to governments who carried out research during the Second World War in consideration of its use as a possible agent for chemical warfare. Since then government interest has been cloaked in secrecy although its properties are thought to be well understood by the powerful intelligence agencies of the great powers.

A major difficulty with some poisons is that they act by damaging one of the vital organs of the body and death results some time later due to the failure of the organ. An obvious example is the use of carcinogenic substances and a case of this sort, fortunately involving animals as opposed to humans, occurred during my forensic days in Africa. A farmer's prize cattle started to drop dead two and three at a time for no obvious reason. The veterinary surgeon who carried out the post-mortems found that the valves in the dead animals' hearts had become swollen and inflamed and stopped the circulation of the blood.

The farmer believed his animals were being poisoned and he set a watch over them at night. In due course, an African was caught red-handed dosing an animal from a bottle containing a milky-looking liquid. The man claimed he had been swindled by the farmer and was killing his prize cattle for revenge. He claimed to be using a poisonous concoction made with juice extracted from a particular type of euphorbia, a plant akin to the cactus but lacking the spikes. A specimen of this plant was sent to me and in a matter of hours I had it identified by Salisbury's foremost botanical experts. They declared it to be completely harmless, an opinion which was endorsed by their leading colleagues in South Africa.

It appeared that our culprit was lying but he stuck to his story, explaining that after being dosed the animals showed no symptoms for ten to fourteen days but then died suddenly. He observed that he had dosed two animals before he was caught and that, therefore, they were due to die in a few days time. He pointed out the two animals which appeared to be perfectly healthy yet, as predicted, both died.

As far as I know the poisonous agent in this case was never found and the deaths of these animals remains a mystery. It might be concluded that the pre-war detective writers with their stories of exotic undetected poisons were nearer the mark than their post-war successors who believed science would easily overcome such trifles.

The chance of a poisoner being caught depends on the effectiveness of the investigation which usually starts with the family doctor. From an analytical point of view, the detection of arsenic, for example, is simple and even elementary analytical laboratories can establish the presence of arsenic in lethal quantities. When a person is given arsenic the poison is excreted from the body by the usual means but it also finds an exit by way of the hair roots. As the hair lengthens so the arsenic grows out. By studying the arsenic distributed along the length of a hair it is possible to determine the course of the poisoning. The hair is a kind of arsenic read-out from which the forensic scientist can plot the course of the poisoning and the nature of the dosing—whether there were several small doses over a long period or just one large dose.

This is made possible by neutron activation analysis (NAA), a technique developed in Canada in the 1950s. Samples are subjected to bombardment by high-density neutrons in a nuclear reactor, which makes the chemical elements radioactive. This irradiation is used to identify and measure the elements present in the sample and has been particularly successful in forensic examination of hair.

In spite of these detection facilities there have been several cases of arsenic poisoning in modern times. In 1952, Marie Bresnard, the 'Black Widow of Loudun', was tried in France on twelve counts of murder. She had been arrested following allegations of poison after her husband's death in 1949. Leon Bresnard's body was exhumed and was found to be riddled with arsenic. Sensation followed sensation and police investigations went back to the death in 1929 of Marie Bresnard's first husband. His body was exhumed after lying in its grave for twenty-two years, and arsenic was found. There followed a series of exhumations—Marie Bresnard's father, her father and mother-in-law, her husband's great aunt and a neighbour and his wife. In none of these cases had the family doctor attached any suspicion to the death; but the exhumed bodies, all of which contained arsenic, were a telling reminder that doctors rarely look for poison. Each death had the effect of contributing to Marie Bresnard's personal gain in the form of various bequests.

Accused of twelve murders by arsenical poisoning, Marie Bresnard was sent for trial. She made no confession and one of France's most extraordinary court cases turned into a trial of toxicology and scientific method. Using theatrical methods in court, the defence was able to cast doubt on discrepancies in the way the toxicological evidence was collected. At a second trial in 1954 the defence again created an atmosphere of doubt over the scientific evidence. It was argued that the arsenic could have been absorbed by the corpses from arsenical soil in the cemetery. Scientific testimony demonstrating this possibility was used to put expert against expert. Analytical findings derived from the use of neutron activation analysis (then a new method) in analysing hair samples was heavily criticized. The second trial was also inconclusive and a third trial was granted to enable a further sifting of the scientific evidence.

Seven years elapsed before the third trial took place in 1961. This was a confrontation of experts and expertise. Despite confirmation by a Nobel Physicist of the neutron activation analysis results showing fatal quantities of arsenic in the hair of some of the corpses, the court concluded that the limits of toxicology had been reached and Marie Bresnard was acquitted.

There have been other cases of arsenical poisoning and even Herbert Rowse Armstrong, the solicitor who was found guilty of murdering his wife with arsenic poisoning, would never have been found out if he had refrained from attempting another such murder. The doctor attending his wife in 1921 was a capable and conscientious physician but did not for one moment imagine his patient was being poisoned. In light of such cases the inevitable question is to ask how many persons have been secretly murdered by poison. How many have murdered once, and having got away with it by a combination of sublety and good fortune, had the sense not to try again? The plain fact is that the science of toxicology and particularly the organization for detecting death by poison has not quite kept pace with the opposition and, generally speaking, the poisoner operates in an unsuspecting climate.

▼▼▼▼▼▼

Forensic science becomes involved in all sorts of odd situations but one of the most unusual I ever met concerned Shumba the lion.

As lions go Shumba was semi-educated and had appeared in films in the course of which he had been taught two words of command. The first was, 'Shumba lie down' and the second was, 'Shumba get up' at which he would rise and canter off.

Normally he was kept with several other lions in an area surrounded by a high, diamond-mesh, wire fence in an open-air zoo near Salisbury. Every evening the owner opened a shed door inside the enclosure and the lions would amble along a path near the fence and bed down for the night.

On one occasion the owner dismissed a black employee who went off with a grudge considering he had been treated unfairly. In revenge he cut one of the wires in the fence and the construction of a diamond-mesh fence is such that if one wire is cut in one place the cut wire can be unthreaded leaving a gap in the fence. On his evening walk back to his shed Shumba noticed the gap and like all cats he was curious and, finding that he could get through the gap, he wandered off.

By the time his absence was discovered it was dark. The owner, using a torch, tracked him to a nearby vlei, a flat valley about two hundred yards across, anything up to a mile in length, covered with tall grass about three or four feet high and surrounded by trees.

There was no sign of Shumba but in the hope that he was lying somewhere in the long grass the worried owner called, 'Shumba, get up'. Up popped Shumba but away he went followed by the frantic cry of, 'Shumba, lie down'. By the time he had complied with this request he was some distance away and again the sequence of orders was repeated and again the lion could not be located. This went on for some time until Shumba, bored with the game, bounded off into the trees. This time his track could not be found immediately but his owner circled 'round the vlei by road and picked up the lion's spoor on a dirt track leading to a farm. In fact while his owner had been running round in circles Shumba had found the farmhouse and had parked himself by a rose bush right by the front door. The farmer's dog either heard or smelled the lion and immediately howled and barked furiously. Rather unwisely the farmer opened the door to discover the cause of the racket just as Shumba's owner drove up in his Land Rover. There was a stretch of lawn between the drive and the door to the farmhouse so Shumba's demented owner stuck his head out of the car window and yelled, 'Get inside quickly there is a lion right beside you'. Partly due to the incessant noise being made by the dog the farmer couldn't hear and shouted back, 'What did you say? I can't hear you'.

The warning was repeated but then the farmer's wife came to the door, heard what was being said, looked down, saw the lion, let out an unholy yell and like a flash grabbed her husband, hauled him inside and slammed the door. This thoroughly unnerved poor old Shumba who went loping off into the darkness.

Eventually he found himself a nice soft sandy patch on a dirt road where, quite exhausted by all the excitement, he settled down for the night. He was next heard of when a black man and woman returning from a beer drinking party at 2.00 a.m. literally tripped over him as he lay in the road peacefully sleeping.

Shumba, as might be expected, did not like being walked on and promptly took a swift swipe at the woman's buttocks with his mighty paw which injured her, but not very severely. If he had really meant business she would not have lived to tell the tale. The man was unharmed and rather ungallantly fled into the bush while the woman made her way to the nearest farmhouse and untruthfully reported that her man had been killed by a lion which had also attacked and injured her—she had her wounds to prove her story.

It was then decided that it had become a matter for the police. Shumba would have to be killed. Three policemen took up the hunt and they finally found the wanted animal quietly standing under a tree. The three policemen lined up armed with F.N. rifles then, with a local farmhand shining a torch on the lion, they all fired, more or less simultaneously. Poor Shumba gave a roar of anguish and, to everyone's amazement, disappeared once more into the night. Nobody fancied the job of stumbling through the African bush in the blackness of the night looking for a lion which, if not dead, could be badly wounded. The hunt was abandoned until first light the next day.

But the hunt was never resumed because when dawn came there was Shumba waiting outside his enclosure by the closed up gap in the fence. Two of the three shots fired at him had missed completely but one had hit him halfway along but just below the spine and it had gone in one side and out of the other without doing any serious harm. The gap in the fence was re-opened and the wounded lion ambled in and settled down on his favourite rock—a large boulder about five feet high and eight feet in diameter with a flat top.

I was called in and as I arrived on the scene the owner decided to give Shumba an injection of penicillin to ensure that the wound would not become infected and I witnessed one of the bravest deeds I have ever seen. Any wounded animal is liable to be ferocious and when the animal is a lion it takes considerable nerve even to approach it, but the owner climbed on to the restricted space on top of the rock and calmly administered the injection.

Shumba had once accidentally stumbled across an ox and instantly killed it with one blow of his paw. To come within striking range of a wounded but still highly efficient killer, relying only on the bond between man and animal, seemed to me to be the ultimate test of faith and confidence.

I came into the case to examine the cut fence wire and I determined that a pair of moderately old fencing pliers had been used. The suspect was found with such a pair of pliers in his possession and the cuts made by these pliers matched those on the fencing wire so he was duly convicted of wilful damage and served two months in prison.

Shumba made a rapid and complete recovery and, to the best of my knowledge, still occupies his favourite rock for most of his waking hours.

▼▼▼▼▼▼

I remarked at the outset that the job of the forensic scientist is to help the courts determine whether or not a particular individual has been involved in criminal offences. Possible traces of criminal activity are gathered by the police as part of their crime scene investigation and sent to the forensic laboratory for examination. These items, which may ultimately be produced as exhibits in court, have first to be identified and then scrutinized for any characteristics which might identify a criminal or provide a clear link with a known suspect. I believe that the future development of forensic science lies mainly in improving the means by which these samples are collected and brought to the laboratory. At present, this operation is the weakest aspect of forensic science organization. Although a useful contribution could be made in about 20 per cent of criminal cases, the laboratories are only involved in about 2 per cent of major crime investigations.

The forensic scientist is equipped for his task by his training and experience and, increasingly is aided by the use of sophisticated laboratory techniques. Those faithful forensic friends, the comparison microscope and the emission spectrograph, have been added to by an arsenal of new methods and equipment. The increased use of drugs and the motor car in the furtherance of crime has forced chemical analysis to new achievements. Gas chromatography and mass spectrometry (GCMS) with computer-assisted data facilities is one of the new breed of specialist tools for identifying drugs, toxic substances and many other compounds in common use. Atomic absorption spectrometry (AAS), which operates on the opposite principle to conventional spectrometry, measuring absorbed radiation instead of emitted radiation, is widely used to determine trace quantities of elements in many materials, including glass and paint. And the scanning electron microscope (SEM), which has the edge over optical instruments for magnification and depth of focus, enables ballistics examinations to probe finer detail.

Of course such equipment—which in the modern fashion for using abbreviations, is known as GCMS, AAS and SEM—requires highly skilled technicians to operate it. Moreover, apart from the mere exercise of technical virtuosity, these sophisticated methods are useless from a forensic point of view unless they are provided with the right materials to investigate. Dr Ray Williams, Director of the Metropolitan Police Forensic Laboratory, put it concisely when he commented that '. . . the technical limitation on forensic science is the ability to pick out the vital item of evidence in the initial search'. The weak link in the forensic chain is the man on the spot—the investigating officer who first reaches the untramelled crime scene. His skilled hands and experienced, searching eyes are paramount factors in spinning the first strands of the web of evidence which will trap the criminal. Once he and his colleagues have collected every conceivably useful piece of evidence, the forensic laboratory has a whole fund of methods for probing and analysing it. But in the US it is reckoned that only between three to ten per cent of potential evidence at a crime scene is actually collected and processed for use in prosecution in serious crimes.

The importance of this initial task is gaining increasing recognition and police forces around the world organize training programmes to meet their particular needs. Evidence Officers or Crime Scene Investigators are a recognized branch of many police forces in the USA. They conduct the search for physical evidence which parallels that for oral information, witnesses' statements and house-to-house inquiries, conducted by plain-clothes or uniformed officers. The use of more efficient methods at the crime scene improves the quality and amount of evidence brought to the forensic laboratory and increases the possibility of obtaining successful prosecutions in serious cases.

It is difficult to see what part Africans will play in the development of forensic science in their own countries. Certainly, their awareness and understanding of African culture and social habits give them advantageous insight into the mentality and behaviour patterns of their own criminal elements. This presupposes that the tremendous primaeval influence of tribal culture on the African mind can be thrown off for the sake of pursuing western ideas of law and order. One of the greatest difficulties is that of language. Many African tongues, for example, have no words corresponding to animal, mineral or vegetable. They divide concepts into active or passive kingdoms. Thus, active agencies are men and ancestral spirits, while living things such as animals and plants are relegated to the passive kingdom. Many English words simply have no equivalent in the African languages and there are corresponding difficulties in going from African words to English. The basic concepts running through African languages are quite different to European ideas. Consequently, the African wishing to learn English has to reshape his conceptual thinking in addition to learning a new vocabulary.

There are other obstacles which also prevent the African obtaining the technical and scientific education necessary to build up a modern society and some of these are by no means obvious. For instance, the ability to look at a picture and mentally translate it into a three-dimensional or solid form is acquired early on in life and is extremely difficult to learn at a later stage. Most Europeans see books and pictures at an early age and pick up this attribute without effort as part of their natural development without even being aware of it. For the majority of Africans, lack of opportunity to absorb this ability is a tremendous handicap in their studies, especially of technical subjects. On the other hand, the African has certain advantages not least of which is his understanding of social and cultural matters. If properly applied to crime investigation he has a major weapon at his disposal—knowing how the criminal thinks. Moreover, the visual element of crime detection is one in which Africans are especially gifted, as I have illustrated elsewhere in this book.

A number of Africans have distinguished themselves in the professions and in administrative and technical spheres, thus demonstrating that the transition from tribal to conceptual thinking is possible. That it is necessary seems self-evident, at least in terms of alleviating the scourges of ignorance, poverty and disease which are the vampires sucking the life-blood of the African continent. Overcoming these is the great challenge, besides which, all else is relatively inconsequential. The task is of monumental proportions and will require generations of effort. Meanwhile, Africa is building highly successful business enterprises, establishing learned institutions and building schools, hospitals, offices and cities. This will not wait for the universal amelioration of the life of the tribal African—it is happening now. And with it are emerging some of the less desirable manifestations of a sophisticated, city-dwelling way of life of which a rising crime rate is one.

The advancing pace of technology, especially of high-technology, puts a premium on adaptibility. Perhaps more than any other innovation the micro-processor is illustrating this. Its impact on people's daily lives and its potential for change is enormous, yet it is accommodated with that spirit of optimism which distinguishes the human from other species. The African, in shrugging off tribal darkness and pessimism, is grasping the fruits of adaptability for his great Continent. He will succeed the quicker if that other precious human commodity, goodwill, permits him to work in constructive partnership with the European so that both may learn and forge their achievements in one world.

▼▼▼▼▼▼

A useful attribute in most walks of life is the ability to improvise. This is certainly advantageous in forensic science but there are dangers in extending its virtues to other fields. As I mentioned in an earlier chapter, I learned at the beginning of my career in Rhodesia of the dangers of insisting on hospital treatment for African workers. Realizing that the fear of hospital is sufficient to result in the death of unwilling patients, I decided the next best thing was to be prepared to deal myself with injuries in cases where someone refused proper treatment. As a result, and not without trepidation on my part, I was able to deal with many quite serious injuries in the bush. I found that some remarkable results can be achieved by the amateur in these circumstances, but there are hidden perils.

When I was growing tobacco in the early 1950s I had an old African worker, named Matope, on the pay-roll. One day the old man accidentally chopped off the ends of three fingers on his right hand. When I saw him, all his finger ends, save that of the little finger, were hanging by threads of skin. I was not at all sure how to deal with such an injury and delivered my cautionary homily about the advisibility of going to hospital. I might have saved my breath, for old Matope refused point blank to go anywhere and simply pronounced his faith in my abilities to restore his hand to its former wholeness.

Feeling a trifle uneasy and in need of a 'second opinion', I took old Matope by the arm and sought the counsel and practical advice of my wife. Despite the fact that she was seven months pregnant at the time, Mollie hardly turned a hair. After a swift look at the injured party and his helper she disappeared and returned quickly with two large brandies. By this time, of course, Matope's hand looked a real mess with blood dripping freely from it and the finger ends dangling like charms on a bracelet. Having been fortified, we filled a bowl with disinfectant and carefully placed Matope's hand and nearly detached finger ends into the solution. In retrospect, I cannot think why we did not simply snip the finger ends off and have done with it. That is probably what most people would have done in the circumstances—but we decided to stick them back on again!

Mollie's practical housewifely instincts came to the fore and out came the bread board. We spread the patient's hand and finger ends on it and applied a generous coating of sulphonamide powder to the stumps and cut ends. Each finger end was then carefully lined up with its finger stump and bandaged in position. After another round of brandies was downed by patient and nurses we drove a somewhat inebriated but incredibly cheerful Matope back to his Kraal.

Twice daily for almost a month we checked the injured hand for any signs of inflammation and examined Matope's armpit for any swelling of the lymphatic gland. We were delighted at the way our patient was progressing and eventually the day arrived when we were able to take off the bandages. For a whole hour Matope sat with his hand in a bowl of water then, gently, we started to ease the bandages off. The bandage on the ring-finger was the first to be removed and to our great joy and satisfaction it had healed beautifully. Then came the middle finger and the forefinger, both equally good. Sighing with relief I exchanged a broad grin with Matope but when I turned to Mollie I caught her look of pleasure change to one of horror. Speechless, she pointed to Matope's rejuvenated hand and I then saw what I had missed in all the excitement of taking the bandages off—the finger ends had been replaced the wrong way round so that the nails were on the inside of the hand.

In stunned silence, joy turned to consternation, we looked at Matope whose wrinkled face creased in a broad smile. Holding up the perfectly healed hand he said, 'Nobody but Matope has fingers inside out. He is a very happy man'. We supplied the old man with a pair of gloves to protect his hands from the cold of the Rhodesian winter and learned later that he fully exploited his unexpected gifts. Dressed in his best clothes and proudly wearing his gloves, Matope would appear at every beer-drinking session for miles around. Raising his right hand and dramatically peeling off the glove to reveal his inside-out fingers was guaranteed to provide his beer free of charge.

Although we were naturally distressed by our mistake we had not perpetrated a disaster. Indeed, the patient had taken on a new lease of life and we provided our doctor friends with a dining-out story which they used to the full. Cynically, we might say that it was no wonder the African is afraid of hospitals and medical treatment, but we reassured ourselves that without the benefits of treatment old Matope would surely have ended up with infected wounds. In any case, to put the matter into a reasonable perspective, we were working in difficult circumstances and simply doing our unqualified best.

This story with its hint of farce does I think illustrate some of the basic needs of Africa. The simple virtues of good will and trust aided by a spirit of practical innovation are perhaps more effective in human terms than certainty of purpose and sophistication of method. It could be that the African would better respect his relationships with Europeans if they included the prospect of fallibility and humility.

INDEX